On My Own Terms

On My Own Terms

John Seymour

Faber & Faber

LONDON   BOSTON

First published in 1963
by Faber and Faber Limited
3 Queen Square London WC1N 3AU
Revised edition published in 1980
Printed in Great Britain by
Latimer Trend & Company Ltd Plymouth
All rights reserved

British Library Cataloguing in Publication Data

Seymour, John, *b. 1914*
    On my own terms. – Revised ed.
    1. Africa – Social life and customs
    I. Title
    960'. 3'0924   DT14

ISBN 0–571–18016–7

Contents

++++++++++++++++++++++++++++++++++◇++++++++++++++++++++++++++++++++++

Preface

✦

Many years ago I wrote a book called *On My Own Terms* which was an autobiographical account of such of my childhood as seemed interesting to me and not too scurrilous or libellous, and of thirteen years of wandering around in Africa and Asia, in peacetime and in war. It was a very bad book and I'm glad it didn't sell very well. I also wrote a book called *One Man's Africa*, to which the same remarks might apply.

But they were at least honest books and what I said in them was true—except, that is, when I had to disguise true facts because my publisher's lawyers thought they were a bit *too* true. Thus I had to call that boring seaside place Frinton-on-Sea by another name, and for some obscure reason I chose the name 'Hexham', not realizing that there really *was* a place called Hexham —a splendid little market town in Northumberland. And not only did I have to change the *name* of my stepfather's business, I had to change the very nature of it, thus altering the making of porridge to the making of chewing-gum. Now, there is nothing wrong with porridge (although there is everything wrong with making it in huge factories and thus knocking all the small country millers out of business) but there is everything wrong with chewing-gum than which surely a more useless and disagreeable substance has never been invented. But where are these books now?—where are the snows of yesteryear?

So now, in 1978, I sit down to write the story again. I can write it now from a more dispassionate standpoint—I can see the wood for the trees. I shall keep in close touch with the trees,

9

though, because I shall simply transcribe large chunks of the original books.

When I read these books now (as I have just done for the first time in a dozen years) they bring back vividly to me things that have long been forgotten. It is a sad man who lives in the past. But it is a sad man, too, who forgets his past. I must confess, that in the urgency of the present and future—my *now* seems ever more pressing and urgent as I get older—my memories tend to lie undisturbed. Now is the time to dig 'em up again.

The life we wandering white men lived in Africa before the Second World War is absolutely inconceivable today. Two whole generations of people have grown up who just cannot imagine it. It is assumed by at least two generations of English people that we white people were in Africa just to 'exploit' it. Well, of course we were. The black people were in Africa just to exploit it—and still are. That is, if exploit means what my dictionary says it means: 'Work, turn to account . . . utilize for one's own ends'. I went to Africa to work, to find adventure and, hopefully, to make a living.

I also had vague, but very honest, ideas about helping the people who already lived there. Was I not a *New Statesman and Nation* reader, and did I not have all sorts of ideas about black people being just as good as white ones and everybody being completely equal? I had been educated to believe that Africans were 'savages'. I expected to find them so. I have to turn to my dictionary again to find what this word means and I find that it can mean two things: uncultivated, wild, in primitive state, etc., and the other is angry, cruel, barbarous, etc. I will not anticipate my narrative by telling what in fact I found. In relating my story I now have the advantage of hindsight—we all know now about General Amin and the Emperor of Central Africa—and the white policemen who torture and murder black prisoners in South African jails. We couldn't even imagine such things then. We knew all about Chaka, though, the Zulu king who had thousands of innocent people stabbed to death with *assegais*. We also knew that old Piet van Tonder over the mountain had flogged an African to death and that the police had done nothing about it.

Indeed I looked upon Africa as a 'savage' continent and that was one of the reasons why I wanted to go there. England was far too 'civilized' for me. England, after the First World War, seemed old, and tired, and sick, and silly. Above all silly. The so-called 'Roaring Twenties' were for me the 'Silly Twenties'. I hated the whole trip. England was following America into an age of vulgarity and stupidity. The honest people—farmers, farm workers, sailors, coal miners, steel workers, men and women who made the true wealth of the world—were unregarded, under-rewarded, flung out of work. A new class, or mish-mash of classes, composed of parasitic, useless, frivolous and bogusly sophisticated people, seemed to inherit the Earth. This process has gone on, until to say 'I make something' or 'I grow something' or 'I dig wealth up out of the ground' is to admit inferiority, but to say 'I manipulate money' or 'I produce lying advertisements' or 'I shuffle papers about' or 'I ponce about in front of a camera' is to claim to be a top person. 'Beeros—beeros!' says my old Welsh farmer-neighbour, tapping his top pocket. This is his way of saying the name of a popular ball-point pen and indicating who the *real* important people of the Earth are now—not people like him and me who work in dirty boots and till the soil.

Anyway, I wanted out of it and out of it I got, and I only came back to it because I believed that I could create my own world within it. I came back on my own terms in fact. And on my own terms I live now.

December 1978   *Fachongle Isaf*
Trefdraeth
Pembrokeshire

Chapter One

✦✦✦✦✦✦✦✦✦✦✦✦✦✦✦✦✦✦✦✦✦✦✦◈✦✦✦✦✦✦✦✦✦✦✦✦✦✦✦✦✦✦✦✦✦✦✦

Bound for Table Bay

We came to a ship. Not a whole ship but part of a ship because she was being broken up.

I was driving through Spain in a little van with my family, before my family itself was broken up, and we came to this ships' graveyard in Barcelona and I noticed her.

Her colour caught my eye at once, for it was a rather sickly puce-purple if you can imagine such a shade. It was the colour which the Union Castle Line always chose to afflict on their vessels. And when I got closer I read the name: *Warwick Castle*.

Immediately, through my head went the strains of that golden oldie of yesteryear—'The Isle of Capri ('. . . she wore a plain golden ring on her finger/So I sailed from the Isle of Capri'). The sight of the poor old ship in her death agonies brought back a flood of memories to me.

I remembered boarding the Royal Mail Motor Vessel *Warwick Castle* in Southampton when I was twenty years old, which must have been in 1934, bound for South Africa. And on the ship's Tannoy system, as they used to call the all-pervading noise-dispensing mechanism that was still an innovation in those days, were being relayed the strains of 'The Isle of Capri'. And this song was played for us over and over again all the way to Cape Town, for three whole weeks. I could have done without it. It lilted away during the strange sentimental symbolism of the throwing from ship to shore of paper streamers, and their subsequent breaking as the huge ship moved away from the quayside, and the cries of 'God Speed!' which, believe it or not, was an expression sometimes heard in those days on such occasions, and during the weeks of voyaging round the curve of the globe.

But I must jump even further back in my narrative, to explain why I happened to be in a ship heading for South Africa.

'You'll be pestered with koodoos,' said the man with the aluminium leg. He was known as Peg-Leg Stacey, and he owned Horsey Island, an island in a backwater of the Essex coast. I had worked for him all summer, helping Mr and Mrs Burroughs, his manager and his wife, look after sheep and cattle and make hay and generally farm the island, and Stacey was trying to talk me into going out to the newly acquired colony of what was then called Northern Rhodesia (now Zambia) to oversee a tobacco farm he owned there.

Stacey had had a leg shot off in the First World War, when he had been flying an aeroplane. Unable to settle down, he had bought a piece of land from the North Charterland Exploration Company in Northern Rhodesia where he had gone to plant tobacco. The price of this questionable substance fell to an uneconomic low and he had been forced to come back to farm in the Old Country, as he called it. He wanted me to go and work the farm in Northern Rhodesia on my own behalf, and at the same time look after it for him, with the option that I would buy it if I found I could possibly make a living out of it. What I was going to buy it with neither he nor I knew, because although I had a stepfather who was an enormously rich man, it was quite evident that none of his wealth was likely to come in my direction.

'You'll be pestered with koodoos,' he said. 'They'll come and make a terrible mess of your seed-beds. But at least you'll be able to shoot them for the pot. One thing I promise you—whatever happens in Africa, you won't starve.'

I was dying to be pestered with koodoos. I couldn't think of anything nicer to be pestered with. I was dying to go to Africa. I *had* to get out of England. I had come to hate the place. It would be hard for a young person in England today to imagine just what it was like then.

It was not *poor*, although working-class people were very poor. Somehow there always seemed to be enough people who could afford to buy Baby Austins, or larger motor cars, and travel down to places like Frinton-on-Sea. The people on the street where we lived were enormously rich. There were a lot of enormously rich people. All my mother's and my stepfather's friends were rich—and they were the unhappiest lot of people I have known, before or since.

But to the disinherited young, such as my brother and myself, the world seemed bleak and hopeless. For the whole of the young generation were made to feel that we were just not wanted. I don't think I speak only for my brother and myself: nearly all middle-class young people were in this situation. As for their working-class counterparts, they just swelled the ever-growing dole queues —two million unemployed. A hundred men lined up for every job: it was a paradise for capitalists no doubt, but a hell for working people. I was offered—and turned down after trying it for a month—a job in my stepfather's business, which was Quaker Oats. I had spent most of my holidays working on farms and had attended an agricultural college. I knew that the one thing the British Isles could grow was oats. And yet here was a firm importing them from the United States. This seemed to me to be completely unacceptable. Our own farms were falling into decay and dereliction. Thousands of acres were tumbling back into rough pasture and often being abandoned altogether. And this American company, of which my stepfather was the representative in Europe, was flooding the stuff into England and foisting it on to the gullible public by means of a massive advertising campaign. 'You can sell anything to anybody,' my stepfather said, 'if you advertise it enough.' And this was sadly the truth, and is sadly the truth today. At least, to *nearly* everybody. He couldn't sell his package to me.

So I left the business and got the job on Horsey Island, and worked for Peg-Leg Stacey, and listened to his tales of Africa. And to Africa, I came to realize, I must go.

But I had to sell the idea to my mother, who alone could find the fare—and the fifty pounds one had to deposit with the South African government—for me to get there. And so I introduced her to Peg-Leg Stacey, and she liked him, and she asked him who, if I went to his farm in Africa, could become responsible for my moral guidance, when out there far from home, with all sorts of temptation on every hand. Personally I was only too keen to be tempted.

Stacey replied to this question with no hesitation. 'Farmer Brown,' he said. 'Farmer Brown, my neighbour there. Excellent man. Thoroughly reliable.'

Alas! My mother caused inquiries to be made to the North Charterland Exploration Company, which had an office in London and another one in Fort Jameson, and the cabled reply came back: 'BROWN GOOD FARMER BUT DEFINITELY UNSUITABLE GUIDANCE YOUNG MAN'.

This so upset my mother that she decided that on no account would she help me to go to Northern Rhodesia. But she saw that nothing would prevent me from going to Africa.

Now I must jump *forward* in my story here, just to complete the history of my relations with the unsuitable Farmer Brown.

I went to Africa. I went to Northern Rhodesia. I went to the Fort Jameson District. I went to the farm of the unsuitable Farmer Brown.

I drove to the latter with a temporary game ranger named George Brent. I was working at that time for the Northern Rhodesia Veterinary Department but had been seconded to the Game Department, also as a temporary game ranger. It was New Year's Eve. George and I, full of whisky, decided to pay a visit to his good old boozing companion, Farmer Brown. We drove many miles through the bush, in a van, and drew up outside the farmer's bungalow. Over the never-ending noises of the African night—tree frogs and honking bull-frogs and the occasional howl of a jackal, and distant drums—we heard a strange fluting music. Approaching the window we looked in and saw a spirited scene.

Clad decorously—if only—in a pair of underpants which failed lamentably to cover his enormous belly, pranced the unsuitable Farmer Brown. He danced, and as he danced he played on a tin whistle. He was quite good at it. He danced round a table on which stood a half-empty bottle of whisky.

He danced as Pan is supposed to dance. Sometimes he pointed the whistle at the ceiling, sometimes at the floor. Sometimes he pointed it backwards, as if beckoning onward nymphs.

He *was* beckoning onward nymphs. Behind him capered, most gracefully and decorously, three lovely black maidens. Except for a few bracelets they had nothing on. The oldest couldn't have been much more than sixteen. They clapped their hands as they danced and they danced with innocent and solemn expressions of enjoyment. Round and round the four of them went, mopping and mowing, as though it was all the most natural and delightful performance in the world.

So much for the unsuitable Farmer Brown.

Well, to get back to England and 1934, my mother, following her disillusion about Farmer Brown, made further inquiries and came up with an organization cumbrously called 'The 1820 Settlers Memorial Association'. The '1820 Settlers' were some people who had sailed out from England and landed on the shores of Africa near the present town of Port Elizabeth. In fact they founded that town, then drove out into the hinterland where they made their homes. There their descendants still are. And these descendants had formed an organization whose purpose was to help and encourage young men such as myself (girls were apparently not thought of) to emigrate to South Africa. *British* young people that is—although I do remember that it was stated in the aims of the organization that other 'North Europeans' would be accepted. There was, in fact, one Dutchman in our party. But of course the whole purpose of the exercise was to try to right the balance between South Africans of British descent and those of Dutch: the Boers as we once called them—Afrikaners as they are called now. The exercise failed: in South Africa the Dutch have inherited the Earth.

My fellow pioneers aboard the ship devoted themselves wholeheartedly to deck games and chatting up the girls. As I was far too shy and inept to do the latter and completely refused to do the former, I developed a sort of holier-than-thou attitude towards my contemporaries. I was amazed that, apparently, they could go half the way round the world on the ocean without seeming to notice it. I got the impression that they were *afraid* to observe that the world was a planet, hurtling through space, and that they were on it, creeping day by day around the great curve of its belly, and that the sea was vast, and hostile, and dangerous, and beautiful, and filled with mysterious life, and that our kind had come out of it, and would no doubt return to it in the end. So they trivialized the whole experience with deck games. Meanwhile I spent the voyage in a sort of trance—gazing out over the ocean, trying to imagine the globe in its wholeness, and to visualize its place among the stars. I still try to do this, but not as often as I ought.

To be woken by the rattle of the anchor cable, and to rush on deck at early dawn and behold Table Mountain, is the sort of experience that a man can have only seldom in his life. It is possible that my thrill at seeing Africa for the first time produced as powerful an effect on me as that experienced by the first man who set foot on the moon.

Africa! How banal and sordid and unhappy it seems now with its welter of politicians, and genocides, and economic reports, and famines, and Cubans, and all the rest of it. In 1934 it seemed to me to be the most romantic continent on Earth. There, across the early-morning bay, was this splendidly sculptured mountain, so aptly named the Table, with the city clinging like moss to its lower slopes and its vertical walls higher up cut off clean and straight by the table-top, the huge mass of it flanked and framed on either side by two minor peaks: Devil's Peak and the Lion's Head. The whole scene was impossibly beautiful—challenging—but somehow hostile and menacing too. I thought of the intrepid spirit of the Portuguese sailors who probed their way southwards, ever southwards, down the apparently endless wall of Africa, until they slotted in, completely unexpectedly, to this magnificent Table Bay. They had only a few more miles to go then to round the Cape of Good Hope and realize that what they must have come to think of as endless was not endless after all. I thought of the Dutch adventurers who had landed in this bay to plant a garden here and to victual their East Indiamen on the long road to the East; and how some of these settlers had turned free-booters and wanderers and, with their great Dutch long-waggons and their oxen and their sheep, and Hottentot slaves, their Bibles in one hand and their rifles in the other, had turned their waggon-poles northward and eastward and forced their ways into the trackless and barren wastes, eventually to build republics in the wilderness. Later, when I had got to know these people, and had, as far as I could, become one of them, I wrote this poem:

Voortrekkers

Iron-bound wheels cut furrows in the soft land
Grind, crunching, the sun-hot rock
Three fathom whip-thongs drive the cattle northward
Slouch-hatted *jonge* gallop after the stock

Poke-hatted women sit in the tented waggons
Pile fires at night, fear not the grunting lion
Voortrekkers—backs to the sea—look finally northwards
Africa cowers before them, beaten by iron

Fire-power of iron, but iron love of freedom
Freedom from domination by another race
Old freedom of Friesland, Zeeland, and the Hollow-land
From feudal arrogance and the servile face

How could the freedom-searchers know the implications
Know the strong logic of their borrowed land
Know that—like rivers in the empty High Veld—
Their search for freedom would perish in the sand?

I did not know it but even then there were *voortrekkers* (the
Dutch word for pioneers) pushing northwards with their waggons into the nearly empty land of South West Africa, taken from
the Germans in the First World War and being settled as quickly
as possible by white South Africans of Dutch extraction. Probably their aim was as much as anything to keep the English out.
This land is now called Namibia, and it is anybody's guess how
long the remaining white people can hang on there.

Now aboard the *Warwick Castle* there was a man named Sir
Ernest Oppenheimer. So far as one man could be said to own
South Africa he was that man. He owned a large share of the gold
mines, all the diamond mines, much of the industry and much of
the trade. He came slumming in the tourist-class part of the ship,
where we would-be pioneers were, and gave us a talk: about how
we were going to a land of opportunity, etc.—a land with prob-
lems, true, but it was our job to solve them and all the rest of it.

Being a young man who, no matter how dreamy, nevertheless
had his eye firmly fixed on the main chance, I went to see him

afterwards. Amazed at my audacity thus to beard such a fantastically great man in his own cabin (I had given his secretaries the slip) he promised me a job. 'Wait,' he said, 'until we dock in Cape Town, and come and see me at the Mount Nelson Hotel. I will be meeting my managers and engineers there. I am sure we can find you the sort of job you want.'

'I want to work down a mine,' I said.

'Working down a mine is dirty, dangerous, and unpleasant. I am sure we can find you something better than that.'

Well, the ship docked in Cape Town. We pioneers went ashore. We were booked in for two nights at a small hotel. I had an appointment to see Sir Ernest Oppenheimer the next afternoon at the Mount Nelson Hotel.

There was a young Jewish man in the hotel who was a fanatical mountain climber. I got talking to him and he offered to take me up Table Mountain, by a beginners' route, the next day. I thought of my appointment with Sir Ernest. I thought of a life of prosperity and ease, as some sort of vaguely-imagined favoured official driving around in a large car. I thought of how proud my stepfather would be of me, when he realized what a *go-getter* I was—how I had, by sheer initiative, sneaked an advantage on the others by actually bearding the great man in his den.

Then I looked up at the slab-side of Table Mountain: it was covered with the famous 'table-cloth' that day—a sheet of white cloud which often pours over the sharp edge of it, falls to a certain altitude and then just disappears. I had to choose between Table Mountain and a new and no doubt privileged career. I am glad I chose Table Mountain.

Chapter Two

❖

The Great Karoo

Our group went to Tarka Training Farm, near Craddock, in the Little Karoo, in what was then called the Cape Province of the Union of South Africa.

This word 'Karoo' could do with some explaining.

Once, many millennia ago, the whole of southern Africa was covered with high rain forest, much as the greater part of Central Africa now is. For some reason the climate became progressively drier. Who knows why? We know that it is dry now because the sea breezes that blow over most of it blow first over cold oceans, and therefore do not pick up much moisture. Why it was wet before we do not know, but then we know very little about the past twistings and turnings of our planet.

But as the climate got drier so the great jungle trees grew smaller and more stunted. Above ground at least—below ground they made up for their lack of height by driving their roots deeper and deeper down into the soil, to find whatever moisture was down there. Smaller and smaller they got until they became what they are now: stunted little bushes, a few inches high, with tiny leaves. These little bushes grow sparsely; there are many yards between each bush in the drier parts of the Karoo, a few feet in the moister parts like Craddock. And they cover the entire countryside quite evenly, stretching as far as the eye can see wherever the observer stands—over the enormous flat plains, up the mountains, on top of the high table lands and in the valleys. They give a speckled, greyish-green appearance to the landscape. The effect is quite unearthly to a person brought up in England. At first I kept imagining I had landed, by mistake, on another planet.

Small though they are, these bushes are tough and immensely long-lived. Their little grey leaves are edible and relished by sheep and cattle. The Karoo is among the healthiest and best sheep country in the world. When the rains come, as they do most years, grass springs up in the spaces between the little bushes, and the cattle get fat on it, but it lasts only a short time and quickly dries up and blows away. The little bushes stay on, though, and sustain stock right through the dry winter when no rain falls at all.

The country was either dead flat like a billiard table or steeply hilly; there was no compromise—no rolling or gently sloping landscape. Hills and plains alike were covered with the little bushes. Except where Man had come with a road or a plough or a house, or where there was a dry river bed, there was no variation at all in the grey-green, shrub-speckled vista, unrelieved by any tree or clearing.

The effect of this on an English boy was devastating. At home I had loved the English countryside. There really *was* some English countryside then, though there is little left to love now. Around Wye, the small town in Kent where I had spent three years at an agricultural college, I had wandered the woods, and the downs, and the marshes, and I knew every inch of the countryside and was familiar with every bird, flower, tree and hill. I had spent those three years in a kind of mystical, magic dream. I had loved the depths of the great beech woods, the great shire horses hauling giant logs out of King's Wood, the flash of a kingfisher across the surface of the Stour, the friendly, slow-speaking farm workers smoking their pipes and drinking their beer in Crundale pub.

Here in the Karoo I could not imagine ever getting used to this enormous emptiness. It seared the soul.

The wire fence had come to South Africa, and the more settled parts of it had been divided up by dead straight, strained wire fences into huge enclosures called camps. Each camp had in it a deep water bore-hole with a steel windmill over it which pumped water into a concrete reservoir. From this it ran into a trough for sheep and cattle to drink from. It was the invention of the ox-waggon, the saddle-horse, the rifle, the wire fence, the rock drill, and the steel pumping windmill which had enabled the white man to conquer southern Africa.

But Tarka Training Farm was in a small irrigated area, below the big new irrigation dam called Lake Arthur. A few thousand acres of the Karoo had been enclosed by fences, ploughed and irrigated. Flood irrigation is an art that is as old as civilization (in fact the first civilizations were the direct result of it). Nowadays, when power is so cheap as to be almost free, farmers in Western countries install expensive and sophisticated piped irrigation systems, with which water is pumped under pressure, spurted up in the air, and allowed to fall down again. But the age-old system of irrigation that was practised at Tarka Training Farm—and, indeed, in most parts of South Africa—was one in which the water was simply allowed to run downhill, through irrigation ditches, then diverted into smaller and yet smaller channels, until finally it was allowed to run out of a channel on to a bed that had been prepared by levelling. Each bed had a *bund* around it, which was a tiny earth wall. Conducting flood irrigation is a delightful occupation. Armed with a spade, you throw up little earth banks in front of the advancing water, break down other ones, wait while the slowly moving water spreads out over the dry earth, driving a flotsam of ants, beetles, small twigs and leaves in front of it, to reach the bottom of the bed. Then you mend the hole in the bank through which it has come and break down a hole into the next bed. You spend the day like this, never in a hurry, mostly standing and watching the slowly creeping water or else just standing. Or, in fact, just sitting. I saw this same process being conducted in Greece last year, on lucerne (what the Americans call alfalfa). It took me back forty-four years, to the lucerne beds at Tarka Training Farm.

Life passed quite pleasantly for me at the training farm. Having worked as a farm labourer on several English farms (for some years I had been spending my holidays doing this) the work came very easily. For the first time in my life I found I was better at doing things than other people were. With the exception of irrigation, there was no job on that farm that I had not already done, having been taught by professional English farm workers, who are (or were then) the most professional people in the world. There was a savage little Jersey bull on the place, of which everybody was scared stiff. I had spent six months looking after a herd of bulls on a Cotswold farm (Cocklebarrow Farm, Aldsworth, then the farm of Mr Arthur Garne), and no bull scared me. This particular bull and I quickly came to an understanding and everybody was most impressed. After a month the manager called me in, asked me if I would like to stay on and ultimately become an instructor, and when I demurred he said that Oscar Southey, a very fine farmer—one of the most famous in South Africa— wanted a pupil. Would I care to be the pupil?

So I found myself on a train heading further north into Africa. The country remained much the same as we went north except that it opened out—the plains were wider, the hills were higher, the farmsteads were much further apart. There was no Lake Arthur irrigation scheme here and so a farm, to give a living to the farmer, had to be several thousand acres in extent.

The hills tended to be flat-topped, like the original Table Mountain at Cape Town. Scattered about the plain there were other things, though, called *kopjes* (pronounced 'koppies'). In Afrikaans the word means a little head. These *kopjes* are the tops of pipes of hard volcanic rock which have welled up from below, and been eroded away much more slowly than the sedimentary rocks of the great plains. The *kopjes* look grey or black—like the jumbled heads of big boulders. All hills, the big mountains and the *kopjes* alike, started up sharp and abrupt from the dead flat plain— there were no gentle gradations as in Europe.

And the farms looked like ships on an ocean. Far away over the plain would be a red-roofed house (all the white men's buildings in South Africa were roofed with corrugated iron) standing among bosky green pepper trees with generally a stand of blue gums near them. Inevitably nearby would be a steel windmill, which pumped out of the deep bore-hole the water which was the lifeblood of every household.

I was met at Schoombie railway station by a Coloured man in a *waanjie*. A *waanjie* (pronounced 'vankie') is a four-wheel small spring waggon. This particular one was pulled by six fine mules. A Coloured man is a man of mixed race: with both black and white blood in him. There seems to be a natural affinity between Coloured men and mules. The Coloured man took my suitcase and threw it into the *waanjie*, I jumped up on the high seat beside him, he cracked a long whip which made a noise like a pistol going off, and the mules broke into a gallop. With superb skill he swerved his long team out of the station yard, on to the dirt track which was the road (there were very few tarmac roads in South Africa then) and, standing up the better to hold his reins and ply his whip, drove at furious speed out into the veld. (Veld is pronounced 'felt' and means the country.)

After a long drive (not all at a gallop I am glad to say) we sighted the farm, far away over the Karoo. This had been named, by the Southey family who owned it, Manor Holme. Previously it had had a Dutch name, *Varkkop*, which meant pig's head. This was considered too unromantic.

Manor Holme was a great farm. Situated in the middle of perhaps thirty thousand acres of veld, all divided into camps of several miles' width, each camp furnished with a bore-hole, steel windmill and reservoir and drinking trough, the homestead itself was palatial. The main farmhouse was a rambling bungalow with the inevitable red-painted tin roof. Double-storied houses were rare in South Africa. There was another bungalow in which I was to live with a fellow pupil, with Oscar Southey's old mother who was over ninety and her lady companion. There were numerous well-built farm buildings. There was a large herd of North Devon beef cattle, a small one of Guernseys kept for milking, about fifty horses bred for police remounts (the South African police were still mounted in those days) and thousands and thousands of Merino sheep.

Oscar Southey was a famous breeder of Merinos. He thought nothing of paying two thousand pounds *in those days* to import a ram from Australia. He sold breeding rams all over South Africa for a high price. Huge consignments of wool were 'ridden' (carried) as the South Africans say on ox-waggons to Schoombie Station.

I spent my waking hours for the next six months on a horse. The job of my fellow pupil and myself was to 'ride camps'. Most mornings, we would both set off mounted on good horses (with a *quidine*, which was the local name for a young native boy, mounted on another horse with us), and ride over the not-quite-boundless veld with the object of inspecting—and counting—the sheep in every fenced camp. As each camp was many miles across and contained several hundred sheep, which were scattered all over it, this took some doing. Sometimes by quietly riding round, and inspecting a bunch of sheep here and there, and counting them, it was possible to get the correct count without rounding the animals up. At other times it was necessary to drive all the sheep over to the boundary fence, and then let them run gently between one's horse and the fence and count them from the saddle.

The chief object of this counting and inspection was to watch for fly-strike—the horrible infestation of maggots that afflicts sheep in Africa as well as in Wales and England. If a sheep looked unhappy, or wiggled its tail, or seemed to be ill at ease, the *quidine* and I would have to catch it. This was easier said than done, but could generally be accomplished by riding quickly at the sheep so as to press it against the throng, and leaping out of the saddle and grabbing hold of it. We would then wash the beastly maggots off the flesh with some disinfectant which we carried in bottles in our saddle-bags.

You might suppose that if you have four hundred and eighty-three sheep in a field (we knew the 'count' from a little book we carried) it mattered little if you only counted, one day, four hundred and eighty-two. It did matter though. If there was a sheep missing you searched for it until you found it. Sometimes you would find it dead, in which case you had to dismount and skin it (actually the *quidine* skinned it—such jobs tended to be the lot of black people). The stinking skin would then be carried back to the farm. But generally all were present and correct.

Southey impressed on me the need to count the sheep accurately, saying that it was the only way to stop the kaffirs, as he (and every other white man in the country) called the Africans, from stealing sheep. Something in my nature made me take him literally and once, soon after I came there, I spent all day searching one camp looking for one missing sheep. I should have inspected three other camps that day but had to leave them. I reported to Southey when I got back.

'You'd better search again tomorrow, hadn't you?' he said.

I searched all next day. The *quidine* and I quartered that camp until we must have seen behind every bush. There was still one sheep missing. I went back and reported to the boss.

'Leave it,' he said, 'Forget about it.'

Next day I rode out and counted the sheep in the next camp. There was one sheep too many. It was that evening that my fellow

pupil told me the truth. Southey always tested his new pupils by
sending a native out to catch a sheep and fling it over the fence
into the next camp. At any rate I had passed *that* test.

This life suited me perfectly. Every morning my *quidine* would
ride up leading a first-class horse ready bridled and saddled. I
would mount and he and I would ride away. If we were riding
nearby camps we would aim to get back at midday to change
horses and have some lunch. If we were to be further away we
would take some rusks and *biltong*. *Biltong* is a traditional South
African food. It is strips of buck meat cut along the grain of the
meat, lightly salted, and then dried in the shade in a breeze. You
can only make it in the dry season when there are no blowflies.
The meat gets as hard as wood. You eat it by paring the end of a
strip off with a sharp knife. It is noble stuff. It has kept many a
man in the veld alive when, without it, he would have died.

There were buck on the farm. This was unusual, for the white
South Africans have remorselessly destroyed nearly every large
wild animal in their country. The enlightened Southeys had, however, preserved some springbok. These gallant little antelope
could often be seen in this camp or that, leaping and bounding
out of sight when they saw us coming. Southey allowed no in-
discriminate shooting but held a few springbok drives a year
when we white chaps would crouch with rifles behind ant-hills
(the veld was speckled with low termite hills about two or three
foot high), while Africans on horseback drove the wild herds past
us. It was the cream of rifle-shooting; the small buck came far and
fast and leapt as they ran. Later on I never shot buck like this,
because I learnt it was a crime to wound one, and I was to shoot
many hundreds of big game animals in Africa without, I am sure,
ever letting one get away wounded. Nowadays shooting big game
has become a most questionable activity, but nobody questioned
it when I roamed Africa. Further north there were hundreds of
thousands of large animals—millions I suppose—and the few
people who had guns could have made no appreciable impression
on their numbers at all. Later, in South West Africa, I was to
'farm' gemsbok in a way of speaking, knowing roughly how
many herds there were in the district and how many buck in each
herd, and simply cropping them when we needed meat and I
knew the herds could afford it.

Bizarrely there were fallow deer on Southey's farm. I know there are meant to be no deer in Africa—but there are. John Cecil Rhodes brought some out from England and turned them loose on the Southey lands, and there their descendants still are and grow to about twice the size of their English cousins. On that farm there were no beasts of prey, only Man. Lions and leopards had long been eliminated, as had wild dogs and hyenas, and the Southey lands were surrounded by a jackal-proof fence. I learnt a fact from this wild life on Southey's farm that I have never forgotten. Here was an enclosed eco-system—the deer and buck could neither get out of it nor into it (surprisingly the springbok, that great jumper, seldom jumps over a wire fence). The grazing animals increased by breeding every year. If we had not shot a suitable number they would quickly have reached the limit of their food supply. Not only would they have starved the sheep and cattle, they would have starved themselves. And—worse even than that—they would have caused deterioration of the veld by over-grazing. They would have killed the little Karoo bushes. The Southeys were good husbandmen, and they maintained both wild buck and tame sheep and cattle at the limit that the grazing could support without deteriorating. Thus they did not deplete the fertility of the land and allowed it to suffer no erosion. People who are opposed to Man killing other animals just do not understand these things. They are city-bred people with no experience of how the world really is nor of how ecology really works.

The Southeys were extremely prosperous and lived in high style at Manor Holme, rather like the aristocrats of Old Virginia in the slave days. There were other rich English-speaking farmers in the neighbourhood, and with these the Southeys had social intercourse. Like some of the other English farmers, they were descendants of the 1820 Settlers. By hard work and industry and good management they had made themselves rich.

Most of the work on the farms was done by black people, but except for my *quidine*, who acted squire to my knight, I had very little to do with the black Africans at Manor Holme. I could not talk with them—they were mostly Xhosa (the X is pronounced as a click in the back of the mouth) and they spoke that language. Although they also spoke Afrikaans I had not yet learnt this language.

28

I saw enough of the Africans, though, to realize that they led
very underprivileged lives. The Southeys were liberal with their
Africans: far more so than other white people. They could afford
to be—they were rich. The Africans had just adequate food. That
is, they had ample 'mealie-meal' (maize meal) which is really what
they lived on, some sugar and coffee, salt, skimmed milk, and
occasionally, but as a special treat and not as a right, some meat.
True, the meat tended to be from animals which had died a
natural death. This last circumstance was a source of great
anxiety to the Southeys, for the Africans—who actually craved
meat—had ways and means of helping nature. If an animal died
it was my unpleasant duty to post-mortem it to see that, first,
the 'natives' had not smothered it (if they had you could tell
by the condition of its lungs) and, second, that they had not
hastened its demise by shoving a wire up its nostril or its anus,
nor assisted nature by any other means. As the Southeys had
some forty thousand sheep that I knew of I wondered, sometimes,
if it would not have been better to have killed a few each week so
as to give the Africans a meat ration and then left the naturally
dead cadavers for the vultures. When I mentioned this idea to
Southey he was fairly contemptuous. 'What? If you give too much
to the kaffirs you only spoil them. Give 'em an inch and they'll
take a mile. If I gave them meat they would *still* steal animals or
kill them so that they could have the flesh. We treat our kaffirs
better than anyone else around here.'

This was true, but they still worked from sun-up to sun-down
six days a week for ten shillings a month if they had rations, or
thirty shillings a month if they did not, and they were still confined to the 'native compound' whenever they were not working.
I likened them to workhorses—they were put away in the stable
when they were not working. No 'native' could leave the farm
without a pass. A pass was a piece of paper scribbled by a white
man and I have scribbled hundreds. It said something like:
'Petrus Mandaba is allowed to leave Manor Holme to visit his
aunt at such and such a farm for twenty-four hours from such and
such a time and date. Signed.' Without such a pass any black man
was liable to be picked up by the police and thrown straight into
gaol. Nor were they allowed to roam about on the farm of which
they were a part, in case they set wire snares for deer or buck or

killed a sheep. Occasionally we were supposed to raid the compound to see if there were any 'strange niggers'. If there were,
they were kicked out, or handed over to the police if they did not
have passes. 'Strange niggers only cause trouble,' the theory was.

The horrible word *apartheid* had not been invented at that time.
The 'pass system' was in its infancy. When I went back to look at
South Africa after the war I found that any African, outside the
'Native Reserves', had to have at least half a dozen passes, each
one up to date and in order, or suffer imprisonment, flogging, and
often worse. But I quickly realized that the Africans working on
the farms in South Africa were kept at about as low a level of life
as it was possible to keep them without them actually dying, and
the amount of liberty allowed them was nil. I have no doubt that
the slaves in the American South, before Liberation, were no
whit worse off.

Of course *in theory* these people had 'homelands' to go to. Thus
the Xhosa had a right to go to the Transkei, which was supposed
to be their country. But in practice they could *not* go to the
Transkei. They had not been born there—they had been born at
Manor Holme. The Transkei, like every other Native Reserve,
was already impossibly overcrowded. It was not possible to practise even a subsistence agriculture there. The people already there
would not let any new person in. Then could they leave Manor
Holme and throw themselves on a free labour market? Well, they
could *not*. They could not leave Manor Holme at all unless
Southey was willing to give them a pass and, except for the odd
Sunday visit to a neighbouring farm, he was not. They were
slaves in everything excepting for one thing: they did not have the
cash value to their master of slaves. If one died it was no financial
loss to Southey. He could easily get another one. A true slave,
who can be turned into cash, is far more likely to be well fed and
properly looked after.

I soon found that there was another class of worker supporting
the Southey empire. Scattered about the country were posts,
which consisted of a small bungalow, one or two pepper trees
beside it (these were just large bosky ornamental trees—nothing
to do with real pepper), a steel windmill, concrete reservoir and
drinking trough, and generally a sheep dip. Besides this there
would be one or two kaffir huts: small conical huts made of mud-

plastered sticks. These posts were manned by white men—not in Southey's class at all—each of whom was responsible for a large area of veld with its occupying sheep. I became very interested in these men because it seemed to me that they were very typical of the land I was in.

They were lean, tough-looking and sun-browned, and they wore, as we all did, khaki drill trousers and shirts. They spent much of their lives in the saddle. Their language was Afrikaans: they hardly spoke English at all. They were all married and had large families of healthy, sun-tanned children. They were paid unbelievably low wages: five pounds *a month* in cash, plus one two-hundred-pound bag of maize meal, one hundred-pound bag of wheat meal (always called boer meal), one sheep for killing, the milk of a cow, some coffee and some sugar. And they were allowed to shoot an occasional springbok. They each had a small irrigated garden in which they grew nothing but pumpkins. They stored the pumpkins on the corrugated-iron roofs of their houses. Their diets consisted of mealie-meal porridge (*mealy pap*), occasional bread, milk, mutton, coffee, butter, *biltong*, pumpkin, and nothing else. They and their families seemed superbly healthy. They never tasted green vegetables, salads, or fruit.

The above wages would have been princely for a black man at that time, but for a white man in South Africa they were absurd. A miner on the Rand might take home seventy pounds a month. And yet these people seemed perfectly contented.

I believe the reason for this was that they came from the old *Veeboere* stock—the people who fanned out from the Cape into the hinterland of Africa in their long ox-waggons, driving their flocks and herds; and they just were not in need of money. Money was something you had to have for rifle ammunition, coffee, a little sugar, some *lamp olie* or paraffin, an occasional dress for the wife, pairs of shorts for the kids, and khaki trousers or a shirt for yourself. The *voortrekkers* did not have a money economy. On Southey's farm these Afrikaners led what was to them a perfect existence: the men at least spent their lives in the open air with horses, sheep and cattle. Their only grudge was that these animals were not their own, and neither was the land on which they grazed. I used to have to ride over to the posts occasionally to help dip sheep, and I was impressed by the friendly, if rough, relationship between the white people and their African helpers there: the little white children played quite happily and unselfconsciously with the black ones.

The narrow Calvinist philosophy that has created apartheid has brought these people into deserved disrepute all over the world, and Afrikaans has become a foul word. How sad this is, because they are no different from any of the rest of us: if *my* ancestors (staunch small 'l' liberal though I consider myself to be) had been *voortrekkers* in South Africa who knows what my views on racial matters might be? During a Communist demonstration in Johannesburg I saw 'workers' (we must not call the faithful just 'people') carrying banners on which were written: 'Workers of the World unite—for a *White* South Africa!'

In the end nearly *all* people work and fight and scheme for the best economic advantage for themselves. Marx was almost right there. Altruism is always shown only by a minority. I did not know it at that time, but there was such a minority in South Africa, and since then this minority, which has grown and is growing, has shown the sort of staunchness and even heroism that redeems the human race.

Meanwhile I was called a *kaffir-boetjie*, which is a term of abuse meaning 'little brother of the black people'. I never once believed what I was constantly told, that 'the kaffirs need keeping in their place, man' and 'give 'em an inch and they'll take a mile' and 'how would you like a nigger to rape your sister?' and 'it'll take 'em a thousand years to reach our stage of development, man.' Later I was to march and fight with kaffirs in the desert and mountains and the jungle and I found, as I had always suspected, that they are just as good as anybody else and in many ways a lot better. At any rate they can *laugh*—and keep on laughing when there really is very little to laugh about.

Meanwhile—back to the Afrikaners. Their ancestors had come out to the Cape in the sailing ships of the Dutch East India Company and these same ships had brought back with them Malay slaves. There is still a community of Malays in Cape Town, still Mohammedans, and with an ancient culture of their own. Surprisingly they do not sing Malay songs nor speak the language, but they have preserved intact seventeenth-century Dutch songs that have been forgotten even in Holland.

The Dutch settlers divided themselves into two groups: one settled on good land in the Western Cape, where their descendants are still, growing good grapes, making good wine, and growing wheat, for which the climate there is suitable; the rest fanned out all over southern Africa.

They left the Cape to get away from government. The government of the Cape was autocratic in the Dutch time, but when the British moved in after taking the Cape from the Dutch they were even more repressive (we English have always been the world's great nannies—and nanny always feels she knows best), and such of the Dutch as were not already settled on good farms moved out. They simply inspanned their oxen in front of their great waggons and headed eastward and northward.

The land they spread out over was virtually uninhabited. It is not true to say they 'drove the African people out of their country'. Southern Africa was not inhabited by black people when the Dutch arrived. Over that vast land was a scattering of two races, one brown and one yellow: the Bushmen and the Hottentots. The Dutch enslaved these peoples when they could, shot them when they could not, and the survivors fled into the Kalahari and Namib Deserts. Meanwhile the true black people, the members of the Bantu race, were slowly driving down from east and central Africa, and they too were killing or enslaving the hunting peoples as they advanced.

Why it was that the Bantu peoples had not spread down into South Africa before is hard to explain. What great dynamic of expansion made them begin the migration southward no one knows. Certainly the *Veeboere*—the Afrikaans *voortrekkers*—met the advance guard of the Bantu race at the Great Fish River, in what is now the Eastern Cape Province, and there they clashed. There was fighting, raids and counter-raids, and when the wave of English settlers landed at Port Elizabeth in 1820, they found they had to fight for their farms and continue to fight to hold on to them.

Meanwhile the English consolidated their hold on the Cape and landed in and took over Natal, on the east coast. The Boers either knuckled down to British rule or crossed the Orange River. There they formed their own country which they named the Orange Free State. They clashed with the Zulus, who were

fanning out from Natal in their hitherto unopposed wave of conquest (they had conquered every other tribe that had stood in their
way, killing the men and turning women and children into Zulus)
and, after several bloody battles, and helped by the English who
were coming inland from Durban, had beaten them. They fanned
out over the great grassy plain of the Free State, set up farms
which were so large and far apart that no man could see the smoke
from his neighbour's chimney, and then, when the land was taken
up, a wave of them crossed the Vaal River (*vaal* means grey) and
set up another free country—the Transvaal Republic.

Then, to cut a long story short, prospectors found gold in a
range of hills in the Transvaal called the Witwatersrand ('ridge of
the white waters'). The end of the republics was in sight. John
Cecil Rhodes outflanked the Boers by settling Rhodesia with
Britons and claiming Bechuanaland for the British Crown. The
English wanted the gold. The Boer War was waged, two gallant
little free countries fought the greatest power then on Earth for
two years before being forced to surrender, and the whole of
South Africa was united under the British Crown. The British
were magnanimous in victory, however, and eventually gave the
whole country over to its white inhabitants (the black ones were
never consulted) and, of course, as the Afrikaners (people mainly
of Dutch descent) were in the majority they simply took over the
government and, after the Second World War in which South
Africa fought reluctantly, kicked the British out and turned the
country into a republic. This gave them a free rein to turn against
the black and Coloured inhabitants of their country with a con-
sistent ferocity which few countries have ever matched. They have
established one of the world's most complete despotisms.

Throughout these events the Dutch settlers forged for themselves their own language which, although Dutch in origin,
differs strongly from modern Dutch. It retains many of the
elements of seventeenth-century Dutch—usages which have
changed in Holland but not in Africa. An Afrikaans poet has said
that the language was 'hammered out by waggon-wheels crashing
on rocks'. It has that feel about it—it is a language of the camp-
fire, the waggon, the rifle, the saddle and the farm. It is a language
much influenced by the Bible, which was early translated into it,
and it was this fact that probably saved it, just as the

translating of the Bible into Welsh saved the Welsh language.

I suppose when I was there the great migration of the Afrikaans people into the cities was just beginning. When I first went to Johannesburg that dreary city was an English place. But all those brown and happy children of the Coetzees and the van Tonders on Southey's farm would have to migrate to the metropolis and become the new sort of Afrikaner: the Afrikaner in the pin-striped suit.

There was no longer any land for the Afrikaners to spread out over. The first huge farms had already been sub-divided—and sub-divided again. Most Free State and Transvaal farmers could see too easily the smoke from their neighbours' chimneys. The British colonies and protectorates to the north and east blocked further advance in those directions. True, there were the 'Angola Boers'—a wave of *voortrekkers* who had, not long before I landed there, made the terrible crossing of the Kalahari Desert with their ox-waggons (their route could be traced afterwards by abandoned waggons and the bones of both oxen and human beings) into the Portuguese-ruled country of Angola where they settled. (I was afterwards to meet them.) But the Afrikaans people had a great many children. They could not stay on the family farms, for there was no more land for them, and so they crowded into the cities. There they learned English, but their own language was saved for them when Afrikanerdom began to take over government and Afrikaans was made one of the two official languages.

I found I liked the Coetzees and the van Tonders and all the rest of them. I got on easily with them. I admired their love of freedom, their adaptability and resourcefulness, their frugality. I liked these 'Dutchmen'. They told me tales of 'transport riding' (carrying goods hundreds of miles up from the coasts in ox-waggons for a living), of lion hunting and buck hunting, of the troubles with *die Kaffirs*, of life in the free and open veld before the days of the wire fence and the motor car and the lust for money came and changed it all.

I read Denys Reitz's *Commando*, the magnificently told story of Smuts' raid into the Cape during the Boer War. I admired those guerrillas who rode their horses a thousand miles through enemy territory until they rode them into the sea. I liked their language and tried to learn it. I loved their songs, of which they had a great number (the hackneyed 'Sarie Marais' is about the only one to have reached England).

I could even tolerate their attitude to the Africans. It was rough but it was human. The Afrikaners on the Southey farms spoke Xhsao better than they spoke English. When a white man worked with Africans, say at putting up a fence or dipping sheep, he led the Africans, worked harder than they did, joked and laughed with them, got them to work with pleasure. The idea of a white man in South Africa standing by with a *sjambok* (rhino hide whip) while the 'boys' laboured in the sun never was, I believe, true. South African white men worked hard, and always have done.

The white South African policemen who so lamentably fail to stop black prisoners from leaping out of fifth-storey windows while under interrogation are drawn from a class of people that every race throws up—natural fascists. I have seen the same sort of people in the Military Police in the British Army. The Japanese, the Germans and the South Africans don't have a monopoly of bullying characters. Such people are divided pretty evenly, I believe, among all the races. It is only that history has forced the white South Africans into a tyrannical position. I pray to God that they may get out of it one day, and take their place in the advance towards a humane and sensible world.

We had never heard of police brutality when I first went to South Africa (I don't doubt there was some but it was some time before I became aware of it) and to me, then, that vast country was a stage on which tanned lean men rode horses over the endless, *kopje*-studded plains, slept at night beside fires with their loaded rifles under the blanket beside them, voyaged over the plains in great ox-waggons much as sailors sail the seas. The principal actors were white men, tough and resourceful, with the look of far-off places in their eyes. The extras in the drama were black men, savage in those days, beautiful, and with great dignity and nobility. I could not see then that all their dignity and nobility was being taken from them by oppressive laws and the hatred of the master race. And the backcloth to this drama was as vast and as savagely beautiful as any country in the world.

Chapter Three

++++++++++++++++++++++++++++++◇++++++++++++++++++++++++++++++

Up North

Oscar Southey told me one day that a cousin of his was coming for a holiday, from a far and savage country called South West Africa. I looked at the map and saw that South West Africa was vast beyond belief—you could have got a couple of British Isles into it and lost them. But it was mostly desert, Southey said. Good for practically nothing. A lot of diamonds up there, mind you, but they had all been grabbed by Sir Ernest Oppenheimer.

The cousin arrived: a sun-tanned, stocky man named Clinton Andrews. I latched on to him and pumped him about the country he lived in. The more he talked about it the more I decided I had to go there.

For one thing, there were *lions!* And *elephants!* And buck galore —real wild buck, not buck confined by any fence. And jackals and hyenas and leopards and packs of ravening wild dogs. And few motor roads—people still travelled, if they travelled at all, on horses, with waggons, or with something called a 'donkeymobile' which, I gathered, was a cart made from an old car axle and pulled by four donkeys.

I asked Clinton if I could go there when he went back. He said that, yes, I could, but he could not pay me any money. Money was absent in South West Africa, because this was the time of the Great Depression. But I could go there and work on his farms, and eat and live, and if I could get some money out from 'Home' I could buy some sheep, up to two hundred, and run them on his farm. Thus I could slowly build up a flock and, in the ripeness of time, perhaps get my own farm and become a farmer. Land was still being practically given away by the government there. Farms were large, some twenty thousand acres in the rainier north, where he was, and vast stretches of one or two hundred thousand acres in the dry south.

I told Southey I was going and he seemed very disappointed and, I realize now, not a little hurt. 'I had hoped you would stick out the year,' he said. He urged me to stay on his farm for a few years and eventually, perhaps, get some money from my parents and buy a small farm in the Karoo. 'The Karoo's the best Merino country in the world,' he said. 'You must prosper here. South West is a savage land, full of vermin [by which he meant, not lice, but lions!] and the veld is not good for sheep. Full of poisonous plants for a start.' But I just had to go. I had been with the Southeys six months, and six months seemed to me then to be about as long as I could stick anything.

I was driven into Schoombie again by the daredevil Coloured man in the *waanjie* drawn by four splendid mules heading over the veld at a fast canter, and, eventually, I changed trains to a place called De Aar, which was a lost and forlorn railway junction in the flat Karoo.

Here Clinton Andrews joined the train (he had been to visit someone else), accompanied by Bessie, his ravishingly beautiful sister. Alas and alack—her brother quickly apprised me of the fact that she was heading to the South West to marry a farmer! Nevertheless we had long and earnest conversations standing close together on the open platforms between the carriages. If only it hadn't been for that bloody farmer—for I fell head over heels in love with her.

I forget whether it took five days or six to get to Clinton's farm on that train and the narrow-gauge train that followed. Certainly it took long enough to give me an idea of the staggering size of Africa. Certainly we passed several stretches that took a full day to traverse without seeing more than one house, one tree, one steel pumping windmill, one little group of kaffir huts, one long waggon. I remember one such homestead—the only dwelling of any sort we saw all that long day's travelling over the dead flat plain (there were no hills or *kopjes* west of De Aar)—and a small white child came out and stood by the waggon and waved to us. What intolerable isolation! Almost certainly that poor Boer father had no motor car. Horse or ox-waggon was his only transport.

Maybe his neighbour was fifty miles away or even more. That child, if an only child, very likely never saw any other children except one or two of the half-breed Hottentots who lived a semi-slave existence in the tiny group of huts beyond the windmill. Clinton told me that the family probably spent every rainy season (say five or six months) travelling the boundless fenceless veld in their ox-waggon, taking their flocks and herds to where the little Karoo bushes had not all been nibbled down to the ground by the sheep in the long desert dry season. During the latter period the stock would be confined to a radius of about five or six miles from the pumping windmill.

Then we came to the Orange River, which was a great contrast to the apparently limitless plain speckled all over with the little greyish-green Karoo bushes, for there were large trees growing near it.

We then came into an even more desert landscape: that of Namaqualand itself. We were in South West Africa.

What a promised land!

The little bushes grew so sparsely there that there were acres of sun-hammered ground in between them. For the first time in my life I knew what real heat was. When the train stopped, as it did occasionally, and we jumped down at some deserted siding (there would be a windmill which pumped water from a deep bore-hole for our engine to drink of, and maybe a Hottentot hut or two), the ground would be far too hot to stand on with bare feet and the heat would come up in waves and hit us in the face. It seemed to me almost frighteningly hot. I asked Bessie if it was as intense at our destination and she said it was. She was a nurse, and gave me a lecture on preventing malaria. It was malaria country where we were going and I would have to swallow five grains of quinine every night and sleep under a mosquito net, at least during the rainy season. I subsequently slept thousands of nights just on the ground, with no mosquito net and no quinine, and I never got malaria, but I saw other people die of it.

We came to the Rehoboth Reserve, where the beautiful Bastard people live. It was not insulting them to call them Bastards for that was the name of their race and they were more than a cut above the Hottentots or black people, in their own opinion at least. I didn't know it then, but had to wait until I became a member of the London Library many years later, after the War, before I found out that these people were the remnants of the strange race of Orlams—a race descended from escaped slaves from the Cape who settled first along the Orange River, and then, when the white men got there, fled further north to conquer practically the whole of South West Africa. Under their Napoleon-like leader, Jonker Afrikander, they conquered the proud Herero people, and the Hottentots, and—very easily—the Berg Damaras or Klip-kaffirs, and even made inroads into the country of the Ovambos to the north. They were enabled to do this by the white traders who landed at Walvis Bay and brought them guns and powder in exchange for the cattle that the Orlams looted from the Hereros and the copper bracelets and ankle rings they wrenched from the limbs of Herero ladies, often cutting off hands or feet to do it. White people have not got a monopoly of brutality and violence.

We were told that we could not leave the train in the Rehoboth Reserve. Only a few trusted traders and missionaries were allowed there. The girls were too beautiful, and white men such as we might not be able to restrain our libidos. I was reminded somewhat of Ulysses' plight when sailing past the Sirens. Certainly the few lassies I saw standing about the station bore out the legend of beautiful people. But people of mixed race, in Africa at least, and often in Asian countries too, are apt to be very beautiful. And the train rumbled on and tore us lecherous but unsatisfied gentlemen away. What with Bessie *and* the fleeting glimpse of the Bastard girls I was in a rare state.

The men with whom we shared our compartment were real old-type Boers. They had battered hats, stained all round the side with sweat, they had drooping moustaches stained with coffee and nicotine, they had large pipes. In the pipes they smoked *skaaplek*: one of them carried a fifty-pound sack of it in the compartment. *Skaaplek* ('sheep-lick') is what its name implies. It is stuff given to sheep to lick. It is, actually, the sweepings from the floors of the tobacco factories, and the sheep like to lick it and it is supposed to keep them free from worms. For the latter reason the government used to allow farmers to buy it duty free. Of course the men smoked it besides giving it to the sheep. To balk this evasion of the excise the government got the idea of mixing bonemeal with it. Good for the sheep, bad for the smokers. The farmers found they could remove at least some of the bonemeal by a process of winnowing. Every weapon has its defence. The next weapon was sulphur. Good for the sheep, bad for the smokers. It says much for the persistence of the latter that some of them smoked on regardless, but at the time Clinton and Bessie and I travelled up to South West Africa the game was at the bonemeal stage. Judging from the appalling smell the stuff had been inadequately winnowed.

Besides the sack of *skaapiek* each man in the carriage had food for the journey—a sack of *biltong*, a sack of home-made rusks and a big old wooden box full of *padkos* ('road food'). Clinton and I had the same. After the war I revisited South West Africa and was delighted to find that the tradition remained unchanged. I travelled in a lorry a few hundred miles across the Namib Desert and there, in the back, was an old wooden box with a lid which wouldn't stay on, and inside it was an indescribable muddle of sticks of *biltong*, goat meat which had gone bad, open tins of rancid butter—and ants—tins of condensed milk with two holes punched in the top and stuffed with twigs—and ants—a huge canister of coffee, a small bag of 'boer-meal' for making *vet-coeke* (flap-jacks)—and ants—and a broken paper bag containing sugar— and ants. All these articles floating in a medium of dust, torn bits of brown paper, loose food, mouldy bread, bits of sack, nameless objects—and ants. I was later to carry on the *padkos* tradition, nobly, for many years, myself.

Such were the passengers and such was the cargo of our compartment. In the evening we availed ourselves of the *padkos*, with great freely offered giving and taking from each other; then we applied ourselves to the neck of a bottle of Cape *dop* (brandy) which was passed round; then we men tactfully withdrew into the corridor while the lovely Bessie prepared herself for the night and disappeared into a top bunk; then we came back, kissed the *dop* bottle again, fell as best we could on the bunks, and went to sleep.

South West Africa had been taken from the Orlams and the Hereros by the Germans and had become part of their empire. It fell quickly to the Allies in the First World War, when Generals Botha and Smuts rode in with their commandos (real commandos on horses—the word commando was an Afrikaans one, borrowed by the British in the Second World War for something quite different). The commandos, as they rode across the veld, were followed by a railway which was laid after them at the rate of a mile a day, and it was along this railway that we were travelling.

After the War the country was awarded to the League of Nations, which appointed South Africa to look after it. It promptly did so, 'opening the country up' as the phrase went. The old Boer economy depended on having an ever-moving frontier, so that the numerous offspring of the farmers (the word *boer* simply means farmer) could trek ever outwards in their never-ceasing struggle to keep out of sight of the smoke from their neighbours' chimneys. No more land could be filched from the natives within South Africa: the only land left to them was useless anyway, so the sudden addition of a country bigger than Spain was welcome to them. A team of surveyors went up to the Territory and the habitable part of it was cut up into 'farms' with the exception of some scraps of useless land here and there which were left for 'Native Reserves'. Huge areas of desert were also declared 'Native Reserve'. This looked good on paper, although nobody could live in them except for a few wandering Bushmen in the rainy season.

The farms varied in size, from blocks of from thirty to fifty thousand hectares in the south to pocket handkerchiefs of a mere seven or eight thousand hectares (fifty-odd square miles), in the north, where Clinton had his farm. And after the surveyors (who travelled on horses with pack-horses) came the settlers. Established farmers would hire a train, load all their belongings including their waggon and oxen on to it, travel to the rail-head, and thereafter trek to their farm.

The Andrews, like the Southeys, were descended from the 1820 Settlers. Clinton's father had been a farmer all his life, but being a gentle and kind man had never made any money. Clinton and his brothers George and Lance had escaped much formal schooling although they had just learned to read. Not having been subjected to the experience of school they had retained their natural originality and resilience and were three of the most stimulating people I have ever come across. They had made some money by contriving a way to build concrete reservoirs more quickly and cheaply than anybody else, had travelled from farm to farm in the Union doing this, and had thereafter bought a herd of North Devon cattle. The boys were capable of working harder than anyone else I have known.

The story of Marshways, as Clinton named his farm, is an interesting one. Clinton had applied for one of the new farms from the new administration of the Mandated Territory of South West Africa. George later applied for another. They had the sense to fill in their applications in Afrikaans and to get only well-known Afrikaners to vouch for them. The two brothers were the only English-speaking people to be allotted farms: all the rest were Afrikaners, although thousands of English-speaking South Africans applied.

Clinton and George, accompanied by Lance, made the enormous and epic drive to their new property in their old T Model Ford, with a black man in the back to do the cooking. (Their cattle followed by train.) It took them months, for the road was a fiction. They arrived at the township of Outjo in the north of the Territory, were shown a map, and drove off into the trackless bush-veld (there are trees up there) for fifty miles, picked up a man of the Bergdama or Klip-kaffir race as a guide, and eventually found what they were looking for: a corner beacon—a little pile of stones with an ant-eaten pole sticking up from it. This was the corner of their new farm.

Striking off on a compass-course they walked seven miles through the bush and found another beacon. Then they found the other two. The farm was seven miles by seven miles.

It was quite level country (although there was a low range of hills in the distance) and all bushed—covered over with small twisted trees (most of them *mopani*—a tree with double leaves) and with dried-up grass and little shrubs like Karoo bushes underneath them. No water. No neighbours. No paths or fences. Enormously hot and terribly dry. No butchers' shops or grocers' shops or Tescos or National Insurance Offices and not a bingo hall in sight.

The first thing to do was to find water. They waited until their cattle arrived from the Union, bought a waggon in Outjo, and inspanned ten oxen in front of it. They were then much better equipped—they could haul things about. They managed, very cheaply, to buy a broken-down drill. This was a large machine, looking like a pile-driver, and driven by an old car engine. They dragged this, with oxen, the fifty miles to their farm and started the long, tedious, back-breaking and often heart-breaking, search for water.

A percussion drill, as this was, has a bit, which is a solid steel cylinder about six inches in diameter with sharpened edges at the bottom and a screw thread at the top. This is screwed into the stem, another solid steel cylinder but longer, weighing about a ton. The stem is screwed into the jars. These are two shapes of interlocking steel and they are used for jarring out the bit if it gets stuck in the hole. These are screwed into the socket, which is shaped to take the steel wire rope. The latter goes up over the pulley on top of the jib, down round a walking-beam which is another pulley on a beam which is made to reciprocate by the old car engine, then is wound on a drum.

The drill is worked by simply bumping the bit up and down so that it bashes a hole into the rock. As the hole deepens, so the drum is released, a few inches at a time, to let it go down further. Water is poured down the hole, for the bit must work in water. As there was no water there the Andrews had to *ride* water in drums on their ox-waggon from an existing bore-hole twelve miles away. The round trip took two days. After some drilling the tools are hauled up and a *baler* is lowered down. This is a pipe with a valve at the bottom, which is hauled up, full of water and rock-paste, and the contents dumped. The bit has to be sharpened from time to time. This is done by heating it red-hot in a fire and slamming at it with sledge-hammers, so as to shape it into cutting edges again.

There is far more to drilling than just this. The bit may—nay, often does—start to wander off-course. The driller holds his hand on the rope, some sixth sense alerting him as to what is going on down there. He may throw stones down and drill through them. He may throw cement and sand down, wait for it to set, and drill through that to straighten his course. He has to exercise uncanny instinct.

In assessing the rights and wrongs of white settlement in Africa the part played by the rock drill must not be forgotten. Before its arrival men could only live near the natural water-holes and these were very few. During the rainy season they could wander out, with sheep, goats or cattle, or just hunting and collecting, but their traversing of the open veld was only temporary. When the rains stopped they had to go back to their water-hole again. The white man, with his rock drill, was able to settle permanently country that had never been settled by man before. He could then provide a living for black people too. The pity of it was that he was so mean: he could easily have provided a much better one. But the role of the rock drill should not be forgotten in considering the history of southern Africa.

The Andrews were lucky—they were 'down' after only a month's drilling. The water-table was unusually near the surface —a mere hundred feet. Many a settler went down to a thousand and failed to find water, and this usually broke him. To get a contractor to do it cost a pound a foot which was an awful lot of money in those days, although the government did give some aid.

The Andrews paid one shilling and sixpence per hectare for their land, but this was an interest-free loan and they had thirty years to pay it off in. Afterwards they ring-fenced their farm, which involved putting up twenty-eight miles of strained wire fencing. For this, again, the government paid. The fence was useless because, firstly, all sheep had to be herded by shepherds and the cattle were limited as to the distance they could go every day by their need to get back to the water; and, secondly, the gemsbok, or oryx, simply laid the fence flat whenever they felt like it. (The gemsbok, with its needle-sharp horns, which grow almost straight up from the head, is said to have given rise to the legend of the unicorn, because when seen from the side the two horns merge into one.) A whole herd of these huge and powerful buck would simply charge the fence—the posts would snap and the six strands of high-tensile wire, strained in quarter-mile stretches with a ton and a half of strain on each wire, would simply be laid flat and then spring up afterwards. I've seen a herd of gemsbok do this and a surprising sight it was.

Well, having found water the Andrews had to get it up to the surface. To do this they needed a windmill.

I often think we contemporary eco-freaks are engaged in trying to re-invent the wheel. The steel pumping windmill was the most efficient machine mankind has ever invented—using efficient in every sense of the word.

It would pump water up from a thousand feet or more (the pump itself was down at the bottom of the bore-hole) and it would go on pumping for two years without being looked at (then the oil in its sump needed to be changed). I have seen wind-mills which were known to be forty years old and were still working. It 'feathered' its blades (turned them sideways to the wind) in strong winds or gales and thus never blew down. It feathered itself completely when a device told it that the reservoir it was filling was full, and thus turned itself off.

The Andrews bought such a mill in Outjo, rode it out in sections on their ox-waggon, and erected it. In England all such jobs would be done by an 'expert': in Africa every man had to be his own expert—there were no others.

Then, of course, there was the little matter of somewhere to live. An African can (with help from his neighbours) build his dwelling in a day, and a day is what is commonly allowed by farmers to a new employee to do just that. A cylinder of sticks is driven into the ground, either thatched with grass or plastered with mud, a cone of sticks is constructed on the ground nearby, thatched with grass, and then lifted up and placed on the cylinder and tied to it with strips of bark. You don't have to conduct elaborate experiments by putting suburban middle-class English young ladies and gentlemen in an English wood so that they can 'go back to the Iron Age' to find out what that era was like. The Iron Age is on today, in many parts of Africa, and so is the Old Stone Age, the New Stone Age, and just about every other age. It is as likely as not that life on this planet will come to a halt when the Nuclear Age finally hits the Dark Continent.

The Andrews first lived under a bush, then in African-type huts, then in rondavels, which are a specifically white-man-in-Africa invention: a rondavel is a cylinder of (usually) mud bricks surmounted by a thatched roof and generally differs from the African hut in having a window. Then they moulded bricks, made charcoal, burnt the bricks with the charcoal, burnt limestone to make mortar, and built a substantial farmhouse which they roofed with timber and corrugated iron which they rode from Outjo.

It did not take you long to read the last paragraph. To do all the things described in it would, though—it would take not only time but a lot of very hard work.

It is not to be supposed that the Andrews did all this work by themselves. They were helped by African labour. A 'boy' (which is what white South Africans call a man—if he is black) worked, at that time, in the Outjo district, from sun-up to sundown (always about twelve hours in the tropics) for a month of thirty days, for which he received eight shillings, plus two pounds a day of mealie-meal, half a pound a month of coffee beans, half a pound per week of sugar, a cup of *skaaplek* tobacco once a week, bone-meal and all. It is not to be supposed that these items came cheaply to the farmer. They *all* had to be imported from the 'Union' (the Union of South Africa, a thousand miles away). The Andrews also gave their 'boys' a ration of separated milk (not obligatory); on the other hand they adopted a completely negative attitude to a meat ration—the one thing that the country itself could have provided.

But my recollection of work on Marshways is not of the white men standing by while the 'nigs', as the Andrews brothers almost invariably called their men, worked in the sun. It is of a white man working frantically hard at the head of a small gang of black men, leading them, exhorting them, making them laugh, always doing himself the more difficult, arduous, or even dangerous tasks. The Africans were, after all, unskilled at anything but Iron Age tasks. They were unused to 'work'. Before the white men came Africans knew neither the word nor the thing itself. They could build their home in a day and needed the barest of utensils; in South West Africa they did not even cultivate the soil (nothing would have grown in it anyway), but lived on hunted animals, *veldkos* (food from the veld—small bulbs, corms, berries and other wild products) and perhaps milk from a few goats with the meat of an occasional slain animal. They could be set to digging holes, cutting down trees, moulding bricks: any job like that they would do well so long as a *baas*, as we white men were called, was there to show them how to do it, encourage them and keep them happy. With the wrong sort of treatment they quickly became sullen and unhappy, and then no *sjambok* in the world would have got good work out of them.

Exploited? Of course they were being exploited. Clinton

47

has since those days left Africa for good and gone to live in New Zealand, a free land, for even he—born and bred in Africa could not be happy with the situation there as it existed and exists.

When the building of Clinton's grand house was complete he moved into it and sent for his old mother and father from the Union. Mrs Andrews quickly made a home of it, and a good home too. The Africans continued to live in their *pondokjies*, or little mud huts, and I have no doubt they are living in these to this day. George Andrews put in for, and obtained, a farm of his own, built three rondavels on it, married a lovely girl, and moved in. Lance continued to live with Clinton and built up his own flock of sheep, about which more later.

Meanwhile I have leapt ahead of my narrative, but what I have been describing is roughly what Clinton Andrews described to me as we sat, day after day, in that train.

The dead flat, arid plain gave way to a hilly land covered with bush-veld. This I had been longing to see, for the England that I had left had been a land full of woods and trees. (It is not now—so many of the woods have been bulldozed out to make room for agribusinesses.) So I longed for trees. But when we got to the bush-veld I found it did not give me the lift that the trees of England did at all. These were miserable little trees. The north of Namibia (as indeed is most of tropical Africa) is bush-veld—like an endless orchard of little trees. Depending on the dryness of the climate the trees grow more or less far apart. They are all about the same height. They are mostly evergreen, but have ways of controlling loss of moisture. The *mopani*, for example, has twin leaves which fold up in the dry season like two hands closed in prayer, thus inhibiting transpiration. Much of the north of Namibia is *mopani* veld—just hundreds and hundreds of miles of country sparsely covered with little stunted trees, all the same, with sparse, dried-up smaller vegetation growing between them. Other huge areas are covered with thorn-veld. Here the trees are a variety of thorn trees, better for sheep, actually, as many of the trees shed seed pods during the rainy season which the sheep eagerly eat. Nothing can eat any product of the *mopani* tree.

So our train rumbled its way into bush country; I was disappointed with it. We had a quick look at the capital, Windhoek (it only took a quick look—there was very little there in this little

German town with its tin-roofed cathedral), and, somewhere to
the north, we changed on to a narrow gauge railway.

This was a childhood dream come true. A little puffing-billy
engine hauled three small and archaic-looking passenger carriages
along the tiny track. The engine was fired with wood, and vast
piles of this stood ready for it every so many miles along the track.
A team of 'boys' would be waiting by each one, ready to load the
stuff into the tender at great speed. On each side of the footplate
was a swinging seat. The driver and fireman (white of course—
this profession was protected for whites by the labour laws)
could sit on these seats and swing themselves out into the wind—
without this the heat of the footplate area would have been un-
endurable. I went up on the footplate—at the invitation of the
driver—and swung myself out too. It was grand. When we came
to a gradient the train couldn't make it. We backed down again,
piled on more wood to make more steam—then charged at it.
Failure again. The fireman walked down the train to order everybody out. Most people were out already—whenever the train
stopped we all got out and walked about on the scorching hot
sand. Finally, after a big head of steam had been built up, the
engine made a final charge and up she went. We all clambered
aboard and on we went again.

Outjo is a whitewashed police station with the Union of South
Africa flag flying outside it and consisting of some rows of whitewashed rocks on the sand, two tiny German-owned hotels (a bar
and four bedrooms each), two 'stores'—large rambling shacks
selling everything from boer-meal and hair curlers to lion traps—
half a dozen bungalows, all scattered higgledy-piggledy about the
bush, with burning hot sand and limestone rock in between. Or
at least it was then: now, for aught I know, it may be a shining
metropolis.

After a night in one of the tiny German hotels (Clinton subsequently married the landlord's daughter) Clinton's father arrived
in the Model T Ford. It was a rakish car with a canvas top which
was rolled back so that one sat in the broiling sun. Off we rattled.
The Model T was a great institution: perhaps the most significant
of the fruits of the early technological era. It was simple—it went.
It got you there and it got you back. If a tyre punctured you
mended it. When a tyre wore out you put a 'gaiter' under the worn

place: a piece of tough canvas or buckskin. When all else failed you stuffed the tyre tight full of *mopani* leaves and rode on that. If a spring went (and springs went!) you cut a piece of wood from a tree and lashed that in to take the shock of it. If the engine stopped you took the whole damn thing to pieces there and then in the veld to see what was wrong with it. I have done all these things. There were no AA boxes to run to for help and the nearest mechanic might be hundreds of miles away.

It was forty-odd miles to Marshways. We drove through a gate (cattle grids had not been invented yet) and there was a surburban-looking whitewashed house and several rows of buildings, a steel windmill (of course), a concrete water reservoir; half a mile out into the bush a little village of mud huts and near them the sheep kraals. The latter were round pens made of thorn bushes in which the sheep were confined for each night.

Mrs Andrews (Clinton's mother) was plump and kindly. Mr Andrews was lean and absent-minded. All white South Africans argue, and I had endless arguments as time went on with Mr Andrews. He was a member of a religious sect called the British Israelites. He believed that the British were the Lost Ten Tribes of Israel. This belief stemmed from readings of the Bible, measurings of the Great Pyramid and all sorts of other esoteric studies, performed by people who had more time than sense. Mr Andrews swallowed the lot. After all—we British must be special mustn't we?—we were so much better, in every way, than the Boers. As for the Blacks—well, the Bible tells us that the Sons of Ham were to be hewers of wood and drawers of water and there is nothing more to be said about that. Of course, when arguing with any fundamentalist, you are arguing not against a man but a book. I have tried to argue with Marxists and have found that, having read Marx myself, I know exactly the answer they are going to give to any of my propositions. When arguing with Mr Andrews I was arguing with the Bible.

Chapter Four

━━━━━━━━━━━━━━━━━━━◇━━━━━━━━━━━━━━━━━━━

The Farm in the Desert

Life was fun at Marshways. Other young white people, English-speaking and Afrikaans, used to visit us, and some of them brought guitars and we sang the fine old Boer songs—and silly American new ones—and all used to run out into the veld at night, if it were the dry season, and flop down on the hot ground, with a blanket, to sleep. There was an old pianola in the house (the strange things that pioneers carry with them into the wilderness!) and Clinton's brother Lance used to belt out on it renderings of everything from the Fifth Symphony to the Cuckoo Waltz.

The system of farming in South West Africa at that time was as old as mankind—as old as Man the Herdsman at any rate. The sheep could not be kept in camps, or paddocks, because in that country there are too many large beasts of prey. So they were divided into flocks of from three to four hundred and each flock was in the charge of a shepherd. In the evening the sheep were allowed to drink water at the trough, and then they were driven into the kraals. At Marshways these were eventually made with post and wire fencing; but many farmers still use thorn bushes laid together with their thorns pointing outwards. The thorns are not so much to keep the sheep in, as to keep beasts of prey out.

As the sun rises in the morning each shepherd goes to his own kraal and walks around among his flock to find any lambs that have been born during the night. There is no tupping season: the rams are always left with the ewes, and lambing takes place all the year round.

The sheep were of the karakul breed, kept for the skins of their new-born lambs. Ram-lambs have a short life if their coats are

51

black and glossy. They must be killed the first or second day, before their little curls begin to open out. Ewe lambs, though, are required to replenish the flock. Desert sheep give little milk, so the ewe lambs that are being reared are suckled on mothers which have lost their lambs, as well as by their own mothers. The shepherd catches the foster mother, holds her by her lower jaw, and allows the lamb to suck. If there is much milk left over, the shepherd milks a few bereft ewes into a tin to feed his own children, but this practice has to be performed when the farmer is not looking.

These things attended to, the shepherd opens the door of the kraal, and the sheep run out into the veld. If the farmer is a good farmer he will be there to count them. If a sheep is missing the shepherd is asked the reason. But perhaps there is a sheep too many in old Simon's flock? Paul walks in amongst his brother-shepherd's sheep and suddenly dives down and catches a ewe by the hind-leg and drags her out. It is his own. He cannot count beyond twenty, but he knows by sight every single one of his three hundred and fifty sheep.

The ewes which are leaving small lambs behind in the kraal are torn between two desires. One is to stay with their lambs, and the other is to get out into the veld and fill their bellies with grass or leaves. The latter desire wins (assisted by the shepherd who throws a well-aimed pebble or two), and the flock moves off into the bush.

Naturally the grazing nearest the water-hole and the kraals gets tramped out and eaten up the soonest, so after a month or two of the dry season the flocks have to walk quite far to find enough grass and bush. Towards the end of the dry season they are probably travelling five miles, which means five miles back as well. So sheep and shepherd cover ten miles during the day, and there is little time for grazing when they reach the grazing grounds.

The shepherd's job is simple, and in a pleasant climate it would be delightful. Who would not love to be a shepherd in the Arcadian tradition, spending his days reclining on some grassy verge, watching his 'seelly sheep', playing on a pipe perhaps, and dallying with some Bonibelle? But in South West Africa, existence out-of-doors can be arduous. The sun glares down like a blow-lamp and the air is like the breath of a blast furnace. Tiny little stingless bees hover endlessly just in front of your nose and eyes, and occasionally creep into your ear cavity. They drive you mad. If you sit down on the ground you will probably sit on a thorn, and you will almost certainly be bitten by ants. (Of course you will search first for scorpions.) The sheep do not stay still to graze, the grazing is so sparse that they are always on the move, and the shepherd must keep up with them. Flocks meet in the veld, and the shepherds *gesels* (Afrikaans for 'chat'). They have a skill of forcing their sheep to stay in one place, in a close mob, not grazing, and then the two shepherds sit and discuss their troubles. That is when the sheep sometimes get mixed up; and that is when the farmer sometimes comes riding up on his horse and lashes out with his tongue, or perhaps with a *sjambok*.

As the sun is setting the flocks return from their day's journey, the mothers which left lambs behind that morning running out in front, bleating loudly, anxious to see their little ones.

Alas! Many of them will never see their lambs again. Their throats have been cut, and their skins taken off, to warm the backs of rich ladies in the tea-shops of Kensington. A sorry trade, but in those days the mainstay of the economy of South West Africa.

Except for the heat, which I found more intense than anything I had ever imagined, I enjoyed life at Marshways. There was always plenty to do. We slept out on the porch, and were awakened by the first rays of the sun. Coffee, and then off to count the sheep out of the kraals.

There is a particular pungent smell connected with sheep kraals in hot dry countries, which one can never forget. As the sheep milled about in their dusty kraals, ankle-deep in dry *mis*, as dung is called in that country, they kicked up a dust that blocked one's nostrils. Ah, but the flies! They soon made you want to go back to the house. African flies have a *clinging* quality which is hard to bear.

Now the sheep on Marshways were dying. Every day, three or four would be sick and would not leave the kraals, and during the day one or two of them would lie down and die.

Clinton blamed this on poisonous plants in the veld. I believe now that this was not the cause; it was worm infestation, despite the fact that every month or two we used to give each sheep a dose of one brand of worm medicine or another. But there undoubtedly *were* poisonous plants in the veld, and it was at this particular time of the year, the dry season, when there was little enough to eat anyway, that the sheep were most likely to fall for the poison.

So Clinton decided to trek. He hired a farm called Edwardsvelde which was just fifty-six miles from Marshways, and made preparations to send his sheep there.

Early one morning, the great trek started.

The six big flocks of sheep were counted out of their kraals as usual, and formed up into a rough oblong, where they were held by their shepherds. In the middle of the oblong stood the waggon —pulled by twenty donkeys.

Most people used oxen to draw their waggons, but some farmers, and Clinton was one of them, preferred donkeys. Donkeys are slower and they don't grow into beef; but they have one big advantage. Lions would rather eat donkeys than any other animal (except zebras) and if you have plenty of donkeys running about on your veld the lions will spare your cattle, and in those days donkeys were five bob a head.

Near to the waggon was a small herd of milk cows, and that was our caravan.

Slowly we started to move off through the veld. There was no track to follow, we simply took a course through the bushes. The waggon, with its heavy iron-tyred wheels, just smashed its way through, avoiding the larger trees and crushing down the small ones.

When we came to the fence we merely halted long enough to knock it down. It could be repaired later, perhaps, if anybody thought of it. Then on we went.

Before nightfall we came to the farm of our neighbour, an Afrikaner named Lombard. He permitted us to water our stock at his trough. We went on for a few miles and then halted for the night.

The flocks were formed up in a rough circle, with the waggon and the camp in the middle. All around the outside of the circle fires were built, and the shepherds did not sleep very much. They kept guard for wild animals. Clinton and I took turns to lie in our

blankets by the big fire in the middle, or roam about with a rifle.
It was not what a wild animal would kill that worried us so much
as the chaos that would ensue should the two thousand sheep be
stampeded.

The first night of that trek was the first time in my life that I had
ever slept on the ground, out in the open, under the stars. Later
I came to do this so often that it was the rule, and not the exception, and it felt strange for me to sleep in a bed. Sleeping in
this manner has never lost its delight for me. Africa, during the
dry season, is a fine place to sleep out in, for you can be quite sure
that it will not rain. It is cold, though; in spite of the great heat
of the day we got frosts at night in South West Africa. You built
a big, long fire, and two of you lay down one on each side of it,
each wrapped in one blanket as a rule, we seldom had more, and
if you were wise you ensured that there was a pile of dry wood
within easy reach.

If there were no sheep to worry about, the same procedure
always used to be followed.

You would wake up. It was extremely cold. The fire had burned
low. It was desirable to put some more wood on it. But you knew
that your companion would wake too. Supposing you pretended
to be asleep? Would he not get up and replenish the fire? And of
course he did wake up, and he also pretended to be asleep, and
had the very same thoughts that you were having. The thing
would turn into a contest to see who could hold out the longer.

At the stroke of dawn one awakes, and shouts for the 'boys'.
Fires are kicked into life, coffee is made, chops are cooked by
being thrown on to the embers. Then breakfast, and off into the
heat of the day.

It took us four days to cover the fifty-six miles, for sheep cannot
be rushed. We were not attacked by any wild animals.

Edwardsvelde!

As we drew up to the little whitewashed bungalow that stood
on the hot sandy ground at the foot of a rocky hill, the first thing
we noticed was a curious erection: a tiny wire fence surrounding
a wooden cross. The cross had written on it, in German: 'Here lie
the brothers Müller'.

We discovered that the brothers Müller occupied Edwardsvelde during the German time, and they both got blackwater

fever. They were deserted by their servants and as they could get no medical help they started to die. One died first, and his brother dragged him as far from the house as he had strength for (which wasn't very far) and buried him. The living brother then crawled back and died himself. Months later he was discovered and buried next to his brother. The brothers Müller were to be my nearest neighbours for a long time.

We got to work and repaired the kraals, the Africans built huts for themselves, Clinton and I made the farmhouse habitable, and we settled down to farm. Clinton stayed for a month or two, to make sure that I knew the ropes. After this I was to look after the farm by myself while Clinton returned to Marshways to get on with some work he was doing there. He took the waggon, but left me a donkeymobile.

There was one thing that Edwardsvelde did for me, and that was to teach me to be alone. The dozen Africans that I had on the farm spoke only their own language and a smattering of Afrikaans, and my own Afrikaans had never amounted to more than a smattering. Also, being shepherd, they were in the veld all day and I only saw them early in the morning and at night. I had a 'boy' to cook for me and keep the house clean, but he was an Ovambo, and spoke no language but his own. His duties were not arduous, for he did not have to practise any very high cuisine. My food consisted of the following: mealie-meal porridge and milk for breakfast, and coffee; mealie-meal porridge (made very stiff) for lunch, and perhaps milk, or sometimes as a treat, goat's meat; mealie-meal porridge (very stiff) for supper, with either goat's meat or milk. Sometimes, as a very special treat, there would be beans. My larder contained: four tons of mealie-meal, a quarter of a ton of sugar, a sack of coffee beans, a sack of split peas (for making beer) and two sacks of *skaaplek* tobacco. If there was anything else I cannot think of it. I also had a considerable quantity of paraffin oil.

Later, during my life in Africa, I became very skilful at shooting buck. If there was a buck in the country I would find him, and if I was short of meat he would end up in the pot. Edwardsvelde was stiff with buck. The noble gemsbok, the most common animal in South West Africa, was there in herds. Also kudu, and zebra, and probably springbok, although I never saw any.

But I could not shoot one. I ranged the veld, with my little seven-millimetre Mauser, and often saw them but never got one. I was too excited. I wanted success too badly. I had been in South West Africa about a year, before I shot one quite by chance. After that my luck altered. Since I was not so desperately keen, I became successful. Later, in central Africa, I was to shoot a buck a day for month after month (in order to supply my carriers with meat) and the thing became simply another chore. But at first at Edwardsvelde if I wanted meat my only recourse was to slaughter a goat.

So I sat alone. I roamed the veld alone.

The house, a little three-roomed bungalow with a corrugated-iron roof, stood by a dry river near the feet of a rugged range of hills. The hills were bush-covered and brown, like the plain. The hills rose abruptly from the flat plain, as most African hills do. The nearest building to my house was fifteen miles away, and it was occupied by a German named Raeder, who had once been an apothecary in New York. Mine was the last habitation before one came to the Kaokoveld, a huge uninhabited stretch of country in which white men were not allowed. I was on the ultimate frontier of civilization. Even though I was occupying Edwardsvelde house, it never really seemed to me to be lived in. It had been given over for years to loneliness, white ants, and the brilliantly coloured lizards, huge chaps with green bodies and red heads, which basked in the roasting sun on the whitewashed walls. And the ghosts of the brothers Müller.

I used to climb the tall hill not far away, and look back over the plain. I could see for a hundred miles in the perfectly clear air over the level plain (one could see the curvature of the earth over it). The plain was entirely covered with the little trees. The otherwise perfect flatness was broken here and there by hills and kopjes. If I climbed to the top of the hill and looked over the other side of it I saw a wild, fantastic ocean. The waves were thousands upon thousands of little hills, all about the same height, all peppered over perfectly evenly with little trees, all brown, all steep, all rocky, all separated by rock-strewn gullies. They tumbled away to the horizon and beyond. Sometimes I would see a herd of zebra standing half-way up a hillside looking intently at me, so well camouflaged that they almost got lost in the background.

One of them would snort and they would scramble away. Near the top of the hillside they would pause for a moment to stare at me again, then turn and clatter out of sight.

I'm not sure how long I stayed at Edwardsvelde—I imagine off and on a couple of years. I know I once went six months without seeing another white man, and I couldn't speak a word of any language that my shepherds could speak. What little communication we had was in our few mutual words of 'Dutch'.

And beyond getting up at sunrise every morning and counting the sheep out of their kraals, I had virtually nothing to do.

Not for me to make improvements to the place, when it did not belong to Clinton anyway, and I had no tools and no material. Anyway—as far as I was concerned—it was perfect as it was. I had a bed, there was a table and two chairs. What on earth more do you want? I slept out of doors. I had a cook 'boy' who fed me on the same sort of food as he fed himself.

I forget also how long I stayed at Keerweder, a post on Clinton's Marshways farm, and very similar to Edwardsvelde—just a shack in the wilderness, where I lived alone, physically as well as spiritually, and where for the first time I found time to think. That is why I say that I look back at Edwardsvelde as my university.

Time to think. Time to read. I sent home for books, and I had found, miraculously, an old box full of books in Clinton's shed— I think they had been his grandfather's. There were the works of Byron, the complete works of Shakespeare, several other classical authors, all in ponderous nineteenth-century volumes and much attacked by termites or white ants, so that often a piece was missing from every page.

For the first time I was able to read all of Shakespeare (who had escaped the ants). I began to make a serious attack on Eng. Lit., one book leading to another. I discovered, with delight, the eighteenth-century novelists. I discovered living writers, people like Clive Bell, Aldous Huxley. For the first time I really began to read seriously, trying to discover what other people had thought, other views of life.

It was as if I had been hustled around all my life, with never a pause to consider, but now for the first time I could sit back, and draw breath, and sum the whole thing up.

From that distance, and that isolation, I could contemplate the civilized world. For the first time I was able to stand back and take a good look at things, see the wood for the trees. I imagine that it is not given to many people who are involved with civilization to do just this.

I thought of my family, my home town, my class, the society I had come from, the schools I had suffered at, the business I had nearly gone into, the farms I had worked on, and I churned all these things over and over in my mind, and weighed them up, and considered what other people whose books I read would have had to say about them, and I thought about life, and the universe, and everything that there was to think about. And, after a year or two had gone by and I was still in the backveld, I began to form some sort of philosophy of life. Also, I began to develop some of the mental ills of the solitary: I began to dread the society of anybody at all. I felt lonely—and yet afraid to go back to the world and mix with people.

I began to feel very strongly that the only good life was a simple one. I reduced the tackle and paraphernalia needed for living to its very minimum. I thought that a man needed some sort of bed, a chair and a table, books, a pen and ink, one knife, one fork, one spoon, one plate, one saucepan and a frying-pan, an enamelled mug, some sort of roof to keep the rain off him, food, water—and practically nothing else. An odd thing or two extra perhaps—a basin to wash in, a bucket, two pairs of khaki trousers, two shirts. Then the wherewithal to get himself food—a rifle, a horse and saddle and bridle, some sort of job or means of subsistence such as a flock of sheep. But nothing beyond this. No complications. I thought of my family's becushioned existence in England and I felt sure that our lives had been bedevilled by belongings. More and more belongings to make you comfortable I believed only made you uncomfortable. Then you had to have servants to keep them all in order, and you had to lie and cheat at some swindling city job to make the money to pay for the things and to pay the servants. I resolved to keep my possessions down to the utter minimum.

I decided to be poor. I remembered all the rich people at home. All those people had been quite obviously unhappy. The rich men were flabby and unhealthy and dissatisfied, they were all unfaithful to their wives, and the women all had that sour discontented look, those pinched-up greedy mouths, those mean eyes, that rich women almost invariably have. You feel when you look at them that they are trying to say all the time: 'Why don't you all do more for me—don't you know I'm rich?—why don't you run around faster, and give me more attention, and make me even more comfortable? I'm not getting all my just dues considering that I've married such a rich man. I'm being cheated by life—short-changed. Help! Give me my money's worth!' However unhappy the poor people in England might have been, this I was sure about: the rich were miserably unhappy. Their lives were futile and a bore. At such a distance I was able to look back and consider England.

It was not until years afterwards that I read the works of Tolstoy, or Thoreau, or Mahatma Gandhi, and discovered that other people had had the same ideas about these things. I thought I had discovered this philosophy of keeping life simple myself.

Then I thought about work, and decided as far as possible to do without it. I didn't like it. I revolted against it. For I wanted my time for thinking and reading. I thought of the work that people have to do in England, and I believed that most of it was arduous and boring in the extreme. I believed that England was a nation of clock-watchers. Nobody had time to think. I have altered my views on work completely since those days: I have found that work can be, and should be, the greatest fun of all, excepting perhaps sex. But in those days I had a revulsion against the whole idea of work. I solved this by thinking: if people are content to live simply and with hardly any belongings there will not be much need to work. Also if everybody does a little work nobody will have to do too much. All we need is the bare minimum of food, shelter and clothing, and everybody to do their share of the necessary work and there won't be very much work to do. I realize now I anticipated the hippies by thirty years.

But what multiple creatures we all are! While I was in other moods other ideas occurred to me. When I considered society I thought—abolish wealth, abolish unnecessary belongings, abolish unnecessary work. But when I considered myself I was quite happy to think—what fun it would be to work hard at something and make a fortune! Or build up a complicated and elaborate farm in the desert! Or something like that. True—the fortune would be spent in helping the needy in some way or other, and the farm in the desert would be a colony of happy Africans learning to be civilized (with me, of course, as the boss). Then I would dream of adventure. All sorts. Whaling in the Antarctic. Elephant-hunting in the Congo. Anything at all. I believe that my thinking could be fairly mature in those days—but it could also drop right back to the *Boy's Own Paper* level. It still can.

I realized at about this time how completely uneducated I was. I had managed to get through no less than eight schools and an agricultural college without learning anything at all. Further, I realized that I wanted to be educated. Or at least cultured. I began to see the fun of knowing about things, particularly the things which are intrinsically fun like the arts. It was difficult to see how I could cultivate the arts other than literature living in a desert; but I decided to try. One day I would go home to England, with just enough money to live on in my newly-discovered simplicity, and really cultivate the arts. Go to plays, to concerts, to opera, to picture galleries, have a gramophone and a wireless, look at buildings; in fact become a real culture-vulture. Here I am back in Britain and have been here for thirty years, and the only place I ever go to is the pub: I could do the other things if I wanted to, so I don't want to.

I did not see any discrepancy between my culture-hunting and my enthusiasm for the simple life. Culture seemed to me to be a thing that you could have and still be poor and without many possessions. But I think that I was a little confused as to what culture was. It did not occur to me to think that an Essex farm worker who had never heard of Beethoven, or a Punjabi ryot who can neither read nor write, can be highly cultured while an erudite man might be a barbarian. I was to learn these things later. Meanwhile I sent home for books and stuffed my head with facts about music, architecture, painting, drama. Culture in a vacuum. Completely meaningless of course, but it gave me the illusion that I was educating myself.

The coming of the rains in a very dry country is orgiastic. The dry season goes on and on, with frightful monotony, the sheep get thin and some die, the cows go dry, no tiny wisp of hay-like grass is left on the mountains; the ground of the plains, between the little bushes or the scrubby trees, is as hard as iron and hot as a furnace. Dogs, on the trek, dash from the shade of one tree to the shade of another and flop down in it panting, unable to stand the hot ground under their pads. The nerves of men become strung up like high-tensile wire—tempers become frayed, you hate your companions, yourself, the world.

Eventually clouds begin to blow in from the west. Small ones at first—then, day by day, larger—then grey and black ones—then huge rain clouds that block out the sky. But no rain. Unbearable heat, unbearable tension, unbearable dryness—and the sight of the rain clouds only seems to make it worse. The rumble of thunder is often heard.

Then, one day (if you are lucky, there are some 'rainy seasons' that bring no rain at all!), you see the south-western horizon black with a big-bellied cloud. This comes up towards you—often *against the wind*. Why like this I do not know. Below the cloud you eventually see a sheet of blackness—rain! A solid curtain of rain. It comes towards you, apparently speeding up as it comes. A cool wind blows. Flashes of lightning play under the black belly of the cloud. The whole experience is frightening and exciting beyond words.

The black curtain comes rushing towards you—thunder crashes —lightning flashes—and suddenly you are almost flung to the ground by the sheer weight of water that is falling from the sky. It seems *solid*. No shower bath on earth is anything like it. You rush about and shout and people often fling their clothes off, for fun.

The hard ground cannot absorb the water and is soon inches deep in it. Dry twigs, ants, insects, debris of all sorts, swirl past on the flood. The plain is one sheet of brown running water. The tension is broken—the rains have come! In a fortnight the whole country is green with luscious new grass.

Chapter Five

++++++++++++++++++++++++++++++◇++++++++++++++++++++++++++

The Death of a Lion

Among my merry men at Edwardsvelde was a man—an old man
—we called the 'Zambezi Boy', although his official name,
among us Europeans, was Paul. The non-white races of South
West Africa included those Stone Age people the Bushmen; the
Hottentots who belong to a race which is surrounded by complete
mystery (theories have been advanced that they are of Asian
origin—certainly they look very Chinese and are quite yellow in
colour); the Berg Damara or Bergdama or Klip-kaffirs, a black
race which had been enslaved for so long by the Hottentots and
the Hereros that they have lost any language they might once
have had and speak Xoisan, the language shared by the Hottentots
and Bushmen and which is all, or nearly all, clicks; the Hereros,
who once were the ruling race until defeated and completely
broken by the Orlams, whose descendants we met at Rehoboth;
and the Ovambos, a race of very black Bantu people who lived
right up in the north, on the Angolan border, in a much greener
and more fertile land than the near-desert we lived in. The
Ovambos were just beginning to wander south to find employment with the white man.

But old Paul, the 'Zambezi Boy', was quite different from any
of these. We had no idea from what tribe or country he came,
except that he would say something about 'the Zambezi'. He
looked different from the other shepherds because for one thing
he had much longer hair. The local Hereros and Bergdamas had
short crinkly curls, but Paul's hair stood up in a frizzy mop like
a fuzzywuzzy's.

Also Paul never wore any covering on the upper part of his

body. The local people would never appear half-naked, they would always put on the tattered remains of a white man's shirt; but Paul just wore a pair of ragged shorts.

Another thing—he was mad.

He was as mad as a hatter. He looked at you with wide-open, staring eyes.

His wife, whom we named Oud Maria, was quite charming. She was thin and she pulled a filthy old piece of rag about her shrivelled breasts and she wore a smoke-blackened cotton-print skirt about her legs. You could not see what colour the cloth had originally been. When she came once a week with the other women to collect the rations of mealie-meal she squatted on the ground and held out a claw of a hand and whined for sugar. If I refused her this she picked up dust and threw it over her head and whined again. When I eventually gave her the sugar (as I always did, of course) she went off and made beer with it and both she and Paul got frightfully drunk and Paul beat her and she screamed and I would have to get up in the middle of the night and go out to the kaffir-compound and tell the pair of them to shut up. But when I looked into Oud Maria's eyes I saw wisdom there, the wisdom that life teaches to some old women the world over, and I saw humour too, and even when she was begging her eyes were laughing at me. She soon found she could twist me round her little finger, but when Clinton was on the farm he used to pretend to be angry with her. 'You naughty old woman!' he used to shout, in Afrikaans, which in any case she did not understand. Nobody knew how she and Paul had ever managed to get across all that desert into South West Africa, nor if they would ever try to get back again. But Paul turned out to be the best shepherd on the farm.

One day he startled me out of my life by coming back to the farm and calling through the window, with an even wilder look than usual in his mad eyes. I went to the window and he immediately started to shower pebbles into the room. Both his hands held pebbles, which he flung in, and he spat pebbles out of his mouth, and then he began to search in old bags and rags around his body for more pebbles. I waited until he had exhausted his supply of pebbles and then asked him if anything was the matter. He explained to me that the pebbles represented the number of his sheep which had turned toes up in the veld and died. I suspected a disease called *gylsiekte* caused by prussic-acid poisoning due to eating withered vegetation. I snatched up some sulphur, which is the remedy for this, and followed Paul off into the veld as fast as we could run. I found that there were four sheep lying down and several others slightly sick. We dosed them with the sulphur and they all recovered. I suppose the large number of pebbles was Paul's way of expressing the urgency of the situation; or maybe he thought that by the time that he got back to the house and back there would indeed be that many dead sheep.

After a few months a series of disasters hit us at Edwardsvelde. First of all we all got 'flu, a particularly virulent kind. The boss-boy got it first and died, and we had a grand funeral with the slaughter of a beautiful white ox which had belonged to the dead man, and a procession and plenty of beer made from sugar and split peas, and singing and dancing. It cheered us all up no end. It cheered Paul and Maria up so much that they were both drunk for two days, but somehow, between them, they always managed to get their sheep out and bring them back again. That was the very serious problem set by the 'flu. The sheep *had* to go to the veld every day. I had little girls of ten taking them out. No sooner had the 'flu got better than another plague of Egypt smote us. A veld fire broke out. As many of us as could get in the donkeymobile rattled off to where we could see the clouds of black smoke, while the rest trailed along behind on foot. It is not so bad as it looks actually, but until the flames are out there can be no respite: a minute's slackness is enough to let the fire-devil escape somewhere and in a few moments spread over a wide front again. We were all a bit wobbly still from 'flu and only one thing kept us going and that was the antics of Paul. Paul danced about like a maniac, waving the old sack he had for beating the flames. His glistening naked back and fuzzy head seemed to be everywhere. He hollered and screamed and cut capers and went wu-wu-wu-wu-wu and put such life into us that we just had to keep going, weak though most of us were from 'flu. Oud Maria worked too and she fairly set the pace. You could not very well flake out when you saw an old crone like that still going strong. After a day and a half we put the fire out and by that time we had forgotten all about 'flu.

The very next day another disaster occurred—perhaps the worst thing that can happen to a farm in the desert. The windmill broke down. The wheel was spinning furiously, but no water was coming out of the spout.

I realized that the connecting-rod which worked the pump had become unscrewed, far down in the seven-hundred-foot bore-hole from which our water came.

The connecting-rod was in lengths which screwed together, and hundreds of feet underground two of these lengths had become unscrewed. Now it seemed to me that if we could lift the top lot of rods—weighing a ton or so I suppose—and drop them again, and keep on doing this for a long enough time, there was a chance that in the end we might drop them so that the two unscrewed ends should come together. Then, by dint of turning the top rods in a clockwise direction with the chain-tongs, we could screw them home again. So I rigged up a block-tackle on the upper lot of rods and we started lifting them—and dropping them—and lifting them—and dropping them.

We kept this up for three days.

There was enough water in the tank for two days. After the second day I wanted to quit, and start the sheep off walking to the next farm—fifteen miles away. But Paul would not let me. He must have had some sixth sense or something, because he just would not let us stop working that tackle. He would become quite vehement, frantic even. So we just went on lifting—and dropping. Sometimes we could feel that the top lot of rods had lodged on the bottom lot and would try to screw them home, but alas, they were only half-lodged and they would fall off again.

On the third day it happened.

The two rods came well and truly together and a few turns with the chain-tongs and the windmill was working.

That night I was woken up with some yarn that murder, rapine and mayhem were taking place. I went out to find that Paul had bashed Oud Maria over the head, chucked her in their hut and set fire to it.

We managed to get Maria out; she was unconscious and seemed to be in a bad way. Paul had run away into the veld.

Next morning Paul was at his sheep kraal as usual but I ordered him back to the farm because I intended to get the police. Where

I thought I was going to get them from I hardly know because the nearest policeman was fifty miles away and I had no means of sending for him. Paul was very contrite and he sorrowfully did as I told him. But just as I was re-entering the door of the house a tornado hit me! Oud Maria had come to! Who was looking after her Paul's sheep? Paul who had never lost so much as a lamb, even. What right had I to talk of police? I was interfering in the sacred contract of matrimony. All this of course in the outlandish Zambezi language which nobody understood—but I understood it. I always did understand Oud Maria. She waved her arms and shouted and wept, and threw dust on her head, and at last I told Paul for heaven's sake to take his old woman away and get back to his sheep. It was all too much for me.

Clinton visited me soon after this to see how things were getting on. 'I suppose you find things a bit quiet here,' he said, as we sat on the back stoep, gazing over at the brothers Müller.

Across the level Namib the Brandberg rises sheer, mountain of mystery, sheer and high and blue and silver. Brandberg, Fire Mountain, she was seen from far away at sea by Portuguese navigators as five hundred years ago they crept down the coast of Africa trying to find an end to it.

I first saw her on an abortive lion hunt. People have been to the Brandberg, and partially explored her. The great Abbé Breuille has made copies of rock-paintings there including the White Lady of the Brandberg, which is part of the mystery of the place. Nobody knows how this painting of a white lady in European clothes came to be painted on this remote and inaccessible rock in the middle of a desert. I could have gone there, one time or another, but I am glad I never did. To approach such a mystery is to destroy it. Mystery recedes as you approach, for mystery is a mirage.

We went on the abortive lion hunt with a buck-waggon.

The South African buck-waggon is eighteen feet long, it will carry eight tons, the handle of the whip that drives the oxen is eighteen feet long, the whip-thong is eighteen feet, the *voorslag* or lash at the end of it is eighteen inches, and often there are eighteen oxen in the span. Sometimes more.

The oxen come plodding up from the water-trough, their jowls dripping. They are chased by a young African boy, who shouts at them in Dutch and whacks them with a stick, an Ariel among a herd of Calibans. The oxen know their places in the span. Each one goes to its yoke, which lies with the others in a long straggling line on the ground out in front of the waggon. The little boy and a grown-up African hoist the heavy wooden yokes one by one on to the necks of the oxen, a yoke to two beasts, with the trek-chain, its thick links polished bright with use, hanging from yoke to yoke down the middle of the span. Piercing each yoke are four *yukskeie*—wooden yoke-pins. They go one each side of each oxen's neck. Beneath the soft and silky dewlaps are fastened raw-hide thongs called *nekrieme*. The two leading oxen are fine beasts chosen for their beauty, with great, spreading horns. The pole oxen—the rear couple—are strong, for they have to support the weight of the *disselboom*, or single shaft of the waggon, on their yoke.

After they are inspanned the oxen do not stand in their places in an orderly fashion. Some turn and half face the wrong way, others lie down, and some engage in friendly jousting with their yoke-mates.

But when the Afrikaner who owns the oxen comes over from the night's bivouac, wiping the remains of his last cup of coffee from his big drooping moustache, and takes the great whip and makes it crack like a gunshot, the oxen straighten themselves out, and lean into the yokes, so that the trek-chain comes up off the ground and straightens like a bar. The long waggon comes to life and lurches forward.

The driver walks along about halfway up the span, and he seems to sense if one of the oxen is slacking behind him, for he will crack the offender on the rump with the whip without even turning his head to look. He can crack the *voorslag* an inch from an ear with a noise like a loud gun, and flick a fly from one of the leaders without touching the ox. He can draw blood if he wants to, he could flay an ox alive if he wanted to, or he can smack a beast with a good loud smack without really hurting him.

All goes well until the waggon lurches down the steep bank of a dry river: the huge, wooden, iron-tyred wheels cut softly through the sand, and the sweating, breathing oxen clamber in a ragged line up the steep bank the other side. The front wheels encounter the bank, begin to lift up it, stay. The waggon will go no further. The oxen heave and strain—some heave their necks into the yoke while others drop back. They feel defeated. They will not pull together.

The Dutchman calms the oxen, then walks up and down the span, calling each ox by name. '*Kom nou jou hoere! Blesbok! Rooiman! Kaffir! Bosman! Trek nou jou blikskottel! Trek nou!*'

At the sound of his voice the frightened cattle straighten themselves out, and lean into the yokes preparatory to taking the strain.

Swinging the great whip rhythmically from side to side over their backs, the driver suddenly cracks it in the air with a tremendous report. The oxen strain into the yokes as one beast, heads right down, legs leaning sharply forward, the whole animal thin and hunched and misshapen with the tremendous effort that it is making: muscles standing up under sweating hides like sharp ridges. The waggon moves forwards and upwards but hesitates. The driver stands in the middle of the span, his besweated hat on the back of his head, his brown, unshaven, moustachioed face in a passion; and he swings the great whip. At the limit of each stroke the *voorslag* slices down on to the hide of one of the oxen, always on one that is not pulling with quite the desperation of its neighbour. Driven, terrified, maddened, the red-eyed cattle make one final frantic effort and the iron-tyred wheels lurch up the steep bank on to the level ground beyond!

'*Hou nou!*' shouts the driver. '*Hou nou! Hou nou!*' and he whistles to make them stand. They must breathe and calm themselves, before going on.

In ox-waggons the *voortrekkers* travelled northward from the Cape, and spread over the empty lands. Sometimes when they crossed over the high mountain passes they were forced to dismantle their waggons, and drag them piece by piece on improvized sledges and assemble them again the other side. If a waggon broke, the men would mend it, cutting suitable pieces of wood out of the veld where they could find them. The women and children and newborn babies rode on the waggons. The young sons rode

out in front on horses, to spy the land, and to shoot fresh meat.
Within living memory a great trek moved across the Kalahari
Desert from the Transvaal in an attempt to reach Angola, which
was under the Portuguese flag and therefore free from the British.
The first wave of the trek succeeded: the second wave came across
water-holes drunk dry by the cattle of the first wave. And all the
people, and all the cattle, left their bones to whiten under the sun.

We travelled towards the Brandberg, with a waggon, to hunt
lions. We heard lions, and smelt lions, but we failed to see any
lions. We were inexperienced, the others smoked and made too
much noise.

The time came though when I did see a lion.

I was staying on Clinton's home farm of Marshways at the time,
and, ironically enough, I was staying there to look after the farm
while Clinton and his brother Lance went away on a lion hunt.
They got no lions . . . .

There was a tame Bushman on Clinton's farm, named Joseph.

The Bushmen, the Stone Age people who roam the desert
living off the wild food that they can pick up, will seldom work
for the white man, but Joseph had been caught as a child by some
Germans and brought up as a servant. He spoke both German
and Afrikaans. He was a good shepherd, and a good poacher.

One day Joseph came back from the veld where he had been
with his sheep and asked to see me. He had left his flock un-
attended, but had sent his wife for it.

Five donkeys had been killed, he said. Three lions had done it,
the night before, a lion and two lionesses. One of the lionesses
was young, but fully-grown; the lion was old and had a bad cut
on the pad of one of his claws. Joseph had seen the vultures, had
gone to investigate, and had built up the story from spoor, or
tracks on the ground.

We made our plans. I gave Joseph my twelve-bore shot-gun,
and took my little seven-millimetre Mauser rifle. We took a
blanket each, a few sticks of *biltong* and a bottle of water, and off
we went into the veld.

After we had gone about a mile, Joseph stopped at a large *wag
n' bietjie* bush. *Wag n' bietjie* means 'wait a bit', and if you touch
one of these bushes you obey this injunction, for it is covered with
little hooked thorns, like tiny fish-hooks. Gingerly Joseph

stretched his arm into the heart of the bush and drew out a spear. 'Natives' were not allowed to own spears in any country administered by the Union of South Africa.

Off we went again, thus further armed, and after another mile or two of hot walking we came across the first kill. The donkey had been disembowelled, and the carcasse had been dragged several yards by the lions. You could see from the spoor how a lion had leapt on the donkey while the latter was at full gallop and brought it down after a yard or two. The vultures had been at work, and bloated birds sat up in the trees round about, looking down at us balefully. Why do carrion birds and animals look so hideous? Is there some law of nature that creatures which live hideously should look hideous?

We found all five of the donkeys. The lions had killed for love of destruction, because they had only eaten small parts of the carcasses. We stopped at the last donkey that we came across.

Now I was completely inexperienced at this sort of work, and I placed my trust entirely with Joseph. I had always read and heard that on these occasions people make skerms (small fortresses of rocks or thorn bushes) or that they spend the night up trees.

Joseph had no such ideas. He just didn't seem to know the first of the traditions of lion-hunting. He walked to a bush some forty yards away from the dead donkey and sat down. 'We'll wait here, Baas,' he said.

It was by then dusk. I sat down beside Joseph, on the hard, hot ground. Behind us was the little bush. In front of us was the dead donkey. We both ate some *biltong* and had a pull at the water flask.

It got dark rapidly, as it does in the tropics (that part of South West Africa is north of Capricorn), and with the dark came the cold. We pulled out meagre blankets over our shoulders.

We arranged to take turns to watch. I took the first turn, and squatted with my rifle, loaded and cocked, over my knees, looking out into the dark towards the dead donkey. Joseph lay wrapped up like a cocoon behind me. I did not feel frightened, simply because I did not expect to see any lions. As I have related, I had been on one abortive lion hunt. I had come to look upon myself as born to be unlucky as far as hunting lions was concerned. But I turned over in my mind all the things that *could* happen! It was a moonless night and quite dark, except for the faintest starlight.

Not that the stars themselves were not bright enough: they were beautiful. We had no torch. I could not see the dead donkey, but I could imagine where it was. If a lion stood over it I might just see a lightish shape, but to shoot at such a shape, with unlit sights, would be madness. Once or twice I questioned the wisdom of our being there, but when I turned my head and looked at Joseph's sleeping form, I felt more confident. He seemed to have complete faith in me. He knew more about lions than I did.

When I could no longer keep awake I woke him, and lay and shivered under my thin blanket, and dreamed bad dreams. After some time he roused me again for my watch, and I squatted as before. I could tell by the progress of the Plough that it was after midnight.

It is good for a man to watch at night, in the open. At sea, or ashore, in peace or in war, it is good. It gives him the chance to be alone, and puts him in the mood to think, and to think about the right things. Part of the unhealth of our society is that too few of us have to spend the night now and again watching under the stars.

I heard a noise. It was the hunting grunt of a lion: a short cough, repeated, in the distance but moving. Whether the lions do it to signal to each other, or to terrify their prey, I do not know. It terrifies me. It is a terrible sound.

Long afterwards I heard a noise coming closer to me. It was some donkeys: I heard one snort now and again, and I could hear their hoofs on the rough stones. They were cantering, then stopping; cantering, then stopping. They passed by behind me, and not far off.

Then I heard another sound, a soft padding. I knew it was a lion.

I strained towards the sound, sitting as I was with my blanket over my shoulder and my rifle actually aimed in the direction of the sound. The sound approached, and I suddenly saw the lion, coming straight towards me! Among the first visual things that I noticed were its two ears, little triangles against the starry sky, making its head look like the head of a toy lion.

The lion trotted straight up to me, completely ignoring the dead donkey, and came to a halt three yards away. Exactly three yards—the distance was measured afterwards.

I had heard nothing from Joseph, and had not had time to wake him. As I thought, I was alone with the lion.

The lion looked at me.

I looked at the lion.

I realized that I had only to squeeze the trigger to have the wounded lion on top of me. The chances of killing it instantaneously in the darkness were remote. On the other hand, supposing I abstained from firing? What would the lion do? It wouldn't just go away, and in any case I did not wish that it should.

After a long time I squeezed the trigger.

The first time you fire a rifle at night you are not prepared for the flash from the muzzle. For several moments after the shot you are blinded by it. I worked my bolt, and tried to see what was happening with my temporarily dazzled eyes. I saw a movement; my finger leapt to the trigger, but stayed. It was not the lion! It was Joseph. He had whipped round from behind me and was holding the muzzle of my shot-gun an inch from the lion's head. The lion was stone dead. My bullet had made a tiny hole between its eyes.

Joseph jumped around and clapped his hands. 'A man need fear nothing if he has a good heart!' he said. It then dawned on me that I had been extremely rash in trusting so implicitly Joseph's judgement about lion-hunting: he was one of those men who glory in taking risks. He told me that he had been awake when the lion had trotted up, had had the shot-gun aimed, and if I had not fired when I did he would have shot at the lion with the shot-gun in spite of the fact that he realized that even at that range the shot-gun might not have been effective. 'But I have my spear!' he said. 'That's my Bushman gun.'

We lit a fire immediately, for we were both numb with cold. By the light of the fire Joseph skinned the lion, there and then. It was a young but fully grown female.

We slung the lion-skin over Joseph's spear—and it was extremely heavy. Soft, thick, warm and heavy. We hung our firearms from our shoulders and started walking. We intended to get to a post of Clinton's, the mud-brick hut that he had built himself when he first arrived on the farm. We were so chilled that we longed for some shelter. We walked about a mile, the spear

73

cutting into our shoulders, then both came to a halt. We could hear a horrible noise! A rhythmical groaning, like a soul in torment. We dropped the skin and snatched our guns off their slings.

We were both frightened. Suddenly Joseph laughed. It was the steel windmill at the post, which needed greasing.

We had arrived at the hut. We built a fire on the floor and went to sleep, in comfort, beside it.

In the morning we ate the rest of our *biltong* and drank some water, and called some old women who lived at the post. We told them to send a child to take word to Mr Andrews about the lion. Then we returned to the dead donkey, and Joseph picked up the spoor. We intended to follow the two survivors of the pride.

To follow a spoor with a Bushman is an almost unbelievable experience.

The ground round about there was very stony: such soil as there was was hard and shallow, and for large stretches there was practically no soil at all, just naked limestone rock, with scrub and bushes growing in pockets of earth or fissures.

Joseph simply walked at full speed, his eyes on the ground.

Several times I stopped him and asked him if he was sure that we were still on the spoor. He would point to a stone which was slightly discoloured, something had inverted it. Or a leaf which had been pressed to the ground, or to some sign that was to me completely invisible. Then, after a time, he would point to a very palpable fresh footprint. And on we went, the hot sweat stinging my eyes and fogging up my glasses and dripping off the end of my nose.

When we got to a really bare patch of rock, Joseph would leave the spoor altogether. He would walk round the circumference of the rocky patch, secure in the knowledge that he must eventually hit the spoor again the other side of it. At no time was he checked for an instant, and at no time did he have to go slower than at a fast walk.

Many Africans are good trackers, but none that I have ever met are in the same class as the real Bushmen. I believe that the latter must have some sense that other humans have lost. I cannot believe that it is all eyesight.

After a few miles Joseph stopped. It had become obvious to him that the lions had decided not to stay around. They were making for the hills to the north of us, beyond which lay the Etosha Pan, the lion paradise of South West Africa. They were passage-making. We gave it up and returned to the farm, to find Mrs Andrews busy boiling down the fat of the dead lion to make soap.

Joseph took me poaching once. He told me to meet him in the veld and not to bring a rifle. It was a clandestine meeting, for he should have been herding his sheep. Again he thrust his arm into the *wag n' bietjie* bush, and this time he had three long, lean kaffir-dogs at his heels. They belonged to the other people in the compound, but followed Joseph because he offered them better sport.

He led me quickly out into the veld. After a long time we sighted a herd of twenty gemsbok—and the dogs were off! A kudu (the corkscrew-horned) will flee from dogs, leaping with a soaring movement over any bushes or fences which may be in the way. The gemsbok will not run. He cannot leap. He is not afraid of dogs. Even the packs of African hunting dogs, the most voracious wild animals of the veld, are chary about tackling gemsbok.

The gemsbok backs himself into a thorn bush and stands at bay. He sweeps the air in front of him with his rapier-like horns. If a dog is too bold it may find itself flying through the air with its belly ripped open. The dogs single out one antelope, keep their distance, but rush in and out barking ferociously.

Joseph slinks away from me like a cat. Just like a cat, making use of cover, silently, glidingly, he threads through the *mopani* bushes. He gets within four yards. His arm flashes up and the spear flies from his hand into the gemsbok's side.

The animal hurls up his head as if shocked by electricity, then bounds into the bush, the enraged dogs hard at his heels. The spear is knocked out of his flank by a bush and falls to the ground. When I get to where it has fallen Joseph is calmly squatting on his heels picking the broken end of the haft out of the iron socket of the spear-head with his knife: the haft has broken off short. Quietly Joseph picks away; and then as quietly pares the remains of the haft with a knife and refits it into the socket.

I ask him if he isn't afraid of losing his buck, but he says that the dogs will never let him go. They will bring him to bay again. And, indeed, we can hear the dogs barking furiously not far away.

The spear is mended, and we proceed. Again the cat-like stalk. Again the spear flung from the bushes, and the buck bounding off. Again the miserable little haft breaking, and the spear dropping out. And again the patient repair.

Next time better luck. The beast has now lost blood. He is tired. The spear is thrown, the buck bounds, then drops. Joseph, more cat-like than ever, leaps over his neck, seizes the nostrils and drives the points of the rapier horns into the ground. Two slashes with the knife open the two jugulars. The dogs lap up the warm blood as it gushes on to the dust.

We have walked a long way and are thirsty. Joseph rips open the belly and bares the great bulging rumen, or paunch. White and enormous. Carefully cutting it open Joseph reveals about a gallon of clear water. He cups his hands and drinks, and so do I, and the water is bitter, but drinkable. The gemsbok, being a desert buck, carries his water supply in his belly. He can go all his life without seeing open water, for he digs in the ground with his hoofs for moist corms and tubers and gets his moisture from these.

By this time I have contrived to light a small fire. Joseph rips out the liver, cuts a slice of the neck-meat which is tender on a freshly killed buck, and throws these meats on to the flames, which is the way we cook in the veld. In a little while our meat is cooked. We fish it out of the fire with a stick, scrape the blackened part away with our knives, and eat it.

The rest of the carcasse is covered with thorn bushes, to keep off jackals and vultures, and a small piece of rag is tied to a tree nearby for the same purpose. We start the long trek home. That night, Joseph and his pals will go and cut the buck up, light a fire and gorge themselves there and then, sling the rest of the heavy meat on to poles, and carry it home to conceal in their huts; and Clinton will wonder why they are late in the morning to let the sheep out of the kraals, and even dopier than usual about the counting.

I became very close friends with Joseph. The Bushmen are a highly intelligent people; Joseph certainly was exceptionally so. They are far quicker-witted than their Bantu neighbours, or than we are for that matter. Joseph's mind worked so much more quickly than mine that he would become impatient long before I had finished a sentence in my halting Afrikaans: he would divine my meaning before I had finished speaking. Bushmen have the most amazing visual memory. An illiterate Bushman will draw for you in the sand the number of a car that has stopped for half a minute at your door and gone off again, when you have been away. He will also give you, if you ask for it, the most minute description of the car and of its driver. If a Bushman played 'Kim's Game' no non-Bushman in the world could beat him.

Joseph and I made a long trip up north with pack-donkeys to see the Etosha Pan. We met other wild Bushmen there, and Joseph introduced me to them: normally they are hard to contact. They will flee from a white man, and if surprised it is said that they hide by turning themselves upside down against a tree. Their own dusty grey colour matches that of the trunk of the tree.

Bushmen don't build huts as a rule. The most elaborate structure they make is a grass lean-to. They live in very small tribes, or large family groups, under the head of the family who is called the *Gei-khoib*. The chief duty of the *Gei-khoib* is the ritual kindling of the fire, which he does by spinning a stick in a hole in another stick. The Bushmen will camp a mile or two away from a water-hole, far enough not to scare the game, and a hunter will conceal himself near the hole with his little bow and arrows. When a buck, or a zebra, or a giraffe comes to drink he gets a little poisoned arrow in his hide. The poison takes an hour or two to work, but the Bushmen follow the animal until it drops. Then they cut away the poisoned meat and eat the rest—flesh, guts, bone-marrow, the lot. Nothing is wasted. Even the skin is often charred and eaten. After such a meal the Bushmen are gorged: their stomachs are enormously distended and they can scarcely stand. This is the time that the troopers of the South West Africa Police are able to arrest them. If a Bushman is taken off to gaol he dies in a few days—from claustrophobia. Many have met their end in this way. The Germans, in their time, never used to put the Bushmen in gaol: they shot them when they found them, like wild animals. Bushmen were classed as vermin, like lions and wild dogs. Anybody could shoot them.

The Bushmen do not only eat meat. They send their women to hunt for *veldkos* (wild food). This includes scorpions, beetles, bulbs, corms and tubers, fruit—around our way we had a pleasant fruit called the *!naras* (! represents a certain click sound in the

Bushmen's language)—flying-ants and their eggs, and larvae, locusts, lizards, snakes, jerboas, anything. 'Bushman grain' is interesting. Certain kinds of ants make large stores of grass-seed in their nests. The Bushmen raid the nests and cook and eat the seed. I have seen them doing it. Is it unreasonable to suppose that man discovered the use of grain in this way?

A Bushman will dig up the ground under an insignificant looking creeper and pull out a tuber the size of a football, full of drinkable though soapy-tasting water. I have been glad enough to suck one. A Bushman will bury a wad of grass yards down in the sand of a 'dry' river and suck for hours with a long hollow reed, getting a mouthful of water each time and spitting the water into an empty ostrich shell, which is afterwards sealed up and buried, a store for future use.

The wild Bushman lives a life of such toughness that one wonders why he doesn't change, and become 'civilized'. But, with the rare exception such as Joseph, he never does. He prefers the veld. He loves to hunt and to follow the *trekbok* (the migrating herds of springbok) across the desert country.

As a Bushman couple grow old a time will come when they can no longer keep up with the ever-moving tribe. A little thorn *boma* will be built for them, food and water for a few days will be put in it, and there they will be left, for ever. They accept this quietly and calmly, as people should.

After my success with the lion I became a good hunter. If Mrs Andrews wanted meat, while I was staying at Marshways, I would sling my little rifle over my shoulder and walk off into the veld by myself, and I would never fail to get a buck. I began to know where to look, and after some years in Africa I began to develop an instinct which told me which way to go for buck.

Oswald, a Coloured man who was building a dam at Edwardsvelde, sold me a horse. A little grey mare, named Popje, meaning 'dolly' (Popje is pronounced Poppy). She was a typical *bosjiekop* or 'bushy-head': a rough little pony, but as tough as iron. I would ride the fifty-six miles from Edwardsvelde to Marshways in twelve hours, and she would still be fresh.

We would leave Edwardsvelde at six o'clock in the evening, ride all night in the cool, and reach Marshways at six the next morning.

Horse-riding is rather different in southern Africa from what it is in Hyde Park. You do not wear special clothes. You will find that the back-veld South African will start on a journey of a hundred miles or so on horseback wearing his ordinary trousers and a pair of city-type walking shoes. He does not find it necessary to put on boots and breeches and special clothes.

South Africans like their horses to 'tripple' (half-canter). Trotting is anathema. Riders in Europe would be horrified if their horses trippled; they force them to trot. However, trotting may look good, but it is exceedingly tiring for both man and horse. Trippling is comfortable, and it was the fact that their ponies trippled that enabled the Boers to ride circles around the well-fed English cavalry during the Boer War.

Popje used to tripple, and she had a very pleasant slow canter, which she would keep up for miles. If I made her walk (which I did very often, so as not to overtire her) I always used to dismount, because this rested both herself and me. If we stopped and rested I would immediately take her saddle off, and rub her back with grass. Normally she lived off the veld alone—she was never fed—and indeed I would only catch sight of her occasionally when she came to the water to drink. But when we were passage-making I would give her a double handful of crushed mealies occasionally. Fastened to her saddle (a 'semi-military') was a pair of hobbles, like large handcuffs, and when we rested I would put these on her fetlocks so that she could not wander far, and let her loose to graze.

Sentimentalizing about horses and dogs is the English vice, and I try to avoid it; but Popje convinced me that a horse can become fond of a man. She used to canter up to me in the veld, and let me groom her, and if I put her in the paddock at Marshways I had only to go to the gate and she would come galloping up. I would jump on her bare back, with no bridle, and she would canter off to the water-trough. Or if I walked away she would follow me, with her nose occasionally touching my shoulder, and I never needed to lead her with a bridle.

I found that it was enormously satisfying to travel about the country on horseback, in the same way that seafaring is. Horse-riding in England is a sorry sport. It is so obviously artificial and unnecessary and it is so much easier to take a bus. Alas, the four-wheel-drive motor vehicle has made the horse an anachronism in southern Africa too, except for 'riding camp' on the big sheep farms in the Karoo. The more's the pity. These 'inventions' do not enrich life: they impoverish. A man will live a life of boredom, rushing in the underground to an office every morning, spending his day in questionable activities to make money, just so that in his tiny scraps of spare time he shall be able to ride horses along petrol-reeking tarmac roads.

We trekked the sheep back from Edwardsvelde, and I lived permanently at Marshways again. With a little money that came to me from home I bought a flock of sheep. Clinton let me live at his post and I could graze my sheep in return for doing certain work for him.

My little flock of karakuls was fruitful and multiplied, and produced sufficient pelts to earn me a living. If I had stayed at karakul sheep-farming I would now be a wealthy man.

It was Oswald, the Coloured man from whom I bought the horse, who diverted me from the path of riches.

He had lived in Walvis Bay, and had been a fisherman. He told me about the snoek fishery. About the schooners and ketches which sail out of Walvis Bay with their holds full of salt, and stay at sea for months at a time, until their cargo is exhausted and their holds are full of fish.

I had spent a couple of years in the desert country, and I felt dry and parched. I longed for the cool blue sea. The more stories that Oswald told me about his fishing days, the more restless I became. So, leaving my livestock in Clinton's care, I took the train to Walvis Bay.

Chapter Six

++++++++++++++++++++++++++++◆++++++++++++++++++++++++++++

Of Fish and the Sea

I arrived at Walvis in the small hours of the morning when I was still asleep stretched out on a seat. As the train went no farther I was able to go on sleeping.

I was aware, though, that it was cold.

At dawn I looked out of the window—and saw sand. Yellow sand and plank shacks. A little town of plank shacks set between a sea of sand-dunes and the real sea. The sand-dunes were enormous—higher than church steeples. For some reason they stopped short of the shore at Walvis Bay, and on the level sandy ground which was left, the town had been built.

Walvis is a mighty bay sheltered from the south-west by a sand spit, at the end of which is a lighthouse. It is not sheltered from the north-west, but then the wind practically never blows from there. It is cool. That never-ending cool wind comes off the sea. The whole of that coast is desert *par excellence*. Desert if there is no other desert in the world. Moving sand-dunes hundreds of feet high—a great ocean of sand. Sand-dunes rolling straight down into the breakers of the sea.

I inquired about the snoeking industry—but who wanted me? The fleet was at sea, and would be for weeks, if not for months. The captains signed their crews on in Cape Town, and did not take on men locally. They only signed seasoned snoekers, or their sons. Very few men were hard enough for the life. The crews were mainly Cape Malays. They worked the six months of the snoeking season, worked fantastically hard every day for six months except Christmas Day, and then sailed south again to spend six months getting rid of their money. I would stand no chance of getting a berth.

I met a man named Max Offen, an old German settler who had owned snoeking schooners, had led expeditions to the Antarctic to kill sea elephants, and even now conducted sealing operations at Cape Cross, a place where the early Portuguese navigators had been the first Europeans to land in South West Africa and had set up a stone cross.

Offen told me that I would never become a snoeker. It just wasn't possible. Not that all the members of all the snoeking crews were Coloured (there was no colour-bar at sea and a few white men lived in the forecastles); but they were all seasoned fishermen and it was a life to which you had to be brought up. They fished on a share basis, and no skipper would dare sign on a man who could not catch his share of the fish. There and then I made up my mind to become a snoeker.

There are times in my life when a kind of stubbornness comes over me, as when I made up my mind that I would not be a fag at my public school. When this happens I will carry out my resolve, whatever it is, no matter what the odds are against it. I wanted to be a snoeker. I determined that if I spent the rest of my life doing it I would become a snoeker.

Why not go and be a crayfishman? asked Offen. He advised me to go to Lüderitz, where the crayfish-canning industry was, and try to get a job aboard a crayfish cutter.

Well, it was no good waiting around in Walvis in case a snoeker might put into port, and as a little coasting steamer happened to be sailing south next day, whose skipper was willing to let me stay in his forecastle for the voyage, to Lüderitz I went.

Lüderitz—a cluster of small German houses like a toy Bavarian village strewn over a jumble of hills of frozen lava. For before you get to Lüderitz from the north the sand-dunes give way to this coast of lava rock devoid of any vegetation; multi-coloured rock, torn, twisted, tortured, piled up and thrown down, cut by an incessant wind of gale force which blows from the Atlantic. The wind blows grit before it across the lava hills, so that the rock is sandpapered—an old bottle left lying about will be cut through; men are driven to drink or sodomy or suicide or insanity. An unhallowed place.

I stayed there a month or two and got a job aboard a crayfish cutter owned by a German.

The 'crayfish' we caught were in reality crawfish, but we called them crayfish. The 'cutters' that we caught them from were, in reality, very powerful diesel-engined motor craft with auxiliary sail.

Thumping great one-cylinder Bolinder diesel shaking the cutter to her keelson: goodbye to wind-cut, sun-scorched toy town on its frozen lava hills, goodbye to Shark Island, to white guano-covered Penguin and Seal Islands—to meet the great rollers and the unfenced wind as we open Dias Point—nothing between us and Antarctica. Howling of wind on deck, thump and thunder of Bolinder downstairs and stink of diesel oil. A day's run to Hottentot Bay or Spencer Bay. Shoot the set-net (a gill net sunk to the bottom) for bait. Drop our anchor amidst the other cutters. Darkness comes, lights pop up around us, guitar music—*Lietjies* and *vas-traps*—played by rough Coloured hands across the calm water. At daybreak—dinghy overboard—pull our nets—in comes the flipping, flopping bait: small sharks, Joseph-fish with long noses, elephant fish with trunks, gurnards with prickles, rough, tough, spiny creatures come trumbling inboard.

Away to the grounds. In close under the rocks on that lee-shore, where the Atlantic water-hills rear up and come spraying down to us. Heavy anchor overboard: the strength of the chain between us and being crayfish-bait ourselves. Overboard dinghies: one man to row in the bow, the other to pull nets in the stern. A loading net laid amidships to take the fish. Eight iron-hooped fish-baited nets shot in a line downwind, the last one horribly close to where the billows rear, for the nearer the rocks the more the fish. The rower pulls those intransigent unyielding oars literally for his life, for if he fails the never-resting wind will blow us to death in a few moments. Back to the first hoop-net—the man in the stern pulls the buoy-rope. Up she comes—two—three—five—maybe eight or ten crayfish. They are shot into the loading-net, the hoop-net is flung again. Oarsman, still rowing upwind, rows a fraction less furiously, and the dinghy is blown astern a few yards and the netsman pulls another net. After half an hour there are several hundredweight of rustling crustaceans in the little boat. Back to the anchored cutter—the German skipper-owner, too old or lazy to take his turn in the dinghies, flings down the halyard with a hook—up goes the great dripping bag of whiskered clawless lobsters to shoot into the wooden hold. Back flops the net, oarsman and netsman change over—the wind blows us in a trice back to our line of hoop-nets.

After an hour or two of this we stand in the dinghy, holding on to the side of the madly plunging cutter, and drink big mugs of hot coffee. Later we eat bread and cold meat or cheese. No time to clamber aboard. Later more coffee. Later tea. It gets dark. We go on. We go on all night. It gets light. We go on. I had never realized before that there are jobs in the world where men go on working—and working fantastically hard—for thirty-six hours without resting. The dinghies are hove up by the great waves like red rags being tossed by bulls, the cutters snatch madly at their heavy cables. One moment you can see your mother cutter riding high on a mountain. The next she plunges right out of sight but for the top of her mast.

'Deck load!' shout the fishermen, spurring themselves on by shouting like cavalrymen in a charge. 'Deck load! Shoes for the babby! *Alle magtig jong.* Money—money—money!' They sing bits of song—but they shout and sing with the hysterical edge of exhausted men. I don't sing. I pull. Oars or ropes—I just pull. I have to concentrate on just keeping going. I can't even think.

Deck load! Deck load it is! The hatches are put on, the deck piled high with crawling rustling whiskered things right up to the tops of the gunwales. Forty—fifty thousand? Big money for all. Up come the embattled dinghies to be hove on top of hundreds of bodies. Engine starts to thunder, we haul on the anchor cable; as the *Königsberg* shoves her head to face the south-west gale we fishers scramble over the rustling fish to the clear place astern, in the lee of the wheelhouse, where the sun shines hot and the wind doesn't come; we flop there and know nothing more until we feel the ship bump alongside the factory wharf at Lüderitz. We are like dead people, and it is difficult to arouse us. Thank God the wind blows too hard even for us next day and the fishermen (my shipmates are all 'Kroo boys', natives of Liberia) go off to the shebeens in the 'location' to drink, gamble, and try for a woman, while I go back to my German-owned boarding-house and lie on a bed and read Shakespeare's plays, one by one, as they come in the book.

After a couple of trips I decided that there was only one thing to do. I must buy a share in a 'cutter'. Owners and fishermen were making money, and in those days I thought it was important to make money.

I went back to Outjo. I sold my sheep. I sold my cart and donkeys. I sold my Popje and the small foal that she had produced, and I turned my head for the sea again. This time Clinton came with me. He wanted a holiday, he decided.

Now if I had returned to Lüderitz and bought a share in a cutter, all would have been well. I would have lived a rough and tough life for a couple of years, made some money, boozed it, sold out, and gone on somewhere else. But I was diverted in Walvis Bay.

When Clinton and I arrived at that port in the desert, we found a schooner tied against the wharf. A genuine, Massachusetts cod schooner: the *Titania*. Although she had an engine she was obviously still a sailing ship rather than a motor-vessel. She looked battered and sea-beaten; and her deck was cluttered with half a dozen huge wooden tanks. Round about the deck lounged a set of the toughest, most piratical-looking characters I had ever seen up to that time.

The man who had appeared to be the captain was a white man who turned out to be a Swede by the name of Oscar Johannsen, and he had an accent which was a cross between Swedish and Scots. Clinton and I asked him if we could come aboard.

We could. We were invited down into the cabin, a spacious compartment in the stern. There we were introduced to the Swedish mate, the Portuguese second officer, and a South African. They were sitting around in the cabin drinking beer.

I told Johannsen of my plans for going into crayfishing. He advised me not to. 'There's a fortune,' he said, 'for the man who starts up a *pilchard* industry here in Walvis Bay.' He went on to explain that the *Titania* was a snoeker—one of a fleet of vessels that sails from Cape Town to Walvis Bay every November, spends six months catching a fish called the snoek and salting it, then sails back to Cape Town, to spend the southern winter resting. But the snoek which they hunted were hunters themselves, and the quarry they hunted was pilchards. 'I've seen five miles of pilchards thick as porridge, half a mile off Pelican Point there!'

said Oscar. 'You guys raise some money, get a ship, send to Sweden for a ring-net, and start catching pilchards. No one has ever tried before: you'll make a mint.'

'What'll we do with the pilchards when we've got 'em?' I asked.

'Make kippers of them,' said Oscar. 'I know a Scotsman in Town named McNaulty who knows all about it. He was a kipperer in Aberdeen. He's been saying for years that these pilchards would make good kippers and that there's a fortune in it. Then, when you can get the machinery, you can can them and also make fishmeal out of them.'

I must now cut a long story short.

Clinton and I got on a German ship and went to Cape Town. We looked out McNaulty. He was indeed a Scotsman, and had been in the fish trade all his life, and what he didn't know he would damned soon make up. He fired us with enthusiasm for kippering. He introduced us to people who might put up money. Clinton decided to put some up. I wrote home to people in England and got them to do likewise. We had a motor fishing vessel laid down in a Cape Town yard: 48 feet long, 15-foot beam, draught 6½ feet. To be fitted with a 66 h.p. Kelvin diesel engine, and called the *Cunene*, after one of the only three South West African rivers that have water in them.

I watched the *Cunene* built, and inspected every piece of timber that went into her. I returned to Walvis Bay after the war and saw her still operating. I had a letter years later from a friend of mine who lives in Walvis Bay, in which he wrote: 'You will I know have some feelings when I tell you that following your visit the *Cunene* has at last packed up. I am not quite sure whether she is a complete write-off, but she went ashore I know; all too many cutters have gone ashore this year, so much so that the insurance companies have increased the Walvis Bay premiums.'

Ah well!

One of the directors of a very big South African company asked us to go and see him, and told us that we were not to go on with our kipper venture. When we asked him why, he said that his firm was importing kippers into the Union from Scotland, and making a very good profit at it, and did not wish for any competition. Clinton and I stood there, in that beautifully appointed director's office, and calmly told him that we would go on with it just the same.

'We will break you,' he said, quite as calmly.

We told him that his kippers were retailed in Johannesburg at tenpence a pair. We were going to retail ours at twopence a pair. What would he say to that?

'I am warning you,' he said. 'If you go into the fishing industry we will break you.'

What innocents we were! We heard later of the fantastic lengths to which the huge firms of South Africa will go to preserve their monopolies. To think that we, with our cockleshell of a boat, our complete lack of experience, our miserable bit of capital, and our drunken Scots kipperer, could fight this Goliath!

So the keel was laid down, a letter was sent off to Sweden for a net which was to cost two hundred pounds, box 'shooks' were ordered, and the rest of it. Clinton returned to his farm, to try to raise some more money by selling sheep and by selling shares to other people, and I settled down to watch the building of the *Cunene*, and attend to 'the business end of it'. Me!

During the three or four months (of 1937) that this took I had a good glimpse of Cape Town, and the people who live in it. Unique among southern African cities, Cape Town is European, by which I mean that it has something of the flavour of Europe about it; the mellowed, sophisticated culture of the Old World. Johannesburg, Durban, Port Elizabeth, East London, are American overlaid on Victorian Colonial; but Cape Town is still, in part, European. The last time I went there I stayed in the Martin Melck Hotel, which is in a building put up in the eighteenth century. There are several (not many) eighteenth-century buildings left in Cape Town, but a lot of the more recent ones have a civilized air about them. Strangely, it is the non-European quarters which are the most European. In parts of the Coloured area of District Six you feel that you must be on the continent of Europe somewhere, though you can't decide just where. The same can be said up in the Malay quarter on the lower slopes of Signal Hill. The sprawling European suburbs, which run right across the peninsula to False Bay, are just bad 'Western' suburban architecture, and the city centre is pure 'modern Western'. But these old parts of Cape Town, in which the twentieth century has not yet shown interest, are unadulterated European.

Cape Town has been a city for a long time now: three hundred years ago there were Europeans living in it, and they were mixing quite happily with people of other races. The Cape Malays are the descendants of slaves whom the old Dutch East India Company brought back from the East, and the Coloured people (who number just under a million in South Africa and a quarter of a million at the Cape) are the product of intercourse between the white people, the Malays, Hottentots and Bushmen, and possibly to a small extent the Bantu, and people from Madagascar.

The result of this admixture is one of the liveliest lot of men and women you could imagine. Cape Coloured people were my ship-mates for over a year, I have come up against them on many other occasions, and I know of few groups of people that I find more amusing or better company. They have enough Hottentot and Bushman blood in them, perhaps, to sharpen their wits and intelligence, for the Bushman in particular (as I found with my friend Joseph) have a quicker, more acute wit than is normal. If one were to generalize about the Cape Coloured race (for it is now a distinct race I believe) one would say that its members are extrovert, lively, musical (in the extreme), brave, hot-tempered, unprovidential. Living in the particular environment in which they do they are inclined to drink a lot, and some of them smoke *dagga*, which is one of the marihuana-type drugs. They will work extremely hard when there is need, or to make money, but when they can they laze in a quite spectacular fashion; and whether working or relaxing they have the knack of getting every drop out of life. They have in full measure something which so many of the rest of us lack sorely, the capacity to enjoy today without worrying about tomorrow. The Westerner never enjoys today because he is always worrying his guts out about what is going to happen tomorrow. And tomorrow never comes. The 'Capie' knows about this, and he enjoys today which alone is his to enjoy.

He is a born gambler, and that makes him a fisherman. The best line fishermen in the world, I believe, are Cape Coloured. They love it, because it is a gamble; they never know what they are going to pull up next. It is a hard and dangerous life, but provides in its off-seasons leisure and money to spend. They spend every penny of it and back they go to catch some more fish.

Human nature being, alas, what it is, the Coloured community until recently had somewhat the same attitude to the African (by which I mean the pure, black, Bantu African) as the white man. When I was first in Cape Town one heard Coloured people say: 'The kaffir must be kept in his place!' just as one heard the white people mouthing this parrot-cry.

The *Cunene* was built, launched, fitted-out and victualled. A skipper was engaged: one Janssen, a Swede, and a friend of Oscar Johannsen the snoeker. A mate was found: one Richie, a South African from the Cape. A crew was mustered: four Coloured men from District Six. I went aboard as a passenger, for until I learnt the trade of fisherman I was to employ myself partly ashore. I did not, I might say, intend to employ myself off the water for very long, but the fishing enterprise had grown out of my hands. So many other people had come into it, with money, that I had to do more or less what I was told.

A sailing date was named, but it was three days after it that we were able to set out. Reason: drunkenness among the crew.

When one man turned up, suffering horribly from alcoholic remorse, he would be sent back to District Six to fetch the others. He would not come back. When the others came they would have to go and fetch him. Then the captain and mate and I would hire a taxi and go and search, and as like as not we too would fall by the wayside.

At midnight on a moonless night we were all aboard, all drunk, but all just capable. Our mooring lines were cast off. A little man named Venter who was with us made one last despairing effort to escape but was recaptured. Richie fired a few rounds off with an old rifle we had aboard and we were away.

We motored out of the harbour into Table Bay and very soon we were feeling the ocean billows which were coming at us from the South Atlantic. We had started on our eight-hundred-mile voyage to Walvis Bay.

The great net had not yet arrived from Sweden, and so it had been decided that when we got to Walvis Bay we should enter into the snoek fishery, and not worry about the pilchards or the kippers until the net arrived.

89

'Wait 'til we strikes the fish!'

It was a refrain.

There was not very much to do on board the *Cunene* as we motored northward along the coast, and most of us spent most of our time lying in the sun. The wind blew consistently from the south-west. It was a cool wind, but we could always get out of it by lying in the lee of one of the big pickling tanks on deck. Jannsen even used to read—paper-backed novelettes.

Richie was not a man for such employment. 'I never reads,' he said one day, with great emphasis. He said everything emphatically, did Richie. He never said anything idly: to whatever he said or did he gave his entire attention. 'Readin's a waste o' time. If you looks after your gear proper on a snoeker there's no time for readin'. It's men what wastes their time with readin' that's always borrowin' dollies and gear from others when we strikes the fish.'

I became more and more intrigued with what would actually happen when we struck the fish, for I was always hearing about it. 'You wait 'til we strikes the fish. There'll be no time for sitting around then!'

The fishermen occupied themselves for part of their time by manufacturing curious fishing gear. Old inner tyre tubes were cut up and the rubber sewn into finger-guards. *Lapjies* they were called—pronounced 'lappies'. Richie made up hundreds of wire traces, by twisting together strands of very thin picture-hanging brass wire. Eleven strands there had to be: no more and no less. Thousands and thousands of objects called 'dollies' were manufactured. These were small lures supposed to look like pilchards as they travelled through the water. They were made out of shark-skin: some scores of these skins had been brought aboard at Cape Town. Men sewed canvas aprons for themselves, or repaired their other garments. Preparations went on apace for the day when we should 'strike the fish'.

At night we would stand three-hour watches: one fisherman and one of the after-guard were always on watch together. You would steer until you were dazed with looking at the lighted, swinging disc of the compass, and then hand over to the other fellow, wedge yourself in the door of the wheel house and look out into the heaving night. Those who were not on watch sat below, and played cards or told stories.

I used to spend a lot of time playing cards with the fishermen down in the fo'c'sle. This was a cramped, wedge-shaped compartment in the nose of the ship, dimly lit by the hatch-opening or by a smoked-up hurricane lantern. It was lined on both sides by tiers of wooden bunks, four a side, and a double-burner Primus stove spat and roared on a little shelf against the after-bulkhead. A narrow bench ran along the bottom bunks and there was a clear space of floor big enough for a couple of men to stand up in. There was hardly enough room for all five of the usual occupants to sit up at the same time, so when they were all below some of them generally got into their bunks. We used to sit around this Hole of Calcutta, everyone smoking, the cook pumping furiously at his Primus stove, while we played cards on an upturned box. The fishermen played with peculiar gusto. They did not just place one of the tattered cards down on the box; they held it up first and then flung it down, in an exaggerated gesture of strength, generally accompanied by an oath or an endearment. When a man took a trick he would seize it up as though it were a thousand pounds, and sometimes even get up and execute a little caper of joy in the cramped space available.

Back aft in the cabin we occupied ourselves more genteelly. The after-guard consisted of Janssen, Richie and myself; but we used to admit into our company two of the fo'c'sle men: a strange Coloured man with Irish blood called Mike, and the little Cape man named Venter.

'Ven fishermen's ashore dey talks of fish,' said Janssen one evening, in his strong Swedish accent. 'But ven dey's afloat dey talks of vimmin.'

Mike had sailed the seven seas in tankers and cargo ships, and what he did not know he would very soon make up. 'Well, talkin' of women,' he said on that occasion, 'Talkin' of women...'

Janssen interrupted that Mike never talked of anything else.

'Well, you know the Queen's Bar in Port Elizabeth, Skip?' said Mike, 'Last time I was in P.E. I goes into the bar wit' a guy named Hendriks. Yous wouldn't know him. We was off a tanker. Well, we starts off wit' gin and stout, 'cos we was t'irsty like. Then we switches to Château brandy. We has about a dozen Châteaus when in walks a guy by the name of Coetze wit' a cow on his arm.'

Janssen listens indulgently, sucking at his pipe, with his usual placid smile. Richie is too busy to listen much; he is twisting wire traces from a hook screwed into the deck-head. Venter sits gazing hard at the speaker. He is fascinated by the story, but is troubled by a sense of Sin. Venter is Saved.

'Well, this here cow was a piece by the name of Elsie,' Mike goes on. 'The tug-master's daughter. Maybe you knows her, Skip?' Janssen nods, and sucks his pipe.

'Blonde piece. Big-built piece. Thighs on her like my waist. Well, I knows this cow so I asks her what she'll have. She calls for a port and lemon. Coetze has a rum, so we goes on to rums. No, no—I'm telling you a lie! I goes on to rums all right but Hendriks sticks to Châteaus.'

'Don't torture us,' says Janssen.

'Well, here we sits quite friendly like, and I'm gettin' on fine wit' this cow, when all of a sudden this fellow Coetze starts calling me all the bastards under the sun! I tells him to go and get fixed and he comes for me wit' a bottle. Old Hendriks gets set into this fellow, and then up comes the barman and gets set into Hendriks, and then the cow gets up and settles it all by laying 'em all out wit' a chair! Great, big-built piece, arms on her like that beam up there. Then me an' she gets away and we goes to her place, but first we goes into the Devon and has one or two, and . . .'

Mike would go on telling such stories for hours. I suspect that he made most of them up as he went along.

Richie never talked about women. When he talked at all he talked about fish. He told me once that he was always completely broke at the beginning of the snoeking season. 'Why don't you put your money in a bank?' I asked.

'Bank!' he said contemptuously. 'The shebeens are my bank!' (Shebeens are low drinking dives.) 'I grafts hard for my money at sea and when I goes ashore I spends it. Then I goes to sea again and grafts for some more. I can always get a berth. They knows me. All the skippers knows me. Last off-season I gets bo'sun of a steam trawler. But when the snoekers sails I sails wit' 'em. Snoekin' beats the lot. You wait 'til we strikes the fish, Mister!'

He had spent his life at sea, Ritchie had. But always as a hunter. He had no interest in cargo ships, or in trading, but only in hunting. He was one of nature's carnivores. He had shipped aboard snoekers and trawlers, line-fishing boats, crayfish 'cutters' and sealers. He had been down to the Antarctic after sea-elephants, and down to the ice with the whaling fleets. He was only at home while at sea.

Many Cape fishermen are lost ashore. They have nothing to do there but tipple and fight, gamble and drug themselves with *dagga* and allow themselves to be robbed by women.

After passing the Orange River mouth we only once saw the coast; a high wall of black lava rock, devoid of vegetation, like a view on Jupiter. Then we ran into a heavy fog, but the strong sou'wester did not abate. The seas off South West Africa are one of the places on the globe where fog and wind habitually go together.

Five days after leaving Cape Town we struck the fish!

Eight lines, one for each man, had been fastened to the gunwale around the stern of the vessel. They were thick lines, nearly as thick as your little finger, and they were blooded.

'We bloods 'em,' said Richie. 'We does 'em in clotted ox's blood and then stretches 'em out to dry. Keeps 'em better.'

At the end of each line was a wire trace, about two feet long, on the end of which was a lead about the size of a straight banana. Linked on to the other end of the lead was a hook. The hook was of heavy steel, kept very sharp; it had no barb, and it was about the size of the outline of a man's hand. To the eye of the hook was wired a dolly, and this was the only bait.

After Janssen said that he reckoned that we were well past Lüderitz (he had no sextant), Richie and one or two of the more ardent members of the crew started 'trying for fish'. They pitched the eight lines overboard and let them trail astern and would stand for hours fruitlessly jerking the lines in the water trying to make the dollies resemble small fish. Sometimes they would ask the helmsman to slow down the engine so as to take way off the ship; but all to no avail.

On the sixth day, towards evening, when we knew that we must be getting close to Walvis Bay, Richie suddenly went stark raving mad.

'SNOEK!' he screamed. In his excitement he broke into Cape Dutch. '*Snoek jou blerrie bastaars*—SNOEK!' As he shouted he leapt up and rushed to the lines.

Sure enough, one of the lines was as straight as a rod, and cutting the water like a knife.

Richie seized it, and began pulling it in hand over hand as fast as he could. I had rushed to the stern and there, in the water, I could see something long and bright and blue snaking furiously as it was dragged by brute force to the vessel. Richie leant down and caught hold of the wire trace near the lead and swung the snoek out—hurled it through the air over his head and let it crash down on the deck behind him. The moment the fish hit the deck the barbless hook clattered free and Richie swung it back over his head to fling it into the water again with unnecessary violence.

And the snoek! It leapt four feet into the air. It battered the deck with its head and its tail—it jumped and it bounded. Often in the months that followed I was broken out of a book while I lay in my bunk below by that mad tattoo of frenzy, a fandango of death, above my head.

Of all the fish I have ever seen, the snoek is the most beautiful. About two feet six inches long, slender and tapering, a gleaming blue back, a burnished silver belly, sharp pointed nose, mouth wide and fierce and set with needle teeth, large eyes set in the centre of its head. The skin looks scaleless and smooth and clean. The tail is large, and broadly fanned. The creature has the most perfect streamlining; it is perfectly evolved for high speed in the water.

By then all was complete turmoil on board the *Cunene*.

Richie had gone raving mad; he was shouting and screaming like a maniac. Fishermen were tumbling up out of the fo'c'sle and rushing aft to their lines. Janssen was standing at the wheel and roaring orders for somebody to back the foresail but nobody was taking any notice. It was pandemonium. We had struck the fish!

By the time we reached our lines every one had a fish on it. I caught my own line and pulled with all my strength—but it might have had a bucking bronco on the end of it. I had not stopped to put my rubber finger-guards on and the line cut painfully into my hands. The fish would slacken for an instant, then give a violent tug which would jerk the line painfully into my fingers, then all at once its resistance slackened and it snaked upwards and broke surface, and I was able to pull it quickly towards the ship. There was only a foot or two between myself and the next man, Venter, and as I swung the heavy fish inboard I narrowly missed Venter's head. However, I soon got the hang of it.

All around me was violent activity.

Every man was either hauling a fish in, or else flinging his hook back into the water, and it seemed that no sooner had the hook hit the water than there was a fish on it! The dexterity with which the fishermen hauled the snoek to the ship and swung them between themselves and their neighbours was remarkable.

The excitement was indescribable. Everyone laughed and shouted: they cursed their neighbours for not pulling in quickly enough and thus risking tangled lines. They seemed like men possessed.

'Clo's for the missus and shoes for the babby!' screamed some-one, with a hysterical note in his voice.

'You mean *dop* for Jenny!' shouted someone else. Furiously we flung the writhing fish inboard, hurling them down to leap in frenzy on the ever-growing pile behind us.

Suddenly there was a complete lull. All was quiet except for the flapping of the fish. There was not a line occupied.

Janssen, who had clamped the wheel so that he could come and fish too, went back and turned the ship on her course to try and enter the school again, but although we tacked about for an hour searching we caught no more.

'Fish's gone down,' said Richie. 'We's better put her round and head on down the coast, Jan.' And Janssen did so. Although the Swede was our skipper, he generally did what Richie suggested when it came to the fishing.

Then came the strange business of 'flecking the fish off the deck'.

Each one of us had a large carving knife stuck in the *latjie* planks that kept the snoek from falling among our feet. We coiled our lines and started to behead the fish.

The space inboard of the *latjies* was now filled with dead or dying fish. The procedure was to grab a snoek by inserting a hand into its gill, place the back of its head over the *latjie* plank, and cut off its head with one firm, crunching slice.

I quickly learnt two things. One was that a snoek has rows of sharp little needles inside its gills. The other was that it is not so easy to cut a snoek's head off with one slice.

The head was then thrown overboard and the headless body, spurting thick red blood like an ox, dropped back among the other fish.

So quickly did we work that in a very few minutes there were no fish left to head, and the deck around the stern was piled high with gory, headless stumps, no longer beautiful.

Water was bucketed from the sea and the fish and deck were swilled clean, then someone gaffed the fish forward out of the way so that the after-deck was clear.

Then the fleckers got to work. Richie and a venerable fisherman named Petrus set up two little tables against the rail of the vessel. I saw Richie pick up a fish by its tail, lay it on his little table, and with four incredibly quick and deft strokes lay it right open along the back like a kipper, but, unlike a kipper, with the backbone partially severed from the body, to form a sort of handle. The guts flew over the side to be snatched before they hit the water by one of the crowd of gulls that had arrived from nowhere as gulls do, and the flecked fish was flying through the air to splash into a tank of sea water. Before it had reached its destination Richie's little knife was ripping into another one.

The fish were then washed, rubbed in salt and thrown into one of the big wooden pickling tanks. There they would lie, pickling in their own juice, for twenty-four hours before being stowed down in the dark belly of the vessel.

During half an hour of fishing the eight of us had killed three hundred snoek. So we carried on 'down the coast' (Cape Town fishermen say: 'down north') while all this was happening, and soon we began to hear the moan of a foghorn. Suddenly the fog lifted and I was delighted to see a tall lighthouse standing on the end of a long, low, spit of sand. Pelican Point: the arm that enfolds Walvis Bay.

We turned in close under the lighthouse and could see the little shanty town of Walvis about six miles away across the bay. When Janssen took the ship in up against the wharf there we were still at work 'flecking the fish off the deck'. A crowd had collected on the wharf, and they cheered to see us come in: the first of the snoeking fleet, and with fish. We flung several snoek up for the people to scramble for. Clinton was waiting for us on the wharf and so was Mr McNaulty. We busied ourselves with unloading the barrels and other impedimenta that we had brought with us.

The wonderful net had not yet arrived from Sweden, and so we spent the next few weeks snoeking. We did not stay at sea like the rest of the snoeking fleet, which began to arrive at Pelican Point as the days went by, but we often came into port at night, to discharge some fresh snoek for McNaulty to practise his arts upon: smoking and the like. The other snoekers would never touch land until they had finished their salt, which, in the case of the big schooners, might take three months. They would not risk losing their crews in the location of Walvis and having the delay and expense of bailing them out of gaol.

For some reason best known to themselves, for the first month of the season the snoek congregate in an area of sea within a few miles of Pelican Point, and during this time the snoeking fleet engages in what is known as the 'Point fishing'. It is more intense than the later fishing, when the shoals scatter far and wide over the ocean, and sometimes there are days when you cannot catch a fish for breakfast. During the Point fishing we felt that we had done badly if the eight of us on board the *Cunene* did not take a thousand fish in a day! One day we took seventeen hundred: starting work at six in the morning we were flecking the last of the catch off the deck at midnight and during that time we had not taken our *vinger-lapjies* off to eat our food, nor once left our places at the latches. The Point fishing had one advantage though, and this was that you could anchor in the shelter of the bay every night. You did not have to leave-to on the ocean.

There is one day, and one day only, during the six-month season, on which the snoekers do not fish. And that is Christmas Day. On Christmas Day we were to rest.

The snoekers do not come into Walvis Bay on Christmas Day, for the same reason that they do not go there any other time, except when they have to go to discharge their fish and take on more salt. They collect behind Pelican Point, and spend their Christmas there. At least they did when I was a snoeker. Nowadays, when there are canning factories at Walvis, and other modern amenities, things are different.

We in the *Cunene* could have spent our Christmas ashore, but

97

we decided that it would be more fun to join the rest of the fleet in the shelter of the Point.

It is the custom for every snoeking skipper to keep a store of liquor securely locked up under his bunk, and this is doled out on Christmas Day. Beyond this no liquor of any sort may go to sea in a snoeker. If the captain finds a bottle it is confiscated. It is a matter of life and death that there should be no drinking at sea.

On Christmas Eve we fished as on any other day, and caught our thousand, but on Christmas morning we were allowed to lie in our bunks. Richie got up a little earlier than usual, however, for he wanted to row ashore and fish for a fish called the *steenbras* off the spit, in the surf. He spent most of the morning at this sport, and then came aboard again and shaved.

'I always shaves on Christmas Day,' he said, as though confessing to an amiable weakness. It is not permissible, normally, either to shave or to wash in a snoeker at sea. The fishermen say: 'It washes the good luck away!' In any case, fresh water is scarce. I never shaved or washed while I was in the *Cunene*, and except for my sea boots I never took my clothes off, and I cannot say that I ever felt the worse for it.

Most of us went ashore that morning. It was nice to stroll about on the sand and look at the fleet of six fine ships—schooners and ketches—lying to anchor, or go over to the other side of the spit and watch the great breakers rolling in. Janssen and I visited the lighthouse. We climbed up and duly marvelled at the lenses, and then we went over to the living quarters of the two keepers and drank bottled beer. They were both South African white men, with strong Dutch accents. They were allowed to go into Walvis once a fortnight, in a motor launch, but they told us they seldom wanted to.

'We don't often go, what,' said one. 'We fishes in the surf, and Piet here's got his fancy leather-work. But I reads westerns. I reads a dozen a week.' And indeed, the place was stocked with them.

Christmas dinner aboard the *Cunene* was not exceptional. There was fried bully-beef, macaroni, tinned peaches and unsweetened canned milk. But the lack of excellence in the food was made up for by the quantity of the drink. There was a bottle of *dop* (Cape brandy) for every man, four bottles of wine, and half a bottle of gin or rum. As all this liquor had to be consumed by the dawn of Boxing Day there had to be some pretty determined drinking.

By five in the afternoon Richie was in a condition to sing his long song in High Dutch about his horse being dead of the rinderpest, and himself being full of tears. Janssen then embarked on a long and tuneless Swedish song which nobody but himself could understand.

Some of us went aboard the *Kernwood*, where we found her Swedish skipper, his Portuguese mate, and the Afrikaans master of the *Star of Africa* all fairly advanced in cheer. There were also one or two others. The master of the *Kernwood* and Janssen weighed in immediately with a Swedish song, the Portuguese played an accordion, and the skipper of the *Star*—quite regardless —bellowed a hymn in Afrikaans.

The skipper of the *Star* was a strong Salvationist, and he then gave out, in English, 'Throw out the Lifeline', and 'The Old Rugged Cross'. After about an hour of solid drinking he began to preach a sermon.

Much of it was in his own language, Afrikaans, but for the benefit of such of us as did not know the *taal* but nevertheless had souls to save, he broke from time to time into English, or a kind of English. The two Swedish captains did not hear the sermon, for they sat on a bench together emptying mug after mug of Cape hock, and singing together in their own language songs that sounded terribly mournful. The Portuguese derived little benefit either, as he lay insensible in a bunk.

But Richie did, for he sat and wept on my shoulder until my shirt was wringing wet where he had been weeping on it.

'T'ink of your little childer and your wives!' bellowed the skipper of the *Star of Africa*. 'Every time yous makes beasts of yous-selves wit' drinkin' an' gamblin' and all horrible forms of bestial wickedness! *O alle magtig! Alle magtig!* T'ink on the yawnin' gates of Hell! Not all the love and mercy of the Lord can save yous from them if yous is marked down to be damned! Oh damned! Damned! Seven and seventy times damned! Cast into the roaring fiery furnace and the flames!'

And he staggered over to the table, and helped himself to another mug of Worcester hock.

Refreshed, he exhorted: 'Every moment yous is sinkin'! Not

D   99

one in twenty is marked down to be saved! One in twenty brothers
—t'ink on it—one in twenty! What if yous was wanted now?
What if yous was taken? Cut off in the midst of your wickedness!
What account would yous render? In the midst of Life we's are
in deat', yet you wilfully sits and drinks, and sins, and lechers.'

Peter the big black Kroo-boy was with us. He sat in a corner
humming happily to himself. Richie wept anew, and had recourse
to the bottle. But poor little Venter sat by himself, his head
forward on his hands, shaken with spasms of sobbing. Venter
was Saved, and a teetotaller, but he had been unable to resist a
drop that day. He had broken his vow, and verily he believed that
he was damned, and would roast in due course in the flames of the
inferno. . . .

After the sermon had been going on about an hour, and was
becoming more and more incoherent, I strolled up on deck to see
what was happening there. A very different scene was to be
witnessed.

A crowd of fishermen had gathered round the bows and were
watching a man dancing a *vastrap*, which is a sort of a Dutch jig.
Several men were playing instruments: a couple of guitars, a
banjo and an accordion. Although they were drunk they played
extremely well, with energy, rhythm and subtlety.

They clapped a bottle of hock into my hand and I sat down.
Everyone sang and yelled and clapped, and sometimes one or two
onlookers would leap up and join in the *vastrap* or a dancer would
sit down exhausted or thirsty and another would leap up to take
his place. In spite of the wildness and abandon of the measure the
complex tripping rhythm remained perfectly even. I think it was
this evenness that made it so effective. The folk music of the
Coloured people of the Cape would hold its own anywhere in the
world, but to be heard at its best it must be performed by drunken
fishermen, on the deck of a snoeker! On a snoeking schooner, in
the shelter of Pelican Point, under the moon.

+++++++++++++++++++++++++++++◇++++++++++++++++++++++++++++

Chapter Seven

Cape Agulhas and Danger Point

We took to the snoeking in earnest. Soon after Christmas the snoek leave the neighbourhood of Pelican Point, and begin to work south 'up' the coast towards Lüderitz, and the snoekers have to range the ocean, far and wide, searching for the shoals. When the snoek ceased to bite in the evening we were no longer able to go back into the shelter of the Point and anchor. It became the practice to stop the engine and heave-to with the sails—point the vessel out to sea, on the port tack, in such a manner that the constant south-west wind would keep her slowly sailing away from the land.

Sometimes the little fleet of six schooners and ketches kept to-gether: at other times we scattered and roamed far and wide. sometimes we did not see the shore for days together, nor any other vessel. Much of the time there was fog about, and we would grow weary standing all day at our lines around the stern in the damp, swirling mist, not always catching very much because, having left the Point, the snoek were not so voracious. But the record for the *Cunene*, when she had seven of a crew, was nineteen hundred snoek: caught, headed, flecked and salted, and the pre-vious day's catch stowed down in the hold. And many a week went by in which we averaged a thousand a day. What this meant in terms of sheer hard *graft* as Cape fishermen call work can hardly be imagined. It meant standing in the *latjies* from dawn until dark; eating our meals standing at our lines without even bother-ing to take our slimy rubber finger-guards off, toiling into the night under the glaring light of a pressure-lamp 'working the fish off the deck'. My privilege as mate, which I became when Janssen left us, was to stow the previous day's catch in the hold, helped by one or other of the fishermen. This would mean working for a couple of hours down in the heaving hold, by the light of a hurricane lamp, carefully stowing the prickly, heavy fish. I would then stagger out on deck, go into the cabin and eat a colossal mound of fried snoek and potatoes, and tumble on to my dirty stinking blankets without even taking my canvas apron or my sea boots off. Wash? Shave? Never! Wash the good luck away.

Cormorants, or *duikers* as we called them, *malagas* or gannets, and penguins would show us where to look for fish. If we saw all the *duikers* flying in a certain direction in the morning that was the way for us to head. The *malagas* would fly high above the waves and sometimes plummet down like an arrow to hit the water with a smack that we could hear from a distance. Penguins would swim up to the ship miles out to sea, thinking she was an island to rest upon I suppose. Once I fished one out of the water with a hoop-net. It waddled about in a charming manner until Richie picked it up and flung it back. 'Penguins!' he said. 'Them's bad-luck birds. Proper Jonahs them birds is, we's don't want no Jonah penguins aboard!' For a long time any bad luck was blamed on the penguin.

Occasionally an albatross would follow us, gliding along effortlessly and apparently quite pointlessly, except that it liked our company. Then there was a bird like a smaller albatross called by the fishermen the *malmok*, and that we used to catch, trailing a line astern with a small fish-hook on it baited with some snoek gut. When a *malmok* took the hook it would be drawn squawking to the taffrail and dispatched with a blow with a fish club. It would be skinned, gutted and hung up in the rigging to dry for a few days. It would then go into stew.

Once we killed a porpoise. Clinton was aboard at the time, and was at the wheel. A friendly German blacksmith ashore had made us a small harpoon, and I took this up in the bows and flung it at a porpoise. There was too much way on the ship and the barbs pulled out, but the porpoise died, and floated belly-upwards on the waves, with his companions leaping around him as if trying to help. We put the ship about, got a strop round the porpoise and heaved him aboard. He was beautifully streamlined, his skin like wet black rubber, but the meat was like butcher's meat, tough and red. It tasted very good, and what we couldn't eat fresh we made *biltong* of. I am now ashamed of having done this but in those days the 'save the whale' campaign had never been thought of.

Once a huge cachalot, or sperm whale, broke surface not three fathoms from our bow. We had a seven-foot Bergdama on board named Bob, and he picked up the porpoise harpoon and was just about to dart it when I stopped him. I didn't quite see what we could do with a seventy-ton sperm whale.

Seals were a constant nuisance. Just when the snoek were biting well a solitary seal would poke his moustachioed head out of the water and splutter at us, and we would know the fishing was temporarily suspended. If a man did hook a snoek he would suddenly feel an irresistible tug on his line and then pull it in to find it broken, and minus hook, fish and sinker! I had my little Mauser on board and used to pot at the seal to scare them away. All snoekers carry rifles for this purpose.

'Them bastards,' said Richie once. 'I've seen me make four hundred quid in a season killing them things! Nowadays there's no price much for the skins.'

He went on to relate how the sealing schooner he was in would sail down the coast (i.e. in the northerly direction) from 'Town' in the winter, anchor off one of the numerous rocky seal islands off the coast of South West, and the men would put off in boats to hunt the seals. First a drift net would be shot on one side of the island, then half the crew would pull round to the other side, land, and rush the seals with clubs. Such as escaped the clubs would get tangled in the nets as they tried to swim away. Only the young seals were taken, the adult Cape seal being no good for fur. Sealing still goes on off the coast of South West Africa, under close government supervision.

Sometimes it would blow a gale when we were fishing, and the wet mist would rush swirling by and spray fly from the tops of the rushing white horses. The *Cunene* would heave and toss, and we had to jam our knees against the gunwales to keep our balance, but we still went on fishing. The ocean outside Walvis Bay is noted for fog. At times we would spend weeks in a fog, and have no idea of our whereabouts, but as long as our salt and water held out and we stayed with the roaming snoek, we did not care. I remember one period of a month during which we never even saw the shore, let alone set foot on it.

Once when we were standing at our lines catching steadily in a dense fog, and had not sighted another ship for a week, we heard the sound of a vessel tramping through the waves towards us. Suddenly the schooner *Kernwood* (like the *Titania*, an old Grand Banks cod schooner) appeared from the wall of mist like a ghost ship; sails set, crew around the stern at their lines, long hull heaving out of the water so that we could see the barnacles and green weed growing on her bottom. Before we could do more than shout a greeting she was gone again, lost in the fog.

In fine weather we would often fish close inshore, and the monotony of the ocean would hardly be broken by the monotony of the endless line of high, shifting, sand dunes. 'If you gets shipwrecked in that lot,' said Richie, 'you dies of t'irst.' But the dunes looked golden in the sunshine.

At night the sea was often phosphorescent, and as we headed and flecked the last lot of fish off the deck, long slender sharks would glide about the ship, their outlines illuminated as with neon lights. They were after the heads and guts that we were flinging overboard.

When our salt was finished and our hold full of fish—so that the deck of the *Cunene* was not very high above the water—we turned for home. We steamed east until we sighted the coast, turned north until we sighted the lighthouse on Pelican Point, and then rounded it and made across the calm bay for Walvis.

The calm bay! How strange it was to feel a steady deck under one's feet, and not have to hold on, day and night, to keep one's balance. How strange to step ashore, and feel firm ground. When one lay on one's shore bed it seemed to heave about more madly than the little *Cunene* at sea!

Richie left us. We could no longer afford to pay his salary. Clinton came aboard as mate and engine driver, and I was promoted to command. We took on more salt and put to sea again.

How well we got to know the ocean! We were so close to it. We spent so much time moving slowly over it. So much time conjecturing what went on underneath its surface. Trying to think like a snoek.

How fine to stand one's watch at night! To stand for one's hour wedged in the door of the wheelhouse, looking out at the inky swell, the mist-wet deck, the water dripping from the foot of the

close-hauled mainsail; to see, quite often, a sea bird, a *malmok* perhaps, asleep on the heavy Atlantic swell, her head under her
wing.

As each voyage wore on we used to get near mutiny. The
trouble was always tobacco.

Before the voyage I would muster the crew and say: 'Have you
all got enough tobacco?' There would be a shout of derision, as
each man would claim that he had enough for twenty voyages.
Nevertheless I would send them off to buy some more. Secretly,
I would buy a store myself, although I did not smoke, and lock it
under my bunk.

After a fortnight of fishing the men would begin grumbling. No
tobacco. Would I sell them some? I would not. I would tell them
that I did not have any. Two days would go by, the last crumbs
had been scraped up from pocket-linings. People were surly. I
would still maintain that I had none. The next day I would relent
and produce my reserve stock. It was gone in a day or two. Then
would come the *tea* phase. People would roll tea up in paper and
try to smoke that. All sorts of reasons would be advanced for
returning to port. The water was foul. (It was: we carried it in old
wine-casks and it had a strange taste.) Once I caught a man, in the
middle of the night, letting water run out into the scuppers. He
was trying to make us short of water so that we would *have* to
return to port.

But the snoeking tradition is that as long as you have salt in
your hold you stay at sea.

The season ended for us dramatically.

One day the whole fleet was fishing together near the coast at a
place called Conception Bay, some seventy miles south of Walvis.
When night fell we lighted our pressure-lamps, and addressed
ourselves to 'working the fish off the deck'. It looked as if we were
in the middle of a small village, with the brilliant lights of the
other snoekers round about us. By ten or eleven o'clock we were
finished, and, leaving one man on watch, we of the *Cunene*
turned in.

At some time after midnight I was awakened by the watch, and
he told me that the wind had altered direction. I went on deck,
found that the wind had veered northerly and that we had veered
with it and were sailing towards the shore.

It was a simple job to put the ship about, so as to head her out to sea again, after which I went back to my bunk.

The next morning the fleet was scattered, and for a fortnight we of the *Cunene* cruised the seas alone. It was not until we had dropped anchor in Walvis Bay again, and gone ashore, that we found out what had happened to the *Titania*.

Her watch had gone to sleep, failed to note the change of wind; she had veered as we had done and sailed into the breakers at three o'clock in the morning.

Skipper Oscar Johannsen, by fine seamanship (and he is a fine seaman) contrived to send a line ashore and get the crew of fourteen through the breakers in the *Titania*'s two boats despite the fact that these had capsized several times in the process. By a lucky chance the schooner *Kernwood* worked close inshore that day in search of snoek. She sighted the *Titania*'s pickling tanks, which had been washed high and dry up on the beach, together with some wreckage. The ship herself had entirely broken up. Realizing what had happened, the skipper of the *Kernwood* worked north along the coast, in the direction of Walvis Bay, and finally sighted the stranded crew sitting by the water's edge, in their stockinged feet, having walked thus far and having decided to walk no further. Fishermen are not good walkers: they seldom have to do it. By another hazardous piece of seamanship a boat was sent ashore, with a line, and the castaways taken aboard the *Kernwood*. This boat capsized no less than seven times during the operation.

After hearing the relation of this heavy tale, we of the *Cunene* set to sea again. The pelagic shoals of snoek took us a couple of hundred miles south, as far as the fabulous island of Mercury, set in Spencer Bay. And on the way there we sighted the *Titania*'s two boats, high and dry on the steep beach where her men had left them, looking sleek and fat like a couple of sea elephants. We put 'em down in our minds as being worth about forty pounds apiece.

Now a lot of money is made from snoek, but it is not made by the people who catch them. We of the *Cunene* were chronically hard up, and after a week or two the snoek 'went down', as we say when they will not bite. We cruised the ocean and could not catch one for our supper.

So one evening we took the *Cunene* in towards the shore south of Conception Bay, stood in as close as we dared, and let go our anchor. Distance is deceptive in that clear air with nothing but sea and sand dunes to look at. We were much further from the shore than we thought. We did not realize the height of the dunes: they looked nearer than they were.

That night we lay at anchor, and early the next morning prepared for the deed that we were to attempt.

I had briefed my third-in-command, a Cape Coloured fisherman in whom I had complete confidence, and Clinton and I got ready to jump overboard. We intended to swim ashore, launch one of the *Titania*'s boats through the surf, and then row out to the *Cunene* again, forty pounds the richer. Clinton put some tobacco, a box of matches and his pipe into the toe of a sea boot, tied the leg of the boot tightly, and hung it round his neck. We stripped to our underpants, put on cork life-jackets, and slipped over the side. We had not had anything to eat that day, only a cup of tea.

The sea was horribly cold. The Benguela Current flows past that coast, straight from the Antarctic. The water was immediately quite numbing.

I was being strangled as well as paralysed. The life-jacket supported my weight by my windpipe. I had to choke for breath. Clinton was similarly inconvenienced, but he had sufficient sense to turn over on his back and he shouted to me to do the same. I did so and the relief was enormous. It was like sinking into a feather bed. I could breathe again.

I could look around me. At one moment I was in the bottom of a wide watery valley, and at the next I lifted high on to a broad crest. The *Cunene* was terribly far away! I realized that the north-going current was much stronger than I had anticipated. It would be difficult to swim against it. It occurred to me, for the first time, that the whole enterprise was most unsound.

I wished that we had stayed aboard the *Cunene*! The waves were enormous, but slow and smooth. They lifted us high up and dropped us down again, without at first doing us any harm. But, after all, they *had* come right across the south Atlantic, with a strong and steady breeze behind them. We could not expect them to be playthings.

We could see the *Cunene* now far away to the southward, and well to seaward of us, but it was plain that we were still a very long way from the shore. A crescent moon was in the sky, although it was day, and it was useful for keeping direction by. Clinton and I kept in touch quite easily, and vied with each other in making facetious remarks. I had never felt less facetious in my life.

After an interminable deal of backward swimming I saw a wave approaching which obviously meant business. It seemed to be coming faster than the others and had a crest on top. It came at me, slapped me hard in the face and forced me downwards, rolling me over and over violently. If one is only used to the waves of the Channel and the North Sea one can have no idea what real ocean combers are like when they begin to feel the bottom.

I broke surface, gasping for breath. I was exhausted by that time with cold and fatigue (I am the world's worst swimmer), but before I could get a lungful another wave hit me. Down I went again.

They seemed to have a sort of wanton, malignant violence, these waves. I felt that they had determined to kill me. They churned me over and over like a pea in a mill-race, they roared in my ears, filled my lungs with seawater, held me down hard on the creeping sand of the bottom. I could not even fight: my legs and arms would not obey me.

I caught sight of Clinton once or twice, but there was no comfort in that; the knowledge that he was there just seemed to accentuate the tragedy of drowning. Then I lost consciousness.

The next thing I noticed was that Clinton was bending over me, rubbing me hard with sand and getting quite a lot of it into my mouth. He had fared much better than I had, and the cold hadn't affected him. He was well-fleshed; I was a skinny fellow in those days. He had dragged me into the shelter of one of the *Titania*'s pickling tanks, where we were out of the cold wind but in the sun. I was quite blue—I remember being amazed when I saw my skin —and I was too weak to stand for some time. But I soon warmed up in the sunshine, and we began wondering what to do next.

Now I had no illusions about launching a boat through that surf, but it was obvious that there was no other way of getting back to the *Cunene*, which we could see at anchor far out near the horizon. We never dreamt that it was possible to walk to the nearest fresh water, which was fifty miles from where we were.

After thinking in a muddle-headed sort of way, we decided to go and *look* at the boats, anyway.

It was five miles to those boats. Five miles—the wrong way, along the soft sand of the beach. It took us until after midday to work one of them, inch by inch, over a ridge of sand and down to the sea. By a great effort we would manhandle one end of her six inches nearer the sea only to find that the other had pivoted five inches back again.

We got her to the water, though, and launched her. Valiantly we pulled her through the first small line of breakers, over a comparative calm into the second line of breakers. A wave swamped us, we were washed back to the beach again, soaked and exhausted. We launched her again. We were swamped again. We tried a third time, with the same result.

We were wet.

We were worn out.

Clinton would have had another try. He hates to be beaten. But I could see that if we tried for ever we would never do it. That second line of breakers was a killer. And we had to conserve what strength we had left for whatever else we decided to try.

There were some rubber boots in one of the boats. We cut these off at the ankles and put them on. We started to walk.

By the time we got back opposite the *Cunene* it was already nightfall. We could see her light, apparently miles out. I had never seen anything I longed for so much.

On board the ship I had always felt acutely uncomfortable. My bunk was a wooden box almost on top of the stinking diesel engine, and there were tools and spare parts under my thin, fishy and oily mattress. There was no room to sit down properly to eat one's meals. During the weeks that we spent at sea it was constantly necessary to hold on to something, for she pitched and rolled like a cow. The drinking water, as I have related, tasted foul. The tea was horrible, and indistinguishable from the coffee. For breakfast we had boiled snoek-heads, and the big eyes goggled up at us from the watery mess in the plate.

But when I looked out at that little light on the ocean, I thought that I would rather be there, in our dear little cabin, than anywhere else on earth.

When we reached the pickling tank in which I had been resuscitated we had walked ten miles already, and done an extremely arduous day's work; but we knew that we still had fifty miles to go for a drink of water. After a short rest we started walking.

You can see the Plough, or Great Bear, at that latitude, and all night I watched it in front of me, slowly swinging over in the sky. On our right were the steep, high sand dunes: on our left crashed the breakers. As the tide rose we had to scramble along the steep side of the dunes, until we thought that one leg would grow longer than the other. When the tide ebbed we could walk along the narrow beach again.

We rested sometimes on account of Clinton's legs. He had suffered from rheumatic fever in his youth. He had beaten me hands down in the sea, but we found that I was the better walker. I had quite recovered and was feeling fine, although I realized the extreme seriousness of our position; but the night was cold, we were not desperately thirsty, and we had forgotten our hunger.

When morning came and the sun rose, we lay down in the sand and slept for a couple of hours. Then we found it very hard to go on. Clinton did not want to. He kept saying that I was to leave him, and go on and send a police camel-patrol back from Walvis to find him.

I pointed out that by the time I had got there, and the patrol had returned, he would be dead. We wasted a lot of energy arguing. But we got up and kept going, in fits and starts.

The day was unpleasant. The sun became hot, thirst began to attack us, our energy seemed to have left us, and Clinton's legs caused him trouble. They went puffy, so that if you pushed your finger into them the indentation remained when you took your finger away again. He was in agony, every step was like a jab with a knife. I, too, had lost much of my sparkle. There was little facetiousness.

The day passed quickly, in a sort of dreary delirium. We walked along, each in his own little hell, with fantasies of *water* churning over and over in our minds. I have often been thirsty, much thirstier than I was then in fact, and I cannot imagine a more terrible sensation. It is not a sensation that one can describe, of course; and as soon as the thirst is satisfied it is forgotten, much as other bodily appetites are when they are satisfied. But while it lasts, it is terrible. The strange thing about it is, that while it is there, you make vow after vow, over and over again, in between the bouts of water-fantasies, that, if you survive, you will never expose yourself to the danger of being thirsty again. Yet, when the thirst is satisfied, next day perhaps, you will cheerfully walk out into the desert.

When night fell we seemed to have got nowhere. On our left the sea still thundered, and on our right rose the senseless, useless sand dunes. Clinton could only proceed by putting his arm around my neck, and every time he lay down it took longer to get him up again.

At about nine o'clock we came to Sandwich Harbour lagoon.

Sandwich Harbour is a big, salt-water lagoon, about thirty miles south of Walvis, with an underground fresh-water river flowing into it. Islands in it are the sleeping and breeding place of sea-birds, notably *duikers*, or cormorants, and there is a house on the bank in which lives a man employed to guard these birds. The birds are valuable because they produce *guano*, which is collected annually, and if they were not guarded people would steal their eggs. The Hottentots around Walvis Bay are not so richly fed that they would turn up their noses at cormorants' eggs.

We knew that we had seven miles to walk to get round the lagoon to the house. But we knew there might be fresh water on the way. Every time we saw a pool away from the lagoon we tried it, but it was always salt, until finally I tested a pool and found the water in it to be sweet. I spat it out. I was not going to have my friend Clinton park down there for the night. I should never have got him up again in the morning: I should have had to walk seven miles for help and seven miles back again, and then—could the bird-watcher and I carry him? So on we went. I knew now, at least, that we could survive.

The last long seven miles! I think they were the worst.

The first thing we came to was the bird-watcher's garden. It was surrounded by a wattle fence, and all he grew were tomatoes, which were irrigated from a well.

The tomatoes were hard and green, but we ate several of them.

Whenever I eat a green tomato now, and taste the tart, throat-rasping flavour, my memory takes me back to that garden, under the Great Bear. We did not hurry on to the house, Clinton and I: we dawdled. We wanted to savour the joy of being safe.

The bird-watcher showed the usual South African hospitality. He dressed us up in long woollen combinations and cooked us a colossal meal of fried eggs, bacon and tomatoes. According to what I remember being told in the *Boy's Own Paper* in my youth we should have been unable to take more than a sip or two of milk at first, but in fact we wolfed everything that was put before us, after distending our stomachs with water and then coffee until they hurt. We ate the lot, and then slept like birds.

Clinton's legs were puffy for several days, and when we got him to Walvis Bay he had to stay in bed. I boasted that I could walk the remaining thirty-odd miles into Walvis, but when the bird-watcher said that I could do so if I wished I very quickly climbed up into the truck.

Well, the snoeking was over. It would be five or six months before another one of these ferocious fish was caught off Walvis Bay. There was only one course left to the *Cunene*. To set sail for Cape Town.

Clinton went back to his farm. I managed to persuade Bob, the seven-foot Bergdama, Alfred, a normal-sized Bergdama who showed a natural aptitude for the engine, and our Hottentot cook whose nose had fallen away owing to syphilis, and a tough character named Joe who might have been a mixture of any combination of races, to sign on for the voyage, and to accept whatever fortune might bring to us at the Cape. I explained to them that I could not pay their fares back to Walvis, and this they accepted.

'On tick' we got some oil by a ruse. We set to sea, and after six days of plugging into a head wind which certainly reached gale force for part of the time, we made that beautiful landfall where you see hazy Table Mountain across the sea with its twin guardians flanking it; the Lion's Head and the Devil's Peak. We steamed into Table Bay harbour.

A big fishing company agreed to charter *Cunene* for twenty-five pounds a month! It should have cost that for a day! But we were dealing with monopoly.

I had my fare up to Johannesburg, but the manager of the fishing company begged me not to go. How could he get another skipper? The company would offer me the magnificent sum of seven pounds ten a month, plus commission, if I would remain in command of the *Cunene*.

I accepted, and for six months—the windy six months of the Cape winter—I fished the waters off Cape Agulhas, the Cape of Storms.

Our fishing grounds were on the continental shelf to the east of Cape Agulhas, and sixty miles from Cape Town. The length of time that our voyage could take was regulated by the running of the fish trains, twice a week, to Johannesburg. This made it so that one voyage would be eight days, and the next ten; and between each voyage we had three days in town. The *Cunene* had an insulated hold, and so we could take ice to preserve the fish.

The fish we caught were bottom-feeding fish, large and small, that feed among the coral and rough rocks off this part of the coast. From pretty little 'seventy-fours' to *steenbras* and *kabeljou* weighing a hundred pounds or more.

The procedure was this. We would cram as many souls and bodies into the little ship as possible: I never sailed with less than twelve of each. Where they slept—when they did sleep—I cannot imagine. The clamour of people begging to be allowed to come at the beginning of each voyage was pathetic. We would round Cape Point and steam east day and night until we got to the fishing grounds, and then start looking for fish. This we did by turning off the engine and drifting, beam on to the wind, while we lined the weather rail and fished with hand-lines that went to just clear of the bottom. Our hooks were baited with *chokka*, or squid, and *maasbanker*, which is a kind of small fish, both commodities supplied us by the company, and brought in by the trawlers.

If we struck good fishing we would anchor, in as many as sixty fathoms of water! We had a hundred fathoms of five-inch coir rope which made a pile in the bows as high as a man, and it had thirty fathoms of chain cable on the ground end of it, and a very heavy anchor. We needed it. At that time of the year you get two sorts of weather off the Cape—north-west wind and south-east wind—and it's often gale force. East of Danger Point there is no shelter from the south-east until you get to Mossel Bay. So, when that gale blew, we just used to ride it out, if we possibly could, and go on fishing. I have lain for days anchored in twenty fathoms of water, close to the lee shore, with the engine ticking over, and a man always up in the madly plunging bows watching the anchor cable, changing its nip, lagging it with gunny-bags, nursing it like a baby, for our lives depended on its holding.

If the wind abated, we fished. We fished all day and we fished all night. And we fished all day again. And so on. For what money we made we made from the fish we caught. I got my tiny 'retainer', but it was my share of the penny halfpenny a pound we got for the fish that kept me going. The men only had the catch money, and after I had deducted from it the amount that I had advanced to them before the voyage, their share of the food, and their share of the fishing-tackle, there was seldom much for them to get drunk on. The fact that they stuck this fantastically tough and comfortless life, and that if one was sacked there were a hundred waiting for his berth, was a measure of the stringency of their economic situation.

The life had compensations. In line fishing on the bottom there is the eternal uncertainty as to what you are going to pull up next. A fish? An octopus? A beautiful piece of pink coral? Or an old boot? We never caught an old boot off Cape Agulhas.

We caught the strangest sharks, though. Hammer-heads, tigers, blue sharks and dozens I never bothered to ask the name of. This is in the believe-it-or-not category, but we caught a ray once: all our lines got fouled in it and as we were at anchor we were fishing from both sides of the ship. When we eventually pulled it up it blanketed the bottom of the *Cunene*, which was fifteen feet wide, and its wings came up each side level with the gunwales! As God is my judge it was twenty feet wide. Before we cut it loose a fisherman took a slice out of its wing and later cooked it, but it was pretty tough.

Sharks were an intolerable nuisance. Whenever we fell into a good school of *kabeljou* the sharks would eventually come and spoil the fishing. Not only would the 'kabs' cease to bite, but every time a man caught a shark it would be pulled up weaving and twisting and everybody's line would be tangled up in a mess.

The fishermen were cruel to the sharks, and would always rip them open, or cut a fin off, before letting them go, to be torn by their companions.

Sometimes we motored seventy miles out from land to the 'seventy-four' banks. These were coral banks in about sixty fathoms of water (a great depth for hand-line fishing), and there we would lower our lines with twenty or thirty small hooks on each line. After five or ten minutes you would heave your line in and, as you looked down into the crystal-clear blue water, you would see what looked like a bunch of silver grapes coming up towards you. This would enlarge into a dozen or so 'seventy-fours' that you had caught. Up they would come, gorgeously coloured, clean little fish, their air-bladders bursting out of their mouths because of the change of pressure.

The coastline was another compensation. Instead of the arid sand dunes we now looked upon a green and beautiful coast. We used to land sometimes in St Sebastian Bay, and trade fish with a farmer there for fresh meat and vegetables. A girl used to flash a mirror at us, in the sun, when we passed Still Bay. I hope that she was beautiful, and believe that she must have been. She wore a red dress.

After a further six months of this bracing but comfortless existence I was ready for the shore. I had had a year of sea. The trouble was finding a successor, for although the company that we were working for had no scruples about taking advantage of our weakness, I still did not like to let the *Cunene* go off with an incompetent skipper.

I tried one man, a white South African, and he nearly wrecked us. He was one of those men who know everything, and I took him as a mate, with the idea that if he was any good he would take over. On the return journey home, after we had rounded Cape Point and turned our course northward, I gave him a course and handed over to him. It was in the night and I had not had much sleep. I went below and fell asleep but was awakened by the feeling that we had altered course. I went up on deck and the first thing I saw was a breaker—to port of us! Going into the wheelhouse I saw that we were steaming due east. Then I saw breakers ahead of us—and to starboard. I put the wheel hard over: we narrowly missed a rock, but by the grace of God we got out safely. My mate had decided that the course I had given him was taking us too far out to sea so he had made the decision to make a leg towards the shore. He had run us straight into a bunch of rocks called the Old Ship just outside of Hout Bay. Needless to say he left us, and eventually I found a man named Carrol. A nice chap, keen fisherman, good seaman and by his own account one of the world's great lovers. His conversation consisted entirely of accounts of his amours, generally with famous film stars, or titled ladies, who had happened to pass his way.

The last voyage I made in *Cunene* was to Port Elizabeth. The company decided to transfer her there. During the voyage it blew a westerly gale (a following wind for us) that did considerable damage to the *Winchester Castle*, which happened to be coming the other way. Before or since I have never seen waves like the ones that came rushing up at us from astern one particular night, when I dared not hand over the wheel at all, even to Carrol— waves which picked us up and hurled us forward and dropped us down into the trough again. Terrifying.

At Port Elizabeth I said goodbye to Carrol, and my fishermen, and the *Cunene*, and set off to Johannesburg. I was to seek my fortune in the city of gold.

During my return to Africa after the War, Clinton and I drove across the Namib Desert with an elderly farmer from British Bechuanaland (which is really a part of the Cape Province and not to be confused with Bechuanaland Protectorate). This man had come up to South West Africa looking for a widow, having recently lost his wife. We persuaded him to drive us down to Walvis Bay.

The road from Swakopmund threads its way through the great sand dunes, and, as we drove along this road, I was surprised to see a smudge of smoke in the sky ahead of us. 'Walvis,' said Clinton. 'The pilchard factories.'

Six high chimneys from six huge factories greeted our gaze as we rounded the last sand dune. The waterfront hummed with activity. A hundred and fifty seventy-ton motor vessels lay at moorings, or chugged backwards and forwards, out to the pilchard grounds near Pelican Point, or back to the factories. As each laden boat came alongside the quay a great hose-was lowered into her hold and sixty or seventy tons of pilchards were pumped out into the insatiable factory, to be made into fish oil and fish meal; some of it was canned. *Our* pilchards.

'This might all have been ours,' said Clinton.

'Would we really be any happier if it was?' I asked him.

Chapter Eight

✦✦✦✦✦✦✦✦✦✦✦✦✦✦✦✦✦✦✦✦✦✦✦✦✦✦◆✦✦✦✦✦✦✦✦✦✦✦✦✦✦✦✦✦✦✦✦✦✦✦✦✦

Down the Mine

The steel floor pressed hard against our feet, so that we felt the weight of our innards. The cage stopped. There was light and we were standing still. I was going down Mindola shaft of Nkana Mine on the Copperbelt in central Africa as a learner miner.

The gate was opened and I followed Jim out into a large cavern, with rough-hewn walls of rock, whitewashed, and illuminated with naked electric-light bulbs.

About the rock floor lay piles of timber, steel girders, various pieces of machinery. I noticed that the rock ceiling above our heads was unsupported by timber: throughout the mine the rock was hard enough to support itself.

Not all the men got out. The gate clanged to, the bell was rung, and the cage dropped away out of sight, leaving in its place the quivering steel rope on which it was suspended.

The high cavern narrowed into a tunnel about the size of a London tube station, and this 'cross-out' as it was called (because it was driven across the grain of the rock) widened out to make room for a great pit with a steel grid over it. As I was looking down the pit, wondering what it was, I was suddenly startled by an awe-inspiring roaring and grumbling coming from its depths, like the sound of an earthquake. 'Have they mined into Hell?' I asked.

Jim explained that this was the ore bin, and that it held twenty thousand tons of ore. The rumbling noise was the ore shifting as it was drawn away from the bottom of the bin to fill the skips that we had seen shooting up out of the shaft on to the surface.

As he was explaining this, a noise like the rumble of an

approaching tube train was heard, and soon an electric locomotive came into sight, a much larger thing than I had expected
to find underground. An African squatted on top of it holding a
pole up to an overhead cable, another sat in the driver's cab, and
several people were hanging on to the top.

The locomotive was drawing ten ten-ton 'Granby' trucks,
loaded high with broken copper ore, and as each truck drew level
with the great pit it was tipped over by a ramp, and ten tons of
ore were sent crashing and rumbling into the depths. In less than
a minute a hundred tons had been deposited in this way. I began
to have an inkling of the gigantic scale of the mine in which I was
to work.

A young white man, wet, muddy and tired after having had
twelve hours of it, handed over to us, said something about 'two
bad runaways and a derailment', and then went off with his gang
of Africans to wait for the cage.

Jim and I and some thirty or forty Africans climbed into the
now empty trucks. 'Don't touch that cable overhead,' said Jim,
'or it'll be the last thing you touch!' I now saw why the members
of the gang that I was to be in charge of had insulated helmets,
instead of the thin steel ones that the other African miners wore.

In the rear truck stood a man with a whistle, a sort of guard. He
blew two blasts and our train jolted off backwards. We lurched
and shuddered along the rough track through the dim galleries of
the mine. We swung round a corner, into another tunnel (called
a 'level' because it ran along the grain of the rock). The headlight
of our locomotive threw its light backwards to illuminate the
rough, bluish-black rock (we were in the ore itself), and in places
where water was running down out of the rock the latter was
stained with strange colours caused by the oxides of various
metals. It was a weird, Disneyesque world that I had come into.

The drive was by no means straight. It snaked around following
the strike of the ore body, but its main direction was north and
south. At intervals we passed steel shoots set up on girders, obviously meant to deliver broken rock into the trucks. There were
also mysterious holes in the side of our tunnel, with ladders
leading up into the darkness. We travelled for two and a half miles
like this, then stopped, and an elaborate process of shunting was
started, with the aid of another 'pole loco', and two squat 'battery

locos' which could go into new parts of the mine where the overhead cable had not yet been fitted.

It all seemed chaos to me: noisy, crashing, shouting chaos. Trucks were coupled and uncoupled, whistles blown, points switched, there was shouting and swearing (the former in 'kitchen kaffir', the rudimentary *lingua franca* of the mines). Trucks were loaded by being drawn under one of the overhead shoots (called 'ore boxes'), a compressed-air cock turned on to open the great steel jaw of the 'box', ten tons of broken ore would come crashing down into the truck, and the jaw was closed again. By this time one train had been filled and assembled and the other had come rumbling back from the shaft to take its place. There was never a moment's let-up.

'Half the jobs in this mine are a piece of cake,' Jim told me. 'The jobs with the big money—stopping and developing—they're nothing at all. You mark out your hot-holes and then sit on your powder-box and let the *munts* get on with it. But this tramming's a headache.'

And indeed there was trouble enough.

Once when Jim turned the lever to close an ore box a great rock the size of a wardrobe jammed in it and prevented it from closing. The smaller 'stuff' (as broken rock was generally called), little rocks and wet mud, continued to pour past and soon the truck was completely buried. Up above in the open stope were hundreds, perhaps thousands, of tons of broken rock, and the stuff only ceased to slide when there was no more space for it to slide into. Jim had to climb up on top of the box, creep inside it among the broken ore, lay a charge of gelignite on the offending rock, light the fuse and come down again. We walked around the corner, the charge went off and blew all our lights out, we lit them again and returned to find the jaw of the box closed. A dozen men were then set to shovelling the 'stuff' away from the buried trucks, and after about an hour the line was clear again.

Then a loco jumped the road, going round a set of points, and had to be laboriously jacked on again. Loaded trucks would sometimes be derailed, but these we would hoist on without ceremony by using a long piece of railway line as a lever and a pile of sleepers as a fulcrum. Battery locos would run out of juice far from the re-charging point, and have to be towed back by another loco. When things were apparently going well the power would cut out, and the pole locos would become becalmed, like ships in the doldrums.

Where most of the work was done there were no electric lights; and we had to do what we did by the dim, shifting beams of our acetylene lamps. We worked in cramped conditions, and in places the water poured down on us like hard, warm rain from the 'hanging' overhead.

To me the night seemed endless, like a nightmare. I tagged along behind Jim, understanding very little of what was going on, but acutely aware that the next night I would have to do it by myself. What I did not realize was that the gang that I was to be in charge of was perfectly capable of doing the work without my direction.

By the end of the twelve-hour shift (for we were working shift-and-a-half) we had trammed twelve thousand tons of ore two and a half miles from the stopes up the north end of the six hundred and fifty foot level to the shaft! We waited for the cage to come, shot up to the surface in it, and walked out into the blinding sun-light. It was like coming out into a sunny afternoon after wasting a couple of hours in a cinema. We went into the changing-room and stood under beautiful hot, then cold, showers, dressed and drank vile coffee from an urn. We then had a weary wait for an ore train back to Nkana, had breakfast in the mess, went back to our Kator huts and lay in a pool of sweat for the rest of the day. (A Kator hut was a corrugated-iron rondavel.)

The next night I faced my gang alone. Only one out of the forty-odd members of it could speak English, and he was the 'boss-boy', or foreman, and his name, so far as Europeans were concerned at least, was Poison. He was a member of the Wemba tribe.

Poison had been mining for eight years, and tramming for most of them. He knew more about the job than I should ever know. Being young and silly and enthusiastic I took my duties seriously, and from the first I tried to impose my will on the gang. After a week or two I succeeded, but only because of the good disposition and good sense of Poison. He realized that I was young and foolish, and made allowances for me, and saw to it that the team worked smoothly in spite of me.

As I got to know Poison better I came to understand his predicament, and that of thousands of other African miners on the Copperbelt.

Here was I, a farmer and a fisherman perhaps, but certainly not a miner, in charge of a gang of forty men, some of whom had been mining for years, and one at least of whom was a highly intelligent man and a master at his job.

I was getting, even as a learner, as many pounds a week as Poison was getting shillings! If Poison worked for another eight years, or for sixteen years, and got to know everything there was to know about mining, he still could not make as much money as I was making, and, worse, he would still be liable to be ruled and ordered about by some pipsqueak of a learner white miner.

Now most of the members of my gang had little to complain about because they were not people who had taken up mining as a profession. They were birds of passage. They lived in remote villages in central Africa, wanted to make some money to pay their taxes and to cut a dash in front of the girls, and so they walked, some of them hundreds of miles, until they reached the Copperbelt and got a job down the mine.

They would work for a year, maybe two, and then walk home again. They would never do more work than they had to, and would be satisfied with what they got paid for it. While they were working they would be fed better than they ever had been before in their lives (all recruits to the mines both in Northern Rhodesia and South Africa put on weight), they would have strange experiences, meet people from other tribes, broaden their minds perhaps, make as much money as they required, and then go back to their villages.

But a minority, people like Poison, took the business seriously. They did not return home, or if they did they returned only temporarily. They learned the trade, and made their homes on the Copperbelt.

I learned how to manage the traffic of my little private railway so that it ran smoothly. I learned to climb up into blocked ore boxes and lay 'mud-blasts' or 'pop-charges' and blow up the offending rocks that were blocking open the jaws. I learned to organize my labour. I learned to re-rail trucks or locomotives that had jumped the road. I worked hard. During the three and a half months that I was a trammer I did not miss a single night: I worked seven nights a week—and twelve hours a night. The twelve hours passed like a flash, for I was busy all the time. I walked miles every night, striding along the sleepers between the tracks. I did not just stand and shout at my men to encourage them; I would take a shovel and set an example. I learned what has since stood me in good stead, particularly during the War. If you want to get a gang of unsophisticated Africans to work hard, get them to sing, get them to laugh, get them to make bawdy jokes. Kid them into working.

I began to find time to explore the mine. The ore body we were working outcrops at the surface somewhere and then slants down into Mother Earth at an angle of about forty-five degrees. It is like a gigantic plank buried in cement, in such a position that one edge of it comes level with the surface of the cement, and the rest of the plank sinks down at a slanting angle. The cement is what we called the 'country rock': the ordinary, valueless, hard rock of Northern Rhodesia. The 'plank', or ore body, was about forty feet thick.

The 'level' along which I worked (six hundred and fifty feet below the surface) ran through the ore against the 'hanging wall', that is against the country rock *above* the slanting ore body. The system of mining was complicated, and was known as 'trailing and benching'. It is now out of date. There was a main level, like the one I was in, about every two hundred feet down in the ore body. These were connected by slanting holes called 'raises'. The ore blocked out between the raises and the main level was further sub-divided by sub-levels—little dark tunnels that you had to stoop in. When all this 'development' was completed (the ore blocked out between raises and levels) the 'stopers' got to work.

These people drilled into the blocks of ore with long-bitted pneumatic drills. They drilled for perhaps a month before they charged up and blasted; that is, before they filled all the holes that they had drilled with gelignite, lit all the fuses, and walked away. There would follow a long and shattering series of explosions and a thousand tons or more of copper-bearing rock would be broken; the whole 'bench' would come down, crashing into the space that had previously been left for it below.

It is impressive to come to the end of a sub-level at the point at which it drops away into the open stope. You look into a huge cavity under the earth—a steeply sloping, rectangular cavern, big enough to build a house in. The beam of your lamp loses itself in the dusty darkness. It is dangerous to enter such places, you constantly hear creaking and groaning of the rock of the 'hanging' and not infrequently a piece comes crashing down. If you walk on the loose rock that fills the lower part of the stope, you stand a chance of its shifting, in which case you may be drawn down with it and buried. You should not need to go into the open stope at all, for the system of mining practised was supposed to render this unnecessary, but we often used to go. Sometimes, in places where the strike of the ore body was not so steep, the broken ore would not flow very well. We would go in and encourage it, by playing on it with a high-pressure water hose. I sometimes used to explore the open stopes for fun.

Before the broken ore got to my ore boxes, from which I let it run into my trucks, it had to go through the grizzlies. These were steel grids, to stop the biggest rocks. As we were short-handed I took on the job of 'grizzlyman', together with my job of trammer.

The ore slid down on to the grizzly through two steeply slanting tunnels, which led up to the open stope. Sometimes the small tunnels got jammed. The grizzlyman's job was to unjam them.

First you tried the high-pressure hose. If this didn't work you were supposed to use a 'pole-charge'—a dozen or so sticks of gelignite tied to the end of a bamboo pole and detonated against the jam. This was seldom effective, because you could never see just where to place your charge. So the method you actually used was this. You climbed up into the 'rock-raise' as the sloping tunnel was called—right up until the jammed rock was poised above your head. Then, with a thing called a pinch-bar, you attacked the rock. When you got the right spot—inserted your pinch-bar and levered and heard a creak—you dropped the pinch-bar and made a mad dash for your life. For the rock (and there were perhaps thousands of tons of it up there) would immediately come charging down the steep slope at you! You would take a flying leap on to one of the steel bars of the grizzly—and another to safety in the sub-level—and there you would watch the crashing, grinding avalanche where a moment before you had been standing!

If you had been caught doing this by a mine official you would, of course, have been sacked but it was by far the quickest way of doing things, and of keeping the rock moving. Also, it was fun.

There were accidents in the mines of the Copperbelt. At the time that I was there, there was at least one fatal accident a week somewhere among the Big Four. The present system of mining is much safer than 'trailing and benching' but, even so, mining must always be a dangerous job. I do not see anything particularly wrong in this: as long as men are not forced underground by the fear of starving on the surface I do not care how dangerous the job is, provided people try to keep it as safe as they can make it. It is a man's job and men undertake it with their eyes open, and accept the risks involved. Some people like a job with some risk in it.

My opposite number in '650 South' (I was a trammer in '650 North') was killed one night. I went down in the cage with him and, as usual, he turned south and I turned north. In the early hours of the morning the shift-boss came and told me that he was dead.

He tried a silly trick shunting. Driving a battery loco himself he towed some trucks behind him with a long chain, over some points. He wanted the loco to go one way and the trucks the other. A man was to throw the points after the loco had passed but before the first truck arrived. It worked perfectly, but my opposite number stopped the loco too soon and the body of the truck pressed him between itself and the body of the loco. The shift-boss said they folded him up like a handkerchief.

As for my hut-mate, the man with whom I had come up from Johannesburg on the train, he ended his Copperbelt career in a spectacular manner. They made him a 'stope scraper'. This involved rigging a scoop on an endless rope in the open stope, where the dip of the ore body was not steep enough for the 'stuff' to flow by gravity. To do this he (or at least his 'boys') had to drill a hole in the face with a jack-hammer to fix an eye bolt. He was watching three of them do this one day when a piece of 'hanging' came down—a lump of rock perhaps the size of a room—and buried the three men and the jack-hammer. It just missed my hut-mate.

He panicked so completely that he didn't stop running and

shouting 'Help!' at the top of his voice until he had reached the shaft where he rang furiously for the cage. There was not much that he could have done for the poor fellows of course, but he might at least have said a prayer over them.

The four great mines of the Copperbelt, Nkana, Nchanga, Mufulira and Roan Antelope, between them produced in 1952 313,000 tons of copper, valued at £75,000,000. Northern Rhodesia was then the third largest producer in the world, the USA being the first, and Chile the second. Zambia, as Northern Rhodesia is now called, is catching the others up. The reserves of ore not yet developed there are colossal.

To give some idea of the scale of these mines, at Mindola No. 1, down which I worked, 175,000 tons of ore were hoisted every month, or over six and a half thousand tons per working day. That is an awful lot of broken rock to come out of one hole. The tonnage of Nkana Central shaft was about the same. To produce this incredible amount of rock from the depths of the earth and refine it required nearly two thousand Europeans and eleven thousand Africans.

When I worked there the tide of Afrikanerdom was only just flowing northward. The language of the Europeans on the Copperbelt was English, and one seldom heard Afrikaans although there was even then a growing minority of Afrikaners. Nowadays, amongst the 'non-officials' one hears more Afrikaans than English.

The European miners were a strangely assorted crew. Afrikaners who had drifted from the back-veld of the Union for better money. 'Cousin Jacks' (as Cornish miners are called) from the tin mines of Cornwall, men whose forefathers worked underground before the Roman conquest and who only felt really at home with a few hundred feet of rock over their heads! Americans, Canadians, Australians, Englishmen and Scotsmen, Welsh coal miners who had drifted into hard-rock mining, and cosmopolitans who wandered about the world looking upon anywhere as their home.

There were sailors who had strayed from the sea, prospectors who had gone broke searching for gold and who had come to the big mines to make the money for another grub-stake, traders who had traded unwisely, elephant hunters driven from their profession by the low price of ivory (five shillings a pound in those days): every type of roamer and adventurer that our strange, global, Ango-Saxon culture has flung about the world. Men who in another age would have been pirates or sea-rovers, explorers, slave-traders or soldiers of fortune: there they were, making money and spending it as fast as they could in the heart of Africa.

After three and a half months at Nkana I asked for, and was given, a transfer to Nchanga Mine. This had just been reopened, having been flooded for eight years.

Eight years before, a miner had blasted into a mud-rush—a pocket of water and mud underground, trapped in the rock. Blasting is carried out at the end of the shift, and so everybody was leaving the mine anyway, but quite a lot of people had to climb up the ladderways in the vertical shaft because the cage could not take them quickly enough. The mine was completely flooded, and remained abandoned for eight years.

When I went there two incline shafts had been sunk down to within a few yards of the old workings, some very powerful pumps installed in one of them, and a hole broken through from the other into the old workings. The two shafts were connected through the rock by pipes, and through these pipes the water was pumped to the surface. In this manner the old workings were emptied of water.

I entered the old workings a few days after they had been broken into and it was an eerie experience. Here were battery locos standing as they had been left, and when new batteries were put in them they worked perfectly. When the electric light system was connected up with the surface the lights went on. At that depth in water things do not corrode. One found miners' helmets, lamps, sandwich-tins where they had been thrown down in their owners' hurry to escape from the rushing water! At first I was given what must be the most perfect job to have underground, for a lazy man at least. I was a 'sump-watcher'.

My job was to sit on a box in a little cubby-hole in the rock, near the enormous sumps which had been excavated down 'B' shaft to take the rush of water if there should be another 'mud-rush'. When the water reached a certain level in the sumps I had to telephone through to 'A' shaft, which was the pump shaft, and tell the pump men to turn another pump on. When the water sank to a certain level I had to telephone through to ask them to turn a pump off. It was necessary to telephone perhaps once in two hours. I had three Africans to help me in this arduous operation: so prodigal can a mine be with labour, if it is cheap enough.

I rigged up a plank to lean against, taught one African to watch the sumps, one to use the telephone (without waking me) and one to watch out for the shift-boss. On night shifts I used to sleep like a lamb, and then have the day for amusing myself. On day shifts I used to improve my mind. I believe that I am the first man to have read all of Shaw's plays in the sump of a copper mine. I also believe (although I cannot be so sure about it) that I am the only man to have habitually gone swimming in the sump of a copper mine. I used to take off my clothes and dive into one of the million-gallon sumps. The water was a clear greenish-blue, and the rock roof hung low overhead, supported by rock pillars, among which I swam.

> Where Alph, the sacred river, ran
> Through caverns measureless to man
> Down to a sunless sea.

Automatic sump-watchers were installed, and so I lost this delightful occupation. I went on to a 'big-end scraper'.

A 'big-end' is the end of a large tunnel which is being driven into the rock: a drive or a cross-cut. A big-end scraper is a machine for scraping up the rock that has been blasted out of the end and loading it into trucks.

When I returned to the Copperbelt after the War I went into a big-end down Mindola Mine, and tried to make a tape-recording of the noise, but no recording machine in the world could cope with it! The din and confusion in an 'end' are indescribable. In my 'end' at Nchanga the air was warm and damp and stagnant, and it smelt strongly of powder fumes. From the roof fell an incessant downpour of water, like a monsoon storm. We worked in this all the time. In order to 'get a move on' we were mining three shifts in this end: that is, ours and the other two shifts were blasting three times in twenty-four hours. When the miner and I went in at the beginning of our eight-hour shift we would have to wait for half an hour or so to allow the fumes of the recent explosion to dissipate. Then we would go in (leaving our gangs of Africans behind us) and connect up a water hose and hose down the 'face', as the rock in the end of the tunnel was called. This was to dissolve the remaining lethal fumes, and wash away dirt so that we could examine the face. We had to make sure there were no misfires—charges that had failed to go off. 'He drilled into a misfire, poor chap,' is a common epitaph for a miner the world over.

We would sound the 'hanging' overhead to make sure there was no 'bad-hanging'—loose rock—and if there was we would prise it down with a pinch-bar. When we were sure that all was safe we would send for the 'boys'.

My gang would trundle up my scraper. This had a ramp big enough to take a five-ton truck underneath it and a scoop holding about half a ton pulled backwards and forwards on an endless rope. I would drill a hole in one side of the face and drive in an eye bolt to take the pulley. An electric motor would then be started on the scraper and the scoop would begin to travel backwards and forwards, dragging the broken rock up the ramp and dumping it in a truck underneath. The rest of my gang, about twenty men, would get to work shovelling rock into the path of the leaping, bounding scoop, in imminent danger of being scooped up themselves. The miner would get his 'machines' in— four jack-hammer drills (like pneumatic road-drills)—with two men to each drill. Each drill had a compressed air hose and a high-pressure water hose dragging behind it, and these hoses straggled like snakes all over my 'stuff' that I was trying so hard to remove.

The scraper made a terrific noise, as did a pneumatic water-pump which pumped away the water that was being dammed up by the great pile of broken rock which had been blasted by the previous shift. When the four drills opened up, the din could not be heard because one's eardrums were numbed; but it could be *felt!* All speech stopped: we communicated by hand signals only. And the confusion—the crashing scoop—the twenty shovelling, half-naked men—the juddering jack-hammers—the men bringing up sharp drill-steel and taking back blunt—the men pushing up empty trucks and taking away full ones—the dim light—the downpour from the roof over our heads—the heat—the humidity!

The 'machine-boys' sat down waist-deep in water to 'get their holes in' in the foot of the face, or sometimes they built a crazy platform up against the rock and two men would stand on it, holding their heavy, juddering jack-hammer at arm's length over their heads, their brown skins bespattered with white rock-paste, their heads down to get more power into their arms, their muscles bulging!

It was *war*.

Near the end of the shift the holes would be complete. The holes are not drilled just anyhow, they have names, and purposes. You have your 'cut holes' in the middle, six holes drilled in the form of a pyramid so as to throw out a wedge-shaped chunk of rock when the charges go off. Around your 'cut' are your 'easers', which throw the rock into the space left by your cut. Lower down are your 'knee-holes', higher up your 'shoulder-holes', right down at the bottom your 'lifters', in your corners your 'corner-holes', and right at the top your 'slipers'.

They were charged by filling them right up with sticks of gelignite—rammed down hard with a wooden stick. The second from end stick was your 'primer': it had a detonator in it, crimped on to the end of a long piece of safety fuse. (Your true miner always crimps a detonator by putting it in his mouth and biting it, although this is against the regulations.) The fuses were so cut that the 'cut holes' went off first, and then the intermediate holes, and then the ones round the edge. The holes would be from four to eight feet long, depending on what the miner had time for. (He was paid by their length.)

When they were all charged up my men would dismantle the scraper and wheel it off round the corner out of harm's way. Everyone but the miner, his 'boss-boy' and myself would be sent away to the shaft. We three would light 'cheesa-sticks' (small fireworks) and with them light the notched safety-fuses. It was most essential not to miss any—for if we did a misfire would result. We would then shout 'CHEESA! CHEESA!' as a warning, and walk—at a dignified speed—towards the shaft. When we had got round a few corners our helmets would be blown off and our lights put out by a shattering series of explosions. We would count them, to make sure that there were no misfires.

Always count your shots! 'Twenty-three, twenty-four, twenty-five. That's the lot! Got eight feet in tonight, thank God! Come on, let's get up that shaft and have some coffee!'

When I had worked for exactly six months underground I went to the office and gave twenty-four hours' notice. I did not dislike mining, in fact in some ways I enjoyed it; but I did not like working for such a very large organization. I just happen to have the wrong sort of temperament for it. Also, six months is quite a long time for a man to stay in any one place.

I went to Ndola and sat for a little examination to obtain my 'Underground Blasting Certificate'. Then I took the train southward.

Chapter Nine

✦✦✦✦✦✦✦✦✦✦✦✦✦✦✦✦✦✦✦✦✦✦✦✦✦✦✦✧✦✦✦✦✦✦✦✦✦✦✦✦✦✦✦✦✦✦✦✦✦✦✦✦✦✦✦

Spider Has the Rats

First there was a furious barking, as from a pack of ravening dogs. Then a loud crash, followed by someone roaring and screaming to the utmost extent of the power of his lungs, and to the limit of what his vocal cords would undergo. Then the violent shrilling of a police-whistle, then more shouting and bangs and crashes, and all the while the frenzied barking of dogs. . . .

I peered through the mosquito netting into the house.

The fattest man I had ever seen, a bulging, sagging-cheeked, blubber-bag of a man, a man-bolster, a man-balloon, stood on his Michelin-tyre-advertisement legs in the middle of the room. Around him, amid upturned furniture, bounded four great wolf-hounds, their barking reaching almost screaming-point in its ferocity.

The man was trying to perform several operations at once.

First, he was trying to lash the dogs with a large *sjambok* (he failed in this, not being mobile enough). Second, he was stamping his huge feet and kicking the fallen furniture. Third, he was shouting and screaming for somebody named Blanket. And fourth, he was trying to blow a police-whistle. He would put the whistle in his mouth and the shout would burble into a screech, while his cheeks would belly out like twin spinnakers. Then he would withdraw the whistle and the shout would follow it through his lips and he would bellow like a maniac. It was difficult to believe that one individual could create such a commotion.

I was looking for a job.

I had taken the train down to Mazabuka, where many of the white farmers of Northern Rhodesia lived, to see if I could get a job managing a farm. I had been told that the only possible vacancy was on the farm of a man whom I will call Biscoe, and here was Biscoe in the room before me. I had been warned, though, that nobody else had ever succeeded in sticking the man for more than a month.

After I had enjoyed several minutes of this interesting spectacle the door inside the room opened and a servant appeared; obviously Blanket. He was a small Mlozi man, with ugly bare legs, and wearing dirty khaki shorts and a blue shirt.

He entered the room with no appearance of urgency, completely ignored his master, and proceeded to catch the three ravening wolf-hounds one by one and push them through an inner door. They suffered this but did not stop their howling, and it was quite clear to me that if they could have got at me (for I was the cause of their disturbance) they would have eaten me.

The servant's arrival made no difference to the master, who continued to roar and shout and whistle and kick and lash the furniture just as before. Only after Blanket had removed the last dog, replaced the fallen furniture (I noticed that he kept well out of reach of the *sjambok*), and taken a good look at me through the mosquito netting, did his master permit himself a moment's respite. Then he grasped the back of a chair to steady himself and stood gasping for breath.

'Blasted niggers!' he wheezed. 'Swine! Swine! Black swine!' And to emphasize this point he banged the *sjambok* down on the table.

Then he turned to me. 'All right, all right, come in. You're safe now. Come in.'

I went in, noticing as I did so a most unwholesome smell in the room. The fat man sat down.

He knew why I had come to see him. 'I'll give you fifteen quid a month,' he said, 'and you buy your own food, and you can live in the shed.'

I said I would take the job. Indeed, I needed the money.

'I'm too fat to get about any more,' he said. 'Got so blasted fat, can't think why. Always been an active man all me life. Came out to Northern Rhodesia fifteen years ago as a carpenter, got this farm from the government, but now I'm so fat I can't leave this room. Have to leave the farming to the blasted niggers.'

Three days after I had begun working for Biscoe I gave him a month's notice. I found that he had countermanded an order that I had given to his 'boss-boy' over my head, a thing I would not put up with. I worked out the month, took my fifteen pounds, and left him.

Biscoe's farm was fairly typical of the cattle and maize farms on the 'railway line' of Northern Rhodesia, except that it had been terribly neglected. It was about five thousand acres. Thirteen years before when the government had given it to Biscoe on a 999-year lease it had been bush-veld; about a hundred acres of the bush had been cleared and ploughed, the only crop grown on the ploughed area was maize, and the rest of the farm was given over for grazing cattle.

Biscoe gave me his cattle tally-book, which indicated that there were over nine hundred cattle. 'I know that's right,' he said, 'because Sixpence, my boss-boy, gives them to me every morning.'

I counted the cattle and found there were just over three hundred. But everywhere I looked I saw cattle bones. I reported this to Biscoe.

'Nonsense!' he shouted. 'Don't be a fool, man! Sixpence gives me the tallies every morning. You can't count.'

I got a neighbour in, a farmer who told me that he wouldn't speak to Biscoe, having quarrelled with him some dozen years before, but who agreed to count the cattle and send Biscoe a note. He got the same count as I had done. 'His damned cattle have been dying of heart water and red water and gall-sickness for years,' he said. 'Because they haven't been dipped. And his niggers have been killing and eating them. Serve him right. Nobody's got any time for him.'

So that was that.

Biscoe at last believed about the cattle, but he pinned his faith on his maize crop. 'The boys say I'll get ten bags to the acre,' he said. 'They say there's a bumper crop this year. I always used to get ten bags to the acre. Something's gone wrong the last year or two, though. But it's going to be O.K. this time.'

'You'll be damned lucky if you get two bags to the acre,' I told him. 'Your land's farmed out, and what little has grown the boys have stolen and what they haven't stolen the baboons have got.'

But I never did succeed in making him believe that he was not going to get ten bags to the acre, and he celebrated my leaving by setting his 'boys' on to building an enormous crib just near his house where he could see it: it was big enough to hold twenty times the maize that he would harvest.

I certainly do not wish to convey the impression that Biscoe was typical of the Northern Rhodesian farmers. He was unique. Most of the farmers I met at Mazabuka and at Chisamba, where I stayed for a while, were most likeable men, and many of them very good farmers. There were only about five hundred farmers all told along the railway line (and maybe about the same number in the Fort Jameson District, the other side of Northern Rhodesia, where I nearly went to manage the farm of the man with the aluminium leg). The 'Fort Jimmie' farmers grew tobacco, the best flue-cured Virginia. The 'railway line' farmers produced mostly cattle and 'mealies' (maize), although further south, at Choma, some tobacco was grown; and cotton was becoming a more important crop.

The land that they farm is typical bush country. Since time immemorial it has been farmed by the natives of the country and has also produced cattle and maize: maize at least for the last three or four hundred years, since the maize plant was brought from America by the Portuguese. Before then, presumably, they grew millet and sorghum. They practised (and still practise) shifting cultivation. A man clears an acre of bush by cutting down trees and burning. His womenfolk hoe the ground and plant the seed. For three or four years they get a good crop. Then the crops begin to tail off (as Biscoe's had already done) and the man goes and chops down some more trees elsewhere and clears some more land.

This form of agriculture is practised in many parts of Africa and in Asia as well, but it is often frowned upon by governments because it is alleged to spoil the land. In fact, if the country is fairly level, as Northern Rhodesia is, and not too overpopulated, it does very little damage to the land. In some countries now (Ceylon is an example) it is being recognized that this form of agriculture is nothing like as damaging as was at one time thought. For when a plot is abandoned it quickly falls back to bush, and will perhaps not be cleared and hoed again for generations.

The system of farming practised by Biscoe is very much more harmful to the land. On Biscoe's farm we ploughed with three-furrow disc ploughs, drawn by oxen. These turned the soil up to a much greater depth than the hoes of the Africans, and therefore Biscoe had been able to go on getting reasonable crops of maize from his cleared fields for far longer than Africans would have done. But the fields were now completely exhausted. He had taken everything out of them, and put nothing back. He would have to abandon them and clear more bush, but it would be many years before they would tumble back to heavy bush, and they would probably erode badly before they did so. He had killed the soil.

When I took my leave of Biscoe (after another interview which, like all meetings with that great man, involved a repetition of the scene described at the beginning of this chapter) I was in a poor way financially. I had just enough money for my ticket back to the Copperbelt. So I decided to go back there, and (brandishing my new 'blasting ticket') take a job at Mufulira or Roan Antelope—one of the mines, in fact, in which I had not already worked.

Alas! Neither of these mines would have me.

After I had been refused a job at Roan Antelope I did not have the money for my return fare to Ndola, where I was staying, and had to walk back along the railway line which took me all of one night.

Ndola was supposed to be the 'capital of the Copperbelt', but it never really came off. It was a sleepy little place in those days, where untarred roads straggled about in the bush searching for the scattered bungalows of civil servants. I had got a room in a home for refugees: Jewish refugees from Hitler's Germany. Northern Rhodesia, like other British colonies, had taken a quota of these, and some of them were living, and I with them, in great squalor in a slummy building in Ndola.

Having walked back from Roan Antelope I went to a flyblown little café kept by a Greek, to spend my last two bob on a meal. After that I realized that I would 'have to make a plan' as people always say in South Africa when they do not quite know what to do next.

Sitting in the café was a man. A smallish, rather wizened little man, but a man with an amused look on his face and a twinkle in his eye.

I joined him at his table (we had not yet got to the stage in Northern Rhodesia where two white men will sit at separate tables in a café because they have not been 'introduced'). He told me his name, but I will call him 'Spider' Webb. He spoke with a Cockney accent, and told me that he came from London.

I noticed that he paid for his meal, not with money, but with a small ticket. I asked him what this was, and he said it was a meal ticket issued to him at the Home for Distressed British Subjects.

I asked him how one qualified for admission to this establishment, and he said that it was all right for a day or two, but the trouble was that if you stayed there too long they shipped you off, either to England or down south if you were a Southern Rhodesian subject, as he in fact was.

'I've boozed me way round the Copperbelt,' he told me. 'I've done the rounds. I come back here every four or five years and booze me way round; they forget you after a time. The trouble is, you see, I'm a dipsomaniac. I'm all right when I'm broke, but the moment I get some money I get drunk. And if I have enough money I get the Rats.'

'What are the Rats?' I asked.

'You get so you see rats,' he said. 'Only I see little men, but it's really all the same. Little men are worse than rats, really.'

When he found that I too was out of work, and knew not where to lay my head (not that this greatly worried me) he suggested that we team up. 'We'll buy bikes,' he said, 'and cycle down to Southern Rhodesia. We can easily get a job in a small gold mine. Damn these ruddy great mines up here. Give me a small mine every time. Just one or two good chaps and a few dozen *munts*.'

'And where do we get the money to buy the bicycles?' I asked.

'You must have some kit? We'll flog it. Have an auction sale.'

We went back to my lodging and looked at my belongings. I had a gramophone, some discs of music by Beethoven and Mozart and other well-known composers, a dinner-jacket, a light suit and some other odds and ends. Spider sent word out around the African location that there was to be, that evening, an auction sale.

By six o'clock a large crowd had collected in the courtyard of my lodging house. The landlord had already tried to disperse it. The 'Emperor' was going full blast on the gramophone, and Spider was shouting above the din, crying the value of my belongings in a curious mixture of 'kitchen kaffir' and Cockney and one or two other languages.

'Come on me hearties!' he bellowed. '*Trousers moushi sterrek! Mena haikona funa shillingi maningi! Mena haikona az danganya wena!* Here, me old sweetheart, just what you want for your old man!' His battered sun-helmet on the back of his head, he held aloft a pair of my trousers. My effects sold like hot cakes. There was much good humour. The Africans enjoyed the sight of the small, scruffy, white man, prancing up and down with various articles of clothing.

'Vat you make on my premises?' demanded the landlord. 'Iss ziss a kaffir location for black men?'

'You shut up,' said Spider. 'Come on, me lucky lads!' he bellowed. 'Here's a pair of underpants to gladden any girl's heart!'

By the time the landlord had gone off to get the police the sale was over, and Spider and I had nearly twenty pounds in our pockets!

We went off to celebrate. Spider belonged to a charmed circle: he was an ex-member of the British South Africa Police—the mounted police force of Southern Rhodesia, originally founded by Cecil John Rhodes. There are a lot of these people in central Africa, and they have a kind of freemasonry between them. We met another 'old B.S.A.P. man' in a pub, and, alas, by the next morning there was not enough of the twenty pounds left over to buy even one bicycle.

'All right, we'll walk!' said Spider.

So we walked.

We rolled up the remains of our belongings in a blanket apiece, tied the blankets over our shoulders like South American bandits and started southward along the Great North Road of Africa. We would have just a hundred and seventy miles to go to get to Lusaka.

It was the rainy season, and the road was closed to motor traffic. Nowadays it is an all-weather road, but it was not in those days, so we had no hope of getting a lift.

Straight and still lay the road, through the untouched virgin forest. On either side of it rose the slender, crooked trunks of the forest trees: not like the timber of an English wood, not like the scrubby little trees of the bush-veld, but tall, slender, crooked-stemmed trees such as are peculiar to the rolling uplands of the Copperbelt country and parts of the Belgian Congo.

Early in the morning we shouldered our blanket-rolls and set off along the road.

As the sun rose higher its rays penetrated the green canopy overhead and the air became hot, but Spider and I padded on in silence, the sweat running down our foreheads and dripping off our chins. We met no one in a day's march, saw no sign of human habitation, heard or saw neither bird nor animal. Under the trees grew green bushes and rank green grass, the product of the current rainy season, and every so often the flatness was broken by a huge dome-shaped ant-hill.

At noon we halted, built a small fire and brewed up some tea in a three-legged iron pot which Spider had insisted we carry. We drank the tea, ate some bully-beef and bread, and after a short rest plodded on.

Late in the afternoon we came to where a track led off from the main road. We went along it, intending to camp, and found that it led to Bwana Mkubwa Mine.

The track climbed a steep rise, and suddenly the ground fell away at our feet and we found ourselves gazing down into a mighty rectangular hole in the earth, a hole that you could have built a dozen churches in and their spires would have come about level with the rest of the country. At least that is how I remember it. There were no buildings in sight, just the bush: but way down at the bottom of the hole was one abandoned rusty steam-shovel. All that remained of a great endeavour.

This was the first of the big copper mines, but it was found that the ore was 'refractory', and that it would be too expensive to refine. So Bwana Mkubwa was abandoned.

The lip of the crater was high, and afforded a good view over the surrounding forest. As far as we could see—even to the horizon—lay an ocean of tree-tops—broken here and there by *kopjes*. It appeared as if no living thing inhabited this wilderness: there was no sign anywhere of a clearing, nor the smoke of a fire, nor a human habitation.

'Miles and miles of sweet Fanny Adams,' was Spider's comment. 'Like the rest of ruddy Africa.'

Where we camped there were flowering shrubs in bloom: shrubs such as are found in gardens, but growing incongruously here amongst the indigenous vegetation. It occurred to us that they must have been planted by the miners.

'I wonder if they'll spread until they cover the whole of Africa,' I said.

'Not them,' said Spider. 'Africa'll spread and cover them.'

I wondered if that would be the fate of other aspects of European culture that have been planted in this continent.

As we were gathering firewood we saw two figures approaching. An old African man wearing a *khansa*, or white robe, and a young boy wearing a loin-cloth. The man had a musket. The interdiction against Africans possessing firearms did not obtain in Northern Rhodesia as it does in South Africa, although it was difficult for them to get a licence to keep a firearm. The restriction of licences was to protect the wild animals, not because the white people felt unsafe if Africans have guns.

The two Africans squatted down not far away and clapped their hands, which is the local form of greeting. Spider asked the man in 'kitchen kaffir' if he had any beer. 'Here, mate,' he added in English. 'Here's a shirt. You could do with a shirt, me old cock o' the jungle! Can't always run around in a nightie.'

The man, a dignified old gentleman with a pointed white beard, took the tattered remains of Spider's spare shirt and examined it carefully. He then put it on the ground beside him. After watching us for a long time the man and the boy got up and walked away.

In half an hour they returned, accompanied by two women. One of the women carried a four-gallon petrol tin full to the brim with native beer, and the other carried two live chickens tied by the legs, a small basket of maize flour, another of sweet potatoes, and four eggs. The women placed these on the ground, squatted down, and clapped their hands. After a time the four Africans got up and left. They had spoken in whispers to each other, but not one of them had spoken to us.

We boiled the two chickens in the three-legged iron pot, and roasted some sweet potatoes in the embers of our fire. We ate what we could of the chickens and kept the rest for the next day.

The heat of the day gave way to a refreshing coolness, which increased until we were glad to wrap our blankets around our shoulders, and throw some more wood on the fire. The tree-frogs had started their monotonous chirping, and we could hear the complex rhythm of the drums in the distance, the sound that is part of the African night.

The beer was thick, like gruel. It was frothy on top, muddy grey-brown in colour, and it tasted gritty and sour. It 'caught' your throat as you drank it. The sourness was a wholesome sourness, and in any case was new to neither of us, and we dipped our mugs into the beer fairly often. We finished the four gallons before we rolled up in our blankets and went to sleep.

We told each other the stories of our lives. I asked Spider if he was married. 'Me? Hooked and landed, mate,' he said. 'Got a wife in Jo'burg; she works as a typist. We never see each other, so that's why we never quarrel. It's the perfect marriage.'

Spider was fairly typical of a type of adventurer who is to be found wandering around in central and eastern Africa. They are not all dipsomaniacs, of course, but most of them drink heavily. Spider may not have been a model citizen, but I liked him very much better than many a more respectable gentleman I have met. He was one of the rebels from the deadening, all-conquering Western way of life: the way of cloying respectability, deadly mediocrity, efficiency for the sake of efficiency, machines for making more machines. Not a way of life at all, but a way of death-in-life. Spider was one of the rebels: his dipsomania was unfortunate, but was part of his revolt.

We travelled on pleasantly for several days, and every night we found that there was a village near to where we made camp, for always some Africans would come, and always, whether we paid them with some cast-off article of clothing or not, they gave us beer and food. It was as though they looked upon it as their responsibility to feed us while we were passing through their territory.

Wherever I have been in Africa, I have found this unquestioning hospitality among the people. When an African goes on a journey, of twenty miles or a thousand, he takes no food with him, and very often no money. He banks on being fed in the villages that he passes through, even if they are inhabited by people of another tribe, who do not speak his language. I think that maybe it was like this in Europe, in the Middle Ages. It is not like it now.

From the road we saw no sign of humanity, but sometimes off the road one would find a village among the trees, surrounded by cleared patches of ground on which millet and sweet potatoes were growing. Owing to tsetse-fly there were no animals.

We came to the township of Broken Hill, and gazed down into the enormous crater of the mine. Men toiling in the bottom of it looked the size of ants. We met a friend, who allowed us to sleep on the floor of his single quarters for a few nights while we looked for jobs, but jobs there were none. We were shown a hole in the side of the crater where the skull of *Homo Rhodesiensis* was found.

We left Broken Hill and continued on south. Often it rained, and we got wet; but we got dry again after it stopped, and the wetting never did us the slightest harm. We thoroughly enjoyed ourselves. We had not a care in the world. We felt bodily as fit as one can be. We longed for our meals, and enjoyed them when they came. We enjoyed our two gallons each of 'kaffir beer' every evening. We longed for our sleep, and slept like birds. And we enjoyed the day's march. After the months of noise and stress and bustle under the ground the journey was a delight. I particularly loved the early mornings. The cold would wake you in the early dawn. You would get the fire to blaze up, then roll up again in your blanket and lie awake, watching the creeping light. A bird that one is told is the 'bush-turkey' (but I believe it is the Greater Bustard) would start his morning hymn. This was a series of notes, starting in a very low note indeed, but getting higher and at the same time fainter, until on about the eighth note the sound faded out. POM, POM, pom, pom, pom. . . . During the couple of years in which I lived in the bush in Northern Rhodesia I do not believe that a single morning passed without my hearing this noise.

Then, as the sky got lighter, other birds woke up, and the day began.

After about a month, which included a week or so of living in an empty hut on a European-owned farm in Chisamba District (a model farm called Golden Valley, belonging to some grand Scots people) we went on to Lusaka. Spider sent a telegram to his wife.

He wanted ten pounds, ostensibly to buy bicycles. 'I send her money when I'm in a job,' he explained, 'so when I'm pushed she sends me some.'

I heard a rumour of the possibility of a job in the Northern Rhodesian Veterinary Department, and so I telephoned the head office, which is at Mazabuka, where I had worked for Biscoe. They asked me to go for an interview. I had just enough money for my fare; no more, no less. Spider went to stay in another refugee lodging-house.

To my surprise I got the job. I was signed on as a government 'Stock Inspector'. Later this high-sounding title was changed to the even higher-sounding one of 'Livestock Officer'. I was to receive twenty-five pounds a month, plus accommodation and certain allowances. I stayed in Mazabuka for several days, and then borrowed the money from my boss to return to Lusaka.

In Lusaka I found that Spider's wife had been forthcoming with the ten pounds for the bicycles. The bicycles had not actually been purchased, though.

Spider was lying on the bed in his doss-house, and there was half a case of Cape brandy beside the bed, and scattered about the floor were several empty bottles.

'Oh John, I've had hell!' he said. 'Little men! Little men on the floor! Little men jumping off the ceiling. *Oh drive them away! Drive them away!*'

Spider was having a go of the Rats.

Chapter Ten

✦

Of Buck, Buffalo and Serowe Ants

After a month's training at Mazabuka I went up to Barotseland, the semi-independent kingdom on the head-waters of the great Zambezi.

For the first time I had found a job which suited me wholly and entirely.

I lived in a pleasant thatched bungalow in beautiful forest country, by the bank of a stream in which I used to catch fish. For the first time I had real furniture, for this was supplied by the government. I would have, perhaps, a week at home, and then a new batch of vaccine would arrive, an attenuated culture of a virus causing a disease known as contagious bovine pleuro-pneumonia. I would then summon up the twenty-four porters allowed me by the government, my two 'Veterinary Messengers', my small 'boy' and my cook, and off we would go, like Stanley looking for David Livingstone, walking twenty miles a day, inoculating thousands of cattle until the vaccine was finished. For the aim was to inoculate—and brand—every beast in Barotseland three times, to protect them from this dread disease that had been wiping them out.

There were no white people in Barotseland, beyond the District Commissioners, the occasional missionary, the odd trader, a couple of government vets and a doctor or two. But vets and doctors were a hundred miles away from me. I was a livestock officer, a sort of vet *manqué*. I got twenty-five pounds a month and various bush allowances that made it up to about thirty-five. I got an allowance to buy meat for my twenty-seven or so men and I used to pocket the lot. They lived practically entirely on meat, but beyond the cost of cartridges it cost me nothing, for I shot it. The country was full of game which I felt quite justified in shooting, because the game could breed faster than the handful of people in the kingdom who had rifles could shoot it. I do not believe that would be the case today, and as African states get independence so the game will disappear completely.

Thus I divided my time between my pleasant bungalow by the little river, and the bush. In the bush I lived in my large and commodious tent, with a camp bed, mosquito net, canvas bath and washstand, chair and table. I had a cook and a 'boy' to look after me. I was welcome in every African village, because my inoculations really *did* save the cattle, and well the inhabitants knew it. I shot a buck nearly every evening and occasionally a buffalo. The life was healthy, useful, pleasant and varied. And in the little Loanja River valley, near my house, I believe there was the best duck- and goose-shooting in the world.

Travel on the Zambezi itself was by barge. The barges were heavy, flat-bottomed boats, thirty feet long, paddled by a dozen or so paddlers who stood up, in the Barotseland fashion, in the bow and the stern. I once made the trip up to Mongu, and beyond, to Kalabo, in a barge. It took three weeks, and we camped on an island, or near a village on the bank, every night. The Zambezi was in flood at the time, and the whole plain for sixty miles wide was under shallow water. For days our barge would nose her way through long grass, leaving a wake of open water astern. The paddlers sang as they paddled and got drunk every night on local beer.

My nearest neighbour at Machili, where my permanent station was, was Jack Martin, a Forestry Officer: in fact the Assistant Conservator of Northern Rhodesia. He was the first really literate and cultured man I ever met. He had a fine library, a collection of records, an open and a lively mind and an interest in everything. Meeting him was a revelation. He taught me to drink—joyously, argumentatively, uproariously and with song. He was a mad fellow—stood on his head on the rail of Victoria Falls Bridge— launched a full-grown crocodile into the swimming-pool of the Victoria Falls Hotel one night—made a complete survey of

Barotseland (a flat, heavily wooded country unsuitable for theo-dolite surveying) by shooting the stars. He had a gorgeous wife and little baby whom he used to carry with him on *ulendo* (walk through the bush) in a basket slung between two porters. As soon as he was allowed to, when the War broke out, he joined the RAF, got his wings, and was killed.

It was at Jack Martin's house that I heard about the War.

I walked down there one day to find three 'White Fathers'—Roman Catholic missionaries, whom we knew very well and had frequently got drunk with—all in the house and everybody very excited. War had broken out. There we were, a hundred miles from a road, in the heart of Africa—if Africa has a heart—and war had broken out. That day.

Of course we all patriotically clamoured to join the forces, secure in the knowledge that we would never be released. Indeed the Veterinary Department had engineered a little war of its own.

Rinderpest was suspected among the buffalo herds of the Luangwa Valley, that great sleeping-sickness area in north-eastern Rhodesia, uninhabited by men but teeming with animals. There was a danger that, if it *was* rinderpest, it would spread south, to the Union, where there were a few million cattle. If it got there ninety per cent of these would die.

I had got to go, post-haste, to the Valley (several hundred miles away, of course—but they gave me a van), with several other people, and carry out a complete survey of the game there. I was given an area, mostly in Petauke District, and this I had to comb completely, searching for rinderpest, but also making as accurate an estimate as I could of all the game in the area. This was being done in conjunction with the Game Department.

Here was a *Boy's Own Paper* job for a bright young man!

I slogged about that torrid jungle with my little seven milli-metre and a string of porters, not forgetting old Saidi who came with me as a guide. Saidi was a veteran who had fought both for and against the British government. He had also worked for the Arabs in slaving caravans. He told me how he came by his first muzzle-loading musket. He had lain in wait for a young girl of the Angoni tribe (he was an M'senga) in a nearby village when she was coming back with water. He had grabbed her, tied her hands, and dragged her off to an Arab *ulendo* that was trading in the

146

vicinity. The Arabs (they were friendly with Saidi's father who was a chief) took the girl and gave him a musket in exchange for her. With this he had shot a number of elephants, whose tusks he also sold to the Arabs, besides engaging, with his father, in a lot more slaving activities. It dates one a bit—that one walked the bush with a man who was, in his youth, a slaver!

The Luangwa Valley! I wanted to live there, in its steamy heat, among its tsetse-fly and mosquitoes, elephants, lions, buck and game, for the rest of my life.

It is something to sit having breakfast outside your tent in the early morning and watch a herd of perhaps a hundred elephants—bull, cows and calves—bathing and drinking in a river down below, unaware of your presence because the wind is blowing in your direction, and then to see them, swinging their trunks and tails lazily as they go, wind their way off into the bush. Quite something when you know that these are *not* animals carefully controlled and protected in some 'game park', but simply wild animals, which are there because nobody has ever been able to get to them to shoot them, and which have probably never been seen by another white man and not often by black; wild, unfenced, unfearful. We were chased up trees on several occasions by elephants—one day we walked slap into the middle of a big herd which panicked, and we found ourselves with screaming monsters crashing down the small trees and bushes all round us: something to remember! Whenever Saidi saw a bull with very good tusks he would beg me to shoot him. But I wouldn't. I liked and respected the elephants. I went within a few yards of several to photograph them, with Saidi leading the way, squeezing ash out of a little bag to see which way the wind was blowing. But I would not reduce a fine thing to a mountain of dead flesh for any tusks and money: not even to please my friend Saidi.

Buffalo were a different thing. You could eat buffalo, and man is a carnivorous and hunting animal, and buffalo savage and dangerous game. Buffalo lived in special country—thick, impassable undergrowth through which they forced surprisingly low, tunnel-like passages: you had to walk doubled up in them. It was fearfully hot and steamy in those tunnels, and the sweat used to run off on to my glasses and drip off them and then off the end of my nose, for the Valley is low and terribly hot. The undergrowth is partly composed of buffalo-bean to keep you out of those tunnels. In you go, like a coal-miner into his roadway, looking for fresh tracks and dung, using your nose, stopping and using your ears. If the buffalo hear or smell you they will either run away or charge. If you are near to them they will charge, and they charge like an express train. (Another man, Green, who was engaged in the same game survey with me, got his rifle jammed on such an occasion; his back and pelvis were broken and he had to be carried a hundred miles on a home-made stretcher.) When the scent gets hot, and you see the fresh dung—cowpats just like the ones in English meadows, steaming hot—you crouch along tensed up, heart beating, and you take trouble to wipe your spectacles. If you see the buffalo first, all you see is a black shape through the bushes, probably lying down. You can't tell which is his back end and which his head. It matters. But you can't wait, you fire at that black shape about a quarter of the way back from the end which you hope is the head. It's easy shooting as he is only a few yards away.

A bullet never kills him. He's up and at you. Always. A terrible snort—the bushes crash aside—and he's there! By this time you have worked the bolt of your rifle and you have worked it calmly and well: nothing is easier to jam than a bolt-action rifle when you are excited, and we British never went in much for Yankee-style repeaters. Not frightened, but steeled up to an intense pitch of nervous action, you hit him as he comes—you hit him with your whole heart and soul through that rifle, and it's as though some vast charge of electric energy passes out of your body, into that steel shard and out with the bullet. He drops. I always used my little seven millimetre, a rifle that most hunters consider too small for 'hard-skinned game', but he always dropped. If you smack a buffalo in the head—on the boss if you like—with a bullet, he will drop. But you haven't killed him, unless you're very lucky. He'll be on his feet again in an instant, and just before that is the time for the careful shot at the brain (very difficult in a buffalo), or the probe behind the shoulder—at the heart.

If you wound him and he gets away, then is the time to look out. He is then the hunter. You are the hunted. He will circle round to place himself in ambush in front of you, wait until you are past him, and have you from behind. Lions, leopards, elephants —all are really dangerous game and every year they claim a surprising number of hunters. But none is so dangerous as the buffalo. He is a killer. A man with a rifle, though, if he can use it, and can keep his head, is a match for any buffalo, even in the densest bush.

The Valley is full of lions, and indeed full of most sorts of game. I never went out to shoot a lion, excepting the one who had been eating Clinton's donkeys. But once, coming home late to my camp from a trek round the bush searching for game and signs of game—all part of my survey—old Saidi and I walked out into a small clearing in which a lioness stood looking at us. Probably if I had been alone, I would not have shot her. But Saidi said: 'Shoot, Baas!' and automatically I shot. I had probably been walking along in a day-dream and—seeing a lion and being told to shoot—I just pulled the trigger.

The lioness went into a frantic flurry of pain and fury; I have never seen—or heard—anything so terrifyingly impressive. But, alas, four biggish cubs ran out from behind her and into the bush. I felt like shooting myself. The old lioness had been doing me no harm. I ran up and put another bullet into her to quiet her, and we walked back to camp. Wanton killing, and I hated myself for it. There is nothing wrong about man killing animals. We must kill to live. If man refuses to kill—if he loses his stomach for it—he gets into the horrible position of men in many parts of India, who must see their children starve while monkeys eat their crops, and who must see their cattle starve because there are too many of them and no way of removing the surplus; worse—who must see the very land ruined and devastated because it is grazed and trampled by too many animals. Man must kill animals. But when he does it he must do it with thought, and with respect for the thing that he kills. He must give thought to it and consider all its implications. He must respect the thing he kills, and remember that it was part of the divine plan, just as is his right and need to kill it. I had no right or need to kill that lioness.

But we travelled the Valley as privateers might cruise the oceans. We forced our way through the trackless bush, shooting our food, sleeping at night in any clearing, crossing the great muddy Luangwa by dugout canoe—we travelled once, in rainy weather, for a month without striking a village. I had to keep sending parties of porters out of the Valley to trade meal for dried buck or buffalo meat, because we could not live on meat alone. It rained, my neck and wrists were festering from the constant bites of tsetse-fly, my boots rotted and I had to wear an old pair of gym shoes, my clothes fell apart. I sent back the tent as being too bulky, and had long shed all the tent furniture. I just had an old bit of canvas that I threw over the branch of a tree. I had four trained game scouts whom I sent out every day in different directions, and went in another direction myself, and so we quartered the country, trying to see, or at least see tracks of, every herd of buck, buff, elephant or zebra, in the country. And I believe we more or less did, too. I had a very complimentary letter afterwards about the report I sent in, which was nothing less than a complete game survey of the area.

I remember one occasion after a month of this when we had crossed the river and were on its western side. We had forgotten that other people existed in the world, my porters were getting short of food and bolshy and I had a job to make them go on. Then we found a tree which had been cut into by a wild honey-seeker. A cheer went up. It was like sighting a land-bird when you have been lost in mid-ocean. Soon we came to a tiny man-made path which took us to a village. How charming an African village can be! The conical grass-thatched huts, the paw-paw trees, the fowls and dogs and warm little black naked children, the blue smoke from the cooking fires, the smiling, happy women. They made us so welcome, feeding us on boiled chicken, fish and paw-paws, grinding more meal for us, brewing us beer: we rested there for days, and my men got drunk, and I got half-drunk, and I would have liked to have stayed there for the rest of my life. But back we had to go—across those miles of forest and swamp, and the broad river, in Petauke.

I believe it's all some sort of a game resort nowadays, and organized parties of rich people are driven down there in Land-Rovers, housed in luxurious tents, fed on caviare, and taken up to the animals they are supposed to shoot by 'white hunters'. Well, I hope they get as great a kick out of it as I did, when I went there, because I was paid to do it, and walked twenty miles a day and slept under a piece of canvas.

It is fun to get back to civilization after a trip like that and find an accumulation of letters waiting for you.

It took me four days to *drive* back from Petauke to Mazabuka. This was because it was the rainy season and I was constantly held up by rivers running across the road, bridges broken down and things like that.

I loved Northern Rhodesia. It is hard to see why, for it is by and large a flat, uninteresting country, the bush is not magnificent by any means, the Africans are not particularly picturesque, the women not particularly beautiful. The climate is bad—very malarial and very hot. But there is some indefinable charm about the bush. The smell of it—that almost overpowering, sickly-sweet smell of the flowering grass during the brief few days when it does flower during the rains. The noises: the ever-nightly chorus of jackals howling (you never lay your head down on your pillow without hearing that), the occasional rabid screaming of a hyena, the coughing hunting grunt of a lion. Above all the drums. There is something of great power and significance about those drums. They speak of deeper layers of consciousness. I have known Europeans—the worse sort of Europeans—being deadly frightened by those drums. Their beat seems to say: 'All your Western magic—your motor-cars and flying machines, jails and tax collectors, policemen and machine-guns and tarred roads—all this seems so secure, but we will go on beating long after all that is gone and forgotten.'

I loved the Africans, their villages and their way of life. I really did not see what we have got of value to teach them. Our Western medicine has harmed them because it has made them increase in numbers and therefore press harder on the land that is available to them. Not that they were then over-crowded. They practise a natural birth-control that is really effective. Their women do not have intercourse when they are suckling a child, or if they do, do not seem to conceive, and as they suckle a child for from two to three years, this spaces their families out. Their family life is much closer, warmer, richer than ours is. Their tribal life, too, gives the individual an emotional security that we can never know. And yet it is not exclusive. A man from any tribe in Africa can go among the people of any other tribe, and if he goes in peace he will be treated with warmth, kindliness and hospitality. A man can leave his home without a penny in his pocket and go a journey of thousands of miles in Africa: provided the whites and their laws don't get him he will be well fed and safe. I always felt happy and at ease with Africans.

I met a young white chap in the Luangwa Valley who was doing the same job as I was: temporary game ranger. He had run away from his home in Salisbury (his father had tried to put him into some blasted office) and had taken to the bush in the Valley. He had lived by hunting. He had shot buck and traded dried meat with the Africans on the borders of the Valley, he had shot eight elephants a year (allowed by his licence) and a further unknown number which were not allowed. He employed an old man to turn the ivory of his illicit tusks into bangles and other ornaments to evade the game department. He married a pretty girl by local law, and had a sweet little baby by her. He spoke Chinsenga so well that an M'senga could not tell that he was a foreigner unless he could see him. He lived in his own little village, of which he was headman, and his advice and judgement in affairs were sought by people from miles around. He was of greater influence in the Bansenga tribe than the District Commissioner. He had this temporary job with the game department and it was his undoing. For his actions became too public. He shot a rhino and was informed on, and summonsed. He was let off—provided that he joined the army. He did so, paid his little wife off, said goodbye to his little child, and went away. He 'went European' again, and never returned to the Valley. I often used to think of ending up as he would have done had he not joined the army. Without the War I might have done.

But there was the War.

At Mazabuka I tried very hard to be allowed to join up, but they would not hear of it. Instead, they were going to send me to take over the job that, of all the jobs in the world, I had probably coveted most.

This was the Angola-Barotse cattle cordon.

In Barotseland we had wiped out contagious bovine pleuro-pneumonia. In Angola (Portuguese West Africa) they had not. People smuggled cattle over the border into Barotseland, thereby bringing in the disease. The Veterinary Department, for which I worked, had established a cordon, eight hundred miles long, to prevent this. There was one white man in the middle of it, and a pair of African policemen every twenty miles or so. The latter had to patrol it every day. The white man had to travel it twice a year. He did this mostly on foot, but also partly by river, in river barges or canoes.

The border was in perhaps the most remote and least explored part of Africa. Very few white people had ever seen it.

I was to go there and relieve the white man who had been running it for the last three years. I was to do a three-year tour there. The War would be over in a few months anyway, the Director of Veterinary Services told me. Hitler was running out of oil.

So up I went, making the three weeks' voyage on the Zambezi by barge. And a marvellous experience it was. Day after day pushing through the reed flats, or paddling over the broad river, or watching the barge being hauled up rapids by a long grass rope. Most days I walked at least half the journey, meeting the barge farther upstream, generally having shot a buck for my sixteen paddlers to feast on. The great river was in flood, and sixty or so miles wide in places, and often at night we would have to camp on an extinct termites' nest that stuck out of the water like an island. Nowadays there are motor roads to Barotseland and regular air services. I wonder if these make for improvement?

At Kalabo, where the headquarters of the cordon was, I was in for a shock.

The news had got worse. The nature of the war had altered. The guns had really begun to go off. The British Army was falling back on a place called Dunkirk. The man whom I had been sent to relieve received a telegram telling him he was not to go. He had already loaded his barges for the trip downriver. He had to unload them again. I was ordered to report to Mongu, the administrative capital of Barotseland. I was to be allowed to join the army.

I travelled downstream again in convoy with two missionary ladies from the Middle West of America. They were of that sect that believes that Sunday is on Saturday. We camped one night on an island—one of those island villages which are evacuated by the Balozi every year when the river comes down in flood. I saw a *mokoro* (narrow dug-out canoe) on the bank and got aboard and pushed off to demonstrate my paddling skills to the ladies.

Too late I noticed the serowe ants. Tiny red ants with stings of fire. They crawled all over me. I leapt to the other end of the *mokoro*, sent her flying back to the bank so that she shot half out of the water, rushed ashore tearing my clothes off as I came, and the two missionary ladies fled into the village with shrill little screams. It was some time before I managed to persuade them that I had not intended to rape them.

Chapter Eleven

+++++++++++++++++++++++++++++++◇+++++++++++++++++++++++++++++++

Gone for a Soldier

Mongu, which might have been so pleasant, was a terrible place.

There is something terrible about British administrative stations in Africa. A little closed community of civil servants and their wives, measuring each other and other people according to a complicated and tedious system of 'salary groups'.

The old-fashioned type of administrative officer was all right. He could be fine. People like Thornycroft, District Commissioner years ago of Petauke. He risked his life going down into the Luangwa Valley in a sleeping-sickness epidemic, to bring out the survivors of the Bansenga tribe back on to the tribal lands from which they had been driven by the company which had 'bought' their country from their drunken chief for a few cases of whisky. Thornycroft then fought a battle with the Home government to make them return some of the Bansengas' lands to them, to save them from starvation. He broke the law whenever he thought it was right, and kept his telescope firmly and almost constantly clapped to his blind eye. A species of giraffe is named after him— and so are large numbers of people of various shades of colour in the Bansenga country.

I met a few of the Thornycroft type, and they were superb. Such a District Commissioner would rule his district like an eccentric king but better than a king for he had been chosen on account of a certain standard of intelligence and a sense of adventure to want to go there in the first place.

But the new kind, the kind which was assuming authority in those days just before the War (and which later completely took over, before being taken over in turn by Africa Emergent), was just a time-serving civil servant, chosen for his 'reliability' (dullness), and he contributed nothing to the people over whom he was sent to administer. For to help people anyhow you must have abounding and overflowing *spirit*, and these time-servers had as much spirit as tame white mice.

I spent a fortnight in Mongu, waiting for an aeroplane to come and take me back to the 'railway line' to join the army.

Luckily the veterinary officer there had two young horses which were unbroken so I whiled away my time doing this job.

Finally, the Dragon Rapide came which was to fly me to Lusaka, and there—along with a couple of dozen assorted heroes—I was sworn in as a soldier.

Never were men keener to fight the foe. Every moment might count, we felt. The news from Europe was terrible. We all expected England to go at any minute. We would fight on in Africa, of course. Let the *panzer* divisions try coming down the Luanga Valley! But the rumours were that the Italians were already moving into Kenya from Abyssinia. If we hurried north we might just get to Nairobi in time to save it from the Fascist hordes. The fate of Africa—nay, of the world—might depend upon our speed.

The twenty of us set off in two hired lorries, driven by African drivers. We started driving northwards and we drove night and day. At various points we changed lorries and drivers, and so managed to keep up the speed. The road was only *just* a road, of course. Probably now it's a boulevard.

I was in a state of great excitement. It was not only the War (I couldn't get out of my mind the picture of me sitting behind a machine-gun on a tripod—I didn't even know what a machine-gun looked like—mowing down Fascists with big feathers in their hats who were rushing at me over the plains north of Nairobi); I was even more excited to be going to new countries.

Tanganyika was tremendous. Huge escarpments, mountain ranges, barren scrub-filled valleys, skin-clad Africans with thin lips and great broad-bladed spears. Quite different to anything I had seen.

Coming down the Iringa escarpment in the middle of the night, driven by a mad African in an Indian-owned lorry which had no brakes, we came a cropper. The driver failed to engage bottom gear. We heard the terrible grinding of the gears, the truck went faster and faster, one man got up and tried to jump, then thought better of it, the trees flashed by at a terrible speed (the man sitting next to the driver afterwards said he saw sixty on the speedometer), and we hit a bridge at the bottom of the valley.

I had been sitting in the front of the box of the truck with my back against the cab. I heard the crash of the collision—saw my companions rise up in a mass and come sailing through the air towards me. They all ended up on my chest. As they landed, the truck turned over and rolled us out in a big ball. Having been at the bottom of the ball before, I now found myself on top. There I was, at the apex of a pyramid of heads, arms and legs. I clambered down and ran back along the road to stop the other lorry, which was coming behind, from crashing into us. Our lorry had cleaned its axles and wheels right off, and also the steel rail of the bridge, and had shot on thirty yards before turning over. While the others were sorting themselves out an old African came along with a spear. He stopped and said the words: '*Haraka haraka haina baraka!*' These were the first Swahili words I had ever heard. They can be translated as 'The more haste the less speed!' Beyond a couple of broken arms and some broken ribs no one was hurt.

The farther north we went the more romantic the country seemed.

Nairobi was an anticlimax. It was terribly English, terribly suburban. We leapt from our trucks ready to take up arms and rush to the front immediately. But it was not like that at all.

We were kept hanging around the base details camp for days. All that happened to us was: we were taught the way to salute and we were dished out with inconceivable garments known as 'long shorts'. These were khaki trousers which, when extended, went halfway down the calf, and when buttoned up flapped about the knees in a kind of plus-fours *manqué* sort of way. I believe that it was 'long shorts' that prevented the East African forces ever taking themselves or the War really seriously. For example, when your commanding officer appears before you in 'long shorts' he can never be anything else but a figure of fun.

We were eventually packed into lorries and sent up to Eldoret, a little town on a wind-swept open plain with fine green grass on it and great prairies of wheat, and Dutch farmers who had trekked up there in the early days with their ox-waggons. (They've mostly trekked away again now—back to the Union. They don't like being governed by African politicians.)

At Eldoret there was a racecourse, and to it we were sent. This was the training depot of the Kenya Regiment.

I cannot pretend that I enjoyed joining the army. It was like going back to school again, and that I had hated. Only one thing —I was no longer vulnerable. I no longer cared a damn what anybody thought of me. Consequently I was thought well of—by my companions at least.

But after five years spent mostly alone, or working with small groups of friends, it was alarming to be flung in suddenly with a thousand men, men who were just numbers, being shouted at and drilled and paraded from dawn until dusk. Alarming and un-pleasant, but I had a feeling that it was salutary.

Our instructors were all from the Brigade of Guards. Most of our training (which was exactly the same as the training at the Guards Depot in England) was directed not at teaching us to kill the enemy, but at breaking down our individuality. We were never 'off parade', really. We hardly had any spare time, and the scraps of it that we did have had to be devoted to getting ready for the next parade.

I remember once sitting on the edge of my bed in my horse-box reading a book when Regimental Sergeant-Major Bloomfield (Grenadier Guards) looked in. 'Now then,' he said. 'I like to see soldiers working on their equipment when they're off parade— not reading books!' And, of course, he was dead right. The sort of soldiers he was trying to make just don't read books. Books might make you think.

And so today we are going on with Lesson Number Three of the Bren gun. And tonight there are 'night ops'—putting barbed wire up in the pitch dark and then taking it down again. And every day there is the great bull-shit parade which wastes half the morning, where we all hang about on the edge of the parade ground with our rifles polished—our ridiculous 'Bombay bashers' (huge sun-helmets)—our ludicrous 'long shorts'—our shiny boots —the polished studs on our 'web equipment'—our bayonet holsters carefully coated with nail varnish—until R.S.M. Bloom-field bellows: 'Battalion—GET ON PARADE!' and we slip our

hands down to the slings of our rifles, spring to attention, slope
(order) arms, and march smartly to our appointed places, where it
takes three-quarters of an hour for us to be 'dressed' from the
right, shuffled about, made to slope arms, stand to attention,
stand easy, stand at ease—never actually stand on our heads—
while the R.S.M. hands over to the Adjutant, the Adjutant to the
Commanding Officer, the C.O. back to the old Guards sweats who
are to regale us, yet again, with Lesson Number Three of the
Bren Gun.

It was all a most monumental *bore*. And when we were inter-
viewed by the Commanding Officer to pick out 'officer material'
to be sent to O.C.T.U. I was not picked. When he asked me what
my 'religion' was I said 'Pagan,' and when he asked me my
favourite sport I said, 'Chess'! I knew as well as anybody else that
the correct answers were 'C. of E.' and 'Rugby Football'.

My attitude, though, to the whole business was ambiguous.
I did not believe in the British Empire, or 'Western Civilization', or 'Free Enterprise' (capitalism), or any other of these
windy conceptions. I did not believe in 'Democracy' because I
knew it was a sham. You cannot have democracy in large
countries. I believed—as I believe now—only in the individual.
And yet I felt I had to fight on the side of 'Democracy' in
this war because I disliked the other side so much.

I believed I knew very well the sort of people who ruled
Hitler's Germany, and Fascist Italy, and Japan. I had met just such
people and such ideas triumphant in my ten days at an English
public school. The idea of the Tribe—triumphant over the Individual. If the Nazis won we would all have to become members
of some bloody Tribe. Or die resisting it. The world would become intolerable if the Nazis won the war and therefore I had to
make common cause with the bogus 'democracies', which I could
only do by joining one of their armies. But I fought as an ally, not
as a subject. I submitted to their discipline of my own free will,
because only thus would I be allowed to fight. And so, for six
months, I plodded up and down the parade ground at Eldoret
racecourse, and if R.S.M. Bloomfield and his assistants didn't
succeed in making a soldier of me it wasn't their fault.

There was one event, though, which singularly failed to endear
some of us recruits to our instructors. And that was a great

regimental shoot on the range, in which officers, W.O.s, N.C.O.s and men took part.

Our Brigade of Guards instructors (who had the job of teaching us to shoot) were well down on the scores list. The three worst irreconcilables, the three scruffiest and bolshiest recruits of the lot (of which I happened to be one) came top! We old bush Africa hands might not be very good at throwing rifles about and presenting arms with them, but it appeared that we knew how to use them for their original purpose.

The rugger players all went to O.C.T.U. to become officers; the people who wouldn't learn Swahili, or Chinyanja to the Kenya Armoured Cars, which was the only all-white fighting unit; the people who had any sense to various cosy little numbers like Royal Army Service Corps, the Pay Corps, the Military Police; the rest of us went off to be 'B.N.C.O.s' (British non-commissioned officers) in African regiments.

I had taken the trouble to learn Swahili, and so I was sent to a Swahili-speaking battalion. The people with whom I had come up from Northern Rhodesia were all sent back to the Northern Rhodesian Regiment and I was happy not to go with them. For these men, although recruited in Northern Rhodesia, were in fact South Africans. Most of them had been born in the Union, all of them had the South African attitude towards 'the natives'. Most were miners or artisans, and they had the white artisan's hatred for the African. To the end of the War many of them did not trouble to learn Chinyanja, the lingua franca of their regiment. 'kitchen kaffir' was good enough for them. To the end of the War they would still shout 'Boy!' when they wanted a soldier. Such people were poison in an African regiment. The best thing I ever did was to teach myself Swahili, and get sent to a regiment in which there were no Rhodesians or South Africans.

The 3rd/4th King's African Rifles was in training at Bomba, in Uganda. Thither five of us were sent, by train.

Uganda was quite different from the sun-and-wind bathed uplands of Eldoret. It was steamy, torrid, tropical. It was densely populated (I had never seen a highly populated part of Africa before). It was close—closed in. Bananas—everywhere banana trees. The people lived in huts lost among the banana palms. The roads were good—most of them were tarred—and lined with villages. One village started where the last left off. And most of the villages on the roads seemed to be made up of small shops owned, not by Africans, but by Indians. And traffic was dense— old ramshackle buses, all Indian-owned, and bicycles, thousands of bicycles. The people were very black, dignified, the men inclining to white cotton robes, the women to bright-coloured dresses. They grew cotton, as well as bananas, right up to the front doors of their houses. I was used to little groups of huts of shifting cultivators in the lonely, dry bush. Here was a country of permanent dwellings, with villages running into each other, and urbane people with a long history of settled living.

It was strange, and rather exciting, arriving at a battalion of the King's African Rifles, and finding a thousand men, mostly from the wild tribes in the north of Uganda, or the Sudan border country—tall, black as black, primitive, ear-lobes expanded to hang down to their shoulders, faces cut into fierce-looking patterns by cicatrization scars. Men of striking appearance, who looked well in their uniforms with their slouch hats and bush shirts. The 'long shorts' somehow didn't look so ludicrous on them.

And there was a great air of purpose about them. They really thought they were going off to war, and they wanted to. They trained hard, and effectively. The officers were all Kenya settler types, with only one or two regulars from England right at the top. I was assigned to 'A' Company, where I was at once put in command of a platoon. A platoon was forty men, with three Bren guns, and, although I was only a sergeant myself, I had a regular African sergeant under me—a Somali named Dagana who was one of the best men I have ever known in my life. I should have had an officer over me, but fortunately I avoided this, for there were not enough to go round.

British N.C.O.s were a terrible mistake in the K.A.R., in my opinion. There should never have been any. It was only confusing to the African to be expected to recognize two sorts of white man—upper-class ones and lower-class ones. And it was unfair on the B.N.C.O.s themselves. However, it never worried me very much. I was always a platoon commander, which was really an officer's job.

We gave our soldiers Lesson Number Three of the Bren gun.

We marched them along the roads through that steamy heat, up and down the little hills, to the delight of the little boys in the villages, and we would start off at the beginning of every route march with every askari wearing his boots upon his feet, and get home with three-quarters of them with their boots around their necks. At night they lit fires in their quarters and beat their drums and drank beer and danced and sang, and sometimes they would break out and put in a little quiet rapine in nearby villages. Our tall fierce Nilotics didn't get on very well with the smooth, more civilized, Bantu Baganda down south.

I had at that time the British imperialist's traditional attitude to 'native' races. I preferred the 'martial tribes', or 'martial races'. Just as British officers in India preferred the Gurkhas, the Jats, the Sikhs and the Pathans to Bombay babus and Calcutta clerks, so we of the K.A.R. preferred the more primitive members of the cattle tribes to the more settled and civilized people. Above all we disliked Africans who could read or write (there were very few), or those who had become Christians. A lot of our askaris had 'R.C.' or 'PROT' stamped on their identity-discs, but they were no more 'R.C.' or 'PROT' than I am. They were just pagans who had been spoken to nicely by a missionary. We used to tell ourselves that pagans and Muslims were better soldiers than Christians were. We were apt to be right, as a matter of fact. There is a kind of sweetly-suffering, holier-than-thou expression on the face of a Christian-ized askari when he finds himself in the presence of his swearing, boozing, fornicating, un-church-going, British officer, which is infuriating. Also, Christian Africans are a little apt to imitate Christ, who was, of course, a pacifist. We used to call the highly civilized, Christianized and sophisticated ruling race of Uganda the 'Bible-bashing, bicycle-riding, banana-eating Buganda Bastards!'

I was agreeably surprised at the Kenya and Tanganyika settler-officers. They had not been tainted by the South African attitude to *die kaffirs*. Most of them were liberal—up to a point—and most had a real affection for the Africans. Always, of course, provided the African 'kept in his place'. African politicians were naturally anathema to them, as were 'camp lawyers' in the battalion for that matter. These had a very thin time. But the 'unspoilt' African they liked.

In spite of the intense boredom of a lot of what we did—the endless, often rather pointless and always repetitive training, the kit inspections, and arms inspections, and lines inspections, and the never-ending preoccupation we always seemed to have about latrines—I enjoyed the life.

Firstly there was almost constant travelling. We very seldom spent long in one place. New scenes, new tribes, new camps, new climates, all the time. There was plenty of time to read: indeed I read more books during my six years in the army than in the rest of my life. Then there was the comradeship with one's fellow N.C.O.s or officers. But strongest of all, for me, was the fascination of the askaris.

I learnt to speak and understand Swahili well. I became friends with the askaris of my platoon, to the extent of getting drunk with them once a week on the mealie-meal beer they were allowed to make and drink on Saturday nights. Never once, in five years in the K.A.R., did I put a man 'on a charge' for any breach of discipline (sometimes one had to, automatically, for loss of kit). I simply took it for granted that my men would do what I told them, and they invariably did. At times, of course, they would be bolshie. But, in the end, they would do what I told them. One secret of leadership I found out for myself, for I have never seen it in any military manual. And that is, if you tell some bolshie subordinate to come after you, you must walk away and *never turn your head to see if he is coming*. And, if you are afraid that he might bash you on the head, still you must not turn round to make sure that he doesn't. You must simply say: 'Come with me,' and walk away. What one would do, in such circumstances, if he did *not* obey you, I have no idea. It never happened to me. I always took it completely for granted that my order would be obeyed, and therefore it always was. But I am quite certain that if you *did* turn your head in such circumstances, you would lose the respect of your subordinates.

I became enormously interested in Africans. I would defend them against all comers. Endless were the arguments that I have had in the mess (which nearly always meant out in the open under the stars, or under some rough grass shelter in the bush) with people who have been running down the African, or the askari, and I have been defending him. For not only did I see that the

African is as good a man as the European, but I also saw that, in many ways, he is a better. He has a freshness, a *naïveté*, a capacity for fun and enjoyment, a lack of dreariness about him. Tribal Africans are spontaneously generous in a way that could not be imagined among Europeans. They have not been defiled—yet—with our beastly grasping notions of property. If you go up to six Africans and hand one of them a cigarette, he will, without thinking, hand it round to each of the others to let them have a puff, and they will each smoke as much as they think is their fair share. It will not occur to one of them that the person to whom you gave the cigarette is the 'owner'.

I found that there are broadly two kinds of African tribes—possibly the same simplification could be made about people everywhere: but, in East Africa, the tribes can be divided roughly into 'cattle' and 'agricultural', with, of course, the majority falling between the two extremes. The 'cattle tribes' are (in my view) aristocrats. The others are peasants. They look different. The cattle people include, at the extreme end of the spectrum, the Masai and Watende of Tanganyika, the Nandi and Lumbwa of the Kenya Highlands, the Merille and Turkana of northern Kenya, the Bashikalumbwe of Northern Rhodesia (I simply pick out the names of tribes at random, there are plenty of others); they are tallish, slender, fine-boned and proud-looking: the men are handsome and the women often very beautiful. At the other end of the spectrum are people like the Luo, the Baganda, and many of the coastal tribes of East Africa, and the tribes of Nyasaland and Northern Rhodesia. These are inclined to be stocky, with sturdy legs and short fingers, their noses snub while those of the cattle people tend to be aquiline, their lips thick, while those of the cattle people are thin. They are happy and laughing and extrovert: the cattle people are thoughtful and introverted. The peasant types take readily to missionaries and to civilization: the Masai, at the extreme cattle end, have resisted both to this day. The cattle people are individualists; the peasants good organization-men.

All this is unforgivable generalization, and yet there is some truth in it. Certainly the members of most tribes belong to somewhere in the middle of my spectrum. And, of course, one gets cases of obvious cattle tribes (the Wakamba and the Wakikuyu of Kenya for example) which have taken to the settled life.

But I found that I had a natural affinity with the cattle-type people. I liked their individualism, their bolshiness and intractability, their refusal to believe everything that was told them.

The platoon commander becomes tremendously involved with his men. He gets to know each as an individual, the weak as well as the strong. If he is given a weak man he will try to get rid of him. If he can't he accepts him loyally and makes the best of him. He defends his men against all comers. I *hated* anybody else in the army to have anything to do with any of my men. I worked enormously hard to turn them into the best fighting platoon in the battalion (I didn't care a damn how they looked), and was helped in this by that fine regular soldier Sergeant Dagana. (I wonder if he is still a soldier?—I picture him living in contented retirement back in his native Somaliland, sitting smoking outside his hut with several wives bustling about.)

And I would have backed my forty men against an equivalent number of Germans, Japanese or Italians, or anybody else on Earth.

Chapter Twelve

The Fall of the Roman Empire

After training for a month in the steam-heat of Bomba, we marched into Kampala, a thousand strong, proud of our warlike mien and mission, and we crammed into a train. At least our askaris crowded—we British officers and N.C.O.s sat comfortably in first-class carriages drinking rum. At Nairobi we got out (the askaris were half-dead after a couple of nights packed like sardines) and got straight into lorries and were driven north into the N.F.D., or Northern Frontier District of Kenya.

First, though, we passed through the green and beautiful Kikuyu country. Kikuyuland is, to me, the loveliest part of all Africa; green hills and valleys, well cultivated, well watered, well wooded. Eroded only because overpopulated: the Kikuyu had had more land grabbed from them to form the 'White Highlands' than any other race, excepting perhaps the Nandi. Then we came to the Equator, and Nanyuki, the white township at the foot of Mount Kenya. Northward we went, into the N.F.D. proper: a howling wilderness if there is one on this planet.

For in that part of Africa climate depends on height. If you are high up it is moist and green and cool. If you are low down it is appallingly hot, dry and barren.

I had seen something like this desert before, in South West Africa, but the N.F.D. was as hot, or even hotter. Scrubby thorn bush (I never saw *mopani*), wispy grass after the rains: I suppose really the whole of the N.F.D., southern Ethiopia, the Horn of Africa, and most of Arabia, is one howling hot hell of a wilderness. Comfort is there none, unless men have made it for themselves. Life is only bearable in those countries for the unbelievably tough, unless men have managed to build luxurious cities and live in them waited upon by slaves. But for the wandering man in the bush there is no comfort, no escape. The heat, even in his tent, is that of the furnace, and the dryness is torture.

Wajir was a *Beau Geste*-type fort, set down in this wilderness at a point where there are several deep wells said to have been dug by the order of the Queen of Sheba. Here my battalion spent several months.

There were the barbed-wired and heavily mined perimeter, the little crumbling mud-brick town inside it, the offices of the District Commissioner (now battalion headquarters) and the castellated fort in the middle. We were expecting to be attacked by the Italians at any moment. Indeed they could not advance into Kenya on that side without reducing Wajir, for there was no other fresh water.

Fresh water, did I say? Sheba's wells did not yield fresh water at all, but a scarcely drinkable brackish liquid, and we all suffered from what we called 'Wajir Clap', a nasty complaint which caused pain when a man passed his water. We were rationed to half a gallon of water per day for all purposes, and we spent our time there (until the glorious rain arrived at last and rescued us) in acute bodily discomfort.

There was a ring of outer defences around Wajir: little one-platoon strongpoints about a mile outside the perimeter wire. Each had a concrete blockhouse, some trenches and weapon pits and wire defences. It was considered a penance to be stationed in one; every platoon was sent there for three days at a time. But after my three days I asked my company commander if I could stay there permanently. Surprised, he agreed, for it saved a lot of messing about. He was amazed that my askaris and I could stick it, but what he didn't know was that, every few days that we were there, I would take a gentle stroll out into the bush, in the direction that the enemy were supposed to be, and shoot an oryx, or gemsbok—one of my old friends from South West Africa days. The exercise kept me fit and the flesh delighted the forty men of my platoon, who craved, above all, fresh meat. Of course it was highly unlawful for me to stir outside the barbed wire, but I have never taken any notice of laws, in the army or out of it, beyond the overriding rule that one mustn't get found out. That is the only one that matters—and, of course, the dictates of your own conscience. Surely it is a poor man who cannot make up his own laws for himself?

As for the Italian enemy, they were a sore disappointment.

At first, as I sat in my tiny fortress, I used to plan what I would do if they attacked, which I really believed was a possibility. I used to long for them to do so. But they never turned up. We heard news of advances by the South Africans, and the West Africans, and battles that weren't really battles. The Allies advanced, the Italians retreated, in spite of the fact that the latter were vastly superior in numbers.

We could not understand this then, any more than I can now. Time and again well-armed Italian garrisons, holding seemingly impregnable positions, surrendered to tiny attacking forces, with hardly a shot being fired. I could only assume that their hearts were not in the war. Maybe they were too sensible to swallow all that gup Mussolini had been feeding them. If they had really wanted to, they could have conquered British East Africa without any trouble at all. They would have swamped us.

We got into lorries again, and moved across the desert to Mega, which is a romantic little town in southern Ethiopia and the gateway to Abyssinia. We had to climb a steep escarpment to reach it. The Italians had surrendered it after a token attack by the South Africans who were very cock-a-hoop—poor devils, they were all handed to the Germans on a plate later on at Tobruk.

For weeks we hopelessly defended Mega. For how can you defend a place against an enemy who never attacks? 'A' Company made one long patrol, in the middle of the rains, to a place called Yavello. For a week we dragged lorries through deep mud, cut down trees to lay corduroy roads and built bridges over streams. We were rationed to a daily half a tin each of bully beef, and the askaris began to get hungry. It was hard work. We would march along, slogging through the mud, until we came to a stranded truck. We would take our packs off (they were very heavy). We would unload the truck and carry the load forward to where our packs were and pick them up. We would then start our muddy march again.

Every evening our officers went off in a noisy party into the bush, to try to shoot a buck. Every evening they came back without one. I waited until I had really seen good signs of buck, and then slipped away quietly by myself. I had not had years of hunting for the pot in Northern Rhodesia and South West Africa for nothing. Within an hour I was back, having shot a Grant's gazelle and three oryx, and there was enough fresh meat for the whole company for three days. Being a humble sergeant it pleased me very much to do this—as much as it must have annoyed the officers.

The expedition, although strenuous and fun, was a fiasco. The enemy was not there. We turned round and marched back again.

Back at Mega I was given the job which pleased me most of any I had in the War.

Our Brigadier (a man named James) was a horse-lover. He had been told that his and our brigade (the 25th East African) was never to go to fight, but was to be kept doing garrison duty in northern Kenya for the rest of the war. Accordingly he decided to buy forty ponies and forty mules. The mules were to carry the three-inch mortars on patrols that we would have to make against the unruly Merille tribesmen. The ponies were for the officers and B.N.C.O.s to play polo with. We were to be stationed at Marsabit, in the middle of the N.F.D.

Having been in the Veterinary Department, I was selected as the sergeant to help buy the animals and later drive them across the desert to Marsabit. A nice second lieutenant named Nick, who had been in the B.S.A. Police, was in charge of the operation.

Nick and I spent an ecstatic few weeks driving about southern Abyssinia in a truck, visiting the wild and unknown Borana tribesmen, haggling with them for horse-flesh and mule-flesh, breaking in sufficient horses to ride and driving the others, and getting ready for the two-hundred-mile trek across the waterless Chalbi Desert.

Our headquarters, just south of Mega, became known as the 'Lazy B' Ranch. We enlisted two young Boranas to help us. The Boranas are the finest horsemen in the world. A Borana boy will jump bareback on an unbroken horse, with a piece of bark for a bit and bridle, and hunt down a giraffe and kill it with a spear! They are cattle people, but horse people too. They breed mules for sale to the Ethiopians.

We broke a dozen ponies to the saddle, and then set off across the howling wilderness driving the others. We rode every day, camped every night. We had water, because this was brought to us in a three-ton lorry and given to the animals in a canvas trough. At night we took turns to patrol for lions.

That country is fantastic, when you get off the road. Most of it is lava rock, just a sea of black lava boulders, lava that has flowed out of some horrible eruption in the past and run over the land. You clamber up a ridge of higher ground and nearly always find yourself looking down at a great flat-bottomed crater, an old volcano, with perhaps sand, perhaps some sparse grass in the bottom of it.

There is one block of hills—the Horris—which are bare and green with good grass as they are high enough to catch the rains. The chief people of that land are the Borana, either white-robed cattle Borana with their huge herds of fine cattle, living in movable tents which they pack on the backs of their cattle, or camel Borana who wear ochre robes, and herd great herds of camels. They live on sour and curdled camel milk. Nothing else. Only if there is a feast for some reason do they kill a beast and eat meat. They never know bread. They make *tej*—beer—out of wild honey. They are still pagans, and nobody knows much about their religion. They are perhaps the least known people on earth, the least touched by civilization. Even Islam has been unable to reach them. Yet they are civilized in their own way—aloof, proud as the devil, dignified, hospitable if you call on them. They know only one way of settling disputes—with the spear.

I have stood by a well in the desert, dug centuries ago by men alternately making fires and then quenching them to split the hard rock. I have watched the Borana bring in their cattle. A living chain of young men and women, stripped to the waist, clings to the rough walls of the well down below and passes leather buckets of water up from one person to the next, the last tipping each bucket into a stone trough. As they work they chant, and their chanting is not of our century, nor of any race that we know.

Beside the trough the tall Borana elders stand, severe white-robed men with high turbans, aquiline noses, thin lips and pointed beards. Coal-black Borana women may stand by, nearly naked, often beautiful. They smile invitingly—but there were those sharp spears to consider! One by one the herds of cattle (each herd several hundred strong, each herd thirsty from four or five waterless days in the veld) are allowed in to drink. A shout from an elder, a command from the young herdsman, and, disciplined, in come the cattle in a cloud of dust, lowing and bellowing, to drink and drink and drink.

And all day the human chain in the well keeps it up, chanting their weird song, slinging up the full leather buckets and slinging back the empty.

I stood on the rim of the mighty crater of El Sod. I heard the weird Borana singing coming up from the dark depths, echoing and reverberating like a pagan chorus. I ran down the zigzag path, to the bottom of the crater in which lies a small, fiercely blue lake. In the bottom of the lake is salt. Half-naked men cut the salt, load it in blocks on the backs of pack oxen and carry it up thousands of feet to trade with the civilized Ethiopians in their far-flung outpost of Mega.

If the Borana seemed to me to be the most mysterious people in the world, the Somalis were perhaps the most beautiful.

You would be lying beside the embers of your camp fire, somewhere in the wilderness, sound asleep, and you would be awakened by the sound of wooden bells.

Camel bells.

Coming towards you, along the track, you would see a warrior, carrying a spear. A Somali, unmistakably robed, turbaned.

Behind him would come a boy leading a camel. The camel would be high-loaded and would look like a ship, for the load would be fixed on to a strange framework of poles sticking into the air like masts. From the camel's tail would be a rope leading to another camel. And another and another—a whole string of them. Then some women, and small children. All walking noiselessly, glidingly. Then another camel leader and another string of camels. Ignoring your camp they would glide past— heading whither? Coming from whence? Ominous, mysterious, beautiful.

And if you saw them during the day, you would realize that the Somali girls are beautiful as no other women in the world are beautiful. Light-skinned, large-eyed, thin, graceful as gazelles, with a perfection of beauty that perhaps can only be bought by

171

living the hardest life in the world. They look at you with wanton eyes. But the Somali curved knives are sharp, and so are the Somali spears.

If there is one thing that I would like to see in Africa it is a Somali country embracing all the Somali lands. Not only what is now known as Somalia, but the Somali parts of the N.F.D. of Kenya, and the Somali parts of Ethiopia. Such a thing must come in the end. The Somalis are not a race to be kept down for ever. Why should that proud race be a minority in anybody's country? They form a solid block in their grazing grounds: let them rule themselves. God knows the country they live in is a hard enough one. Surely nobody could covet it.

Well, in three weeks Nick and I drove our thundering herd to Marsabit, that high block of hills which catches the rains so as to form an oasis of rain-forest in the desert—only to hear that they would not be needed. The brigade was not to stay there doing garrison duty after all. We were bound for Gondar, in northern Abyssinia, where the Italians were still holding out.

Brigadier James sent the ponies and mules down to Kenya to be sold to farmers, and made a handsome profit out of it.

It was then that he told me that he had recommended me for O.C.T.U. I was officer material after all. But I refused to go. What —miss going to northern Abyssinia? Seeing the lost city of Gondar? Not for any 'pip'. I had to go on a short course, however, and thus the battalion went away without me. But I followed on the next convoy from Mombasa. The troop-ship was full of bugs and cockroaches and impertinent whipper-snappers of officers from 'Home'. I then felt the rigours of being only an N.C.O. We lived in the troop decks, the officers in cabins. But I slept every night on deck, under the glorious stars, and it was beautiful.

Massawa, where we disembarked, was marvellous. An ancient Arab port on the shores of the Red Sea, it had been partly turned into an Italian watering place. There were casinos there, open-air cinemas, lidos and plages. But also winding streets full of old Arab houses, with huge teak iron-bound doors and veiled women occasionally sneaking a look at you from high, small, barred windows.

Needless to say we got drunk. If there was one thing the

Europeans in the K.A.R. could be relied upon to do it was to get drunk, which we did on spumante. The weather was appallingly hot. We lay down, sweating spumante, in the cattle trucks that were to take us up-country. We sank into a drunken slumber.

I woke up some hours later to find that, first, I was lying an inch away from the open door of the truck and we were lurching around the most incredible hairpin bends and precipices; second, that I was freezing cold! The train had climbed seven thousand feet.

Asmara was cold and clear, an Italian city crowded with Italian soldiers in gorgeous uniforms. They were supposed to be the conquered, we the conquerors. But we slouched along in our faded bush-shirts and worn equipment, and they swaggered about with many lanyards over their shoulders, wearing plumed hats and grandiose belts. They sat outside cafés sipping wine. We, poor sods, were crowded into trucks and sent packing southwards toward Gondar, where an Italian strangely named General Nazi was still holding out with an enormous army (compared to ours): sixteen thousand crack Italian troops and ten thousand colonial infantry. These were the irreconcilables, who had refused to surrender when the Viceroy—the Duke of Aosta—did.

The open plain gave way to more broken country, with small trees and scrub; and eventually we came into sight of what must be the most impressive escarpment in the world, thousands of feet high, its face fantastically eroded—great chunks split off like giant slices of cake. It looked as if it was going to bar our way to the south. We stopped before this cosmic wall at a village called Addi Arcai, which was deserted except for some Ethiopian patriots and some R.A.S.C. men and a field hospital. None of us had ever seen such country, for more of that country is vertical than horizontal.

I examined an Italian church in the village: the nave had been put to use by the R.A.M.C. men as a store, but the tower was deserted and gave a tremendous view. Scattered about in the tower were exercise books, in which Tigrean children had been trying to learn Italian. The cover of each book had on it a picture of Death and Glory: a machine-gun wrecked amidst its dead Fascist crew, soldiers wearing extravagant uniforms charging with bayonets, the crew of a mountain gun in heroic attitudes, or sometimes a picture of the great Duce himself, looking just like a cartoon character.

Next morning we pulled out in the thundering rain and drove slowly through the most dreadful country to ever challenge an engineer. I kept my hand on the door handle most of the way, ready to leap should we go too near the edge of the terrible precipices that we constantly skirted. The road ceased to be tarred, but was still metalled with broken stone and well drained and graded.

This day brought our convoy, soaking wet, to the bottom of the famous Wolchefit Escarpment, which had fallen to the K.A.R. only a week before, the defenders having first been cut off from their base at Gondar by Ethiopian irregulars under Ringrose.

We spent that night in a lonely and deserted Italian house—possibly a district commissioner's—and the next morning negotiated the forty-odd hairpin bends by which the Italian-built road climbed the almost vertical escarpment. This took us right out of the broken bush country up on to another great plateau: the northern Abyssinian plain—nearly ten thousand feet above sea level! The land up there was green, treeless and fertile; most of it was ploughed up by the Ethiopians to grow their ancient breeds of bearded wheat, oats, barley, rye and lentils. The fields were not fenced, just ploughed out of the rolling grassland, and they showed a very high standard of farming, with a proper rotation of crops, plenty of legumes such as peas and beans and gram, etc., thorough cultivation and a complete absence of weeds. The farmers looked medieval: except for the blackness of their fine, thin-lipped, bearded faces they reminded one of people depicted in English pictures of the fourteenth century. They broke the ground with primitive ploughs drawn by from two to four oxen.

We soon found our battalion encamped beneath a high, bare, conical hill, near the edge of the plateau from where you could look thousands and thousands of feet down to a jumbled mass of hills and bushy gullies: it made one dizzy to look at the view. The battalion was engaged in intensive mountain training, for in a week or two we expected to embark on the assault on Gondar. I took over my platoon (No. 7 of 'A' Company) and we spent the next few days climbing in full kit up dizzy-making mountains, waiting through miserably cold nights (hard frosts) with no more protection than a gas cape over our shivering shoulders: the C.O. was determined that, if we were to die, we should die tough.

One morning we packed into lorries and drove off southward in the direction of Gondar. The lorries were open three-ton Chevs, filled with slouch-hatted askaris, each with a Bren gun mounted in the middle pointing up at the skies. We joined a stream of miscellaneous traffic going the same way: the brigade was on the move.

After travelling some twenty miles through rolling, very fertile country (an interesting feature was a series of fortified farm-houses built by the Fascists for some of Mussolini's settlers), a country waving with wheat and corn, we came to Amba Georgis, some miles north of the main Gondar defences. It was occupied by a force of irregulars, and as we waited in our lorries a band of Ethiopians came swinging in, some of them wounded, from the Gondar direction. They wore riding-breeches, either Italian soldiers' jackets or white cotton robes, either khaki sun-helmets or their long black fuzzy hair fell free, and their feet were bare. Each had several cartridge belts and a belt full of Italian hand-grenades round him, and each carried either a long-barrelled Italian rifle or a Breda light machine-gun. The little whitewashed village had an air of looting and desolation about it.

We left the main road here and turned off left along a muddy track.

I subsequently heard that our engineers discovered this track by studying the maps drawn up by early Portuguese road-builders. It was the track of a road built by one Peter Paez in the seven-teenth century. It soon became evident that the lorries would go no farther, and so we debussed and started marching.

After about four hours' march along the muddy track 'Mustard' Campbell called a halt, and we threw down our packs under some trees, in a pleasant green valley. We were then told that each company had been allotted a few miles of track to turn into a usable road. After a time our 'first line' lorries came churning up through the mud, bringing us food, tools, ammunition and equipment, and we made camp: tents for the Europeans, ground sheet 'bivvies' for the Africans.

The next few days, during which it often rained and was very cold, were occupied in supervising parties working on the road.

One evening I wandered away from the camp, in defiance, of course, of standing orders and every other sort of order, with the intention of going for a stroll. I followed the course of a little stream, from which flew several pairs of mallard, along the bed of a grassy valley. There were a few stone-built Ethiopian houses (always circular) and several fine herds of cattle, also a few ponies grazing on the hillside. The little valley was too wet to cultivate, but the slopes on either side were ploughed. After about a mile I came to the tree-lined edge of an escarpment: the ground fell away below me for fifteen hundred feet, into a bush-filled valley. The floor of the valley was broken by small hills and gullies, all bushed, and the other side of it was formed by a range of bare grass mountains as high as the place I was on. The tops of these hills were approximately four thousand yards away from me, and on them I could plainly see the earthworks made by the enemy.

Looking south, the valley appeared to open out into what one might call a hilly plain. To the south-west of this plain was another great range of mountains, and to the south lay—so far away that it merged with the sky—a great glistening expanse of blue water—Lake Tana, the source of the Blue Nile. And lo, at the foot of the far hills was a city, gleaming brilliant and white in the sunshine, with towers and battlements and castellated fortresses— the fairest city in the world. The city of Gondar, which we had come to conquer.

I stayed there until the sun went down, gazing at this stupendous view, which is certainly one of the most dramatic and romantic sights in the world.

Day by day we repaired the old Portuguese track farther, and every few days shifted our camp farther southwards. We were slowly working our way round the eastern flank of the defences to the north of Gondar. Every evening, regularly, the enemy shelled us, but always ineffectually. We began to develop a contempt for shellfire, which I still have. A man is terribly unlucky if he gets killed by a shell.

One day Mustard called his platoon commanders, and took us to the edge of the escarpment at a point known as 'O.P. 4 '(O.P. stands for 'observation point'). He pointed out to us the tremendous view of the valley, the backdrop of the mountains occupied by well-dug-in Italians, the plain of Gondar with that glimmering city, and blue Lake Tana beyond. I had seen it all before, but dared not say so, of course. In fact I had made several more evening hunting excursions to the edge of the escarpment.

We were to go on a fighting patrol the next day. At O.P. 4 a battery of Indian mountain artillery was even then digging in. They were to open fire on the enemy positions on the opposing hills, while 'A' Company was to make a feint attack in the valley below, in order to draw the enemy fire and make them disclose their positions even further. My platoon, however, and Number Eight, under Captain Holmes, the second-in-command of the company, were to sit on a low hill down in the valley and act as a firm base for Mustard and the other two platoons to fall back on.

Accordingly we set off at three in the morning. We walked to O.P.4 and then set off to descend the escarpment in single file down a steep and difficult goat-track.

By dawn we found ourselves on the floor of the valley. This consisted of eroded land, cut by steep gullies, and grown over with thick thorn scrub. We struggled through this wilderness, and as the sun got up it became very hot, much hotter than it had been up on the hills.

When we reached the foot of the chosen small hill in the valley floor the company split, Mustard and his half going on, and Holmes and the half I was in clambering up the hill. There we took up defensive positions.

No sooner had we got into position than a whining over our heads followed by a bang from behind us told us that the Indian mountain battery had opened up. After half a minute there was a puff of white smoke on the steep bare hillside opposite us with several smaller puffs simultaneously in the vicinity (dust kicked up by shell splinters) and then, after a longish interval, a vicious *crack*. I saw two men, who had obviously been sunbathing near to where the shell had fallen, jump up and run for one of the holes in the hillside. The Italians had dug their guns in deep inside artificial caves.

There were one or two more sighting shots and then, when a shell had landed near to one of the dark marks on the hillside which denoted a gun emplacement, the battery started firing 'gun

fire' (every gun firing on one target), and the air above us re-
sounded with the roaring, whirring sound of the shells, and Deva
(the name of the enemy hill opposite us) burst out into strange
white flowers.

Then we heard a new noise, that of shells going the other way.
The Italian guns were ranging on our battery position. These
shells sounded much bigger than ours, and they passed close
overhead. I thought I could make out six Italian gun positions,
but they were well hidden and hard to see. The Indian gunners,
who were firing at four thousand yards, which was an extreme
range for their little guns, claimed at the end of the day to have
put two Italian guns out of action. No damage was done to them,
although an Italian shell landed in one of their shell dumps.
Fortunately, like a lot of Italian shells, it did not go off.

All this was entrancing. We sat there, well hidden by trees and
small bushes, watching this artillery duel as though we were
spectators at a circus.

Suddenly our attention was drawn to nine small aeroplanes of
the kind known as Mohawks—trainers actually, but adapted for
bombing. They were flying from the north in the Gondar direction. They circled Gondar once or twice, and then started dive-
bombing various enemy positions. The enemy fired at them with
machine-guns but to no effect. The enemy only had one plane left,
a fighter, but it was kept hidden in a cave in the hillside and only
came out when the sky was clear. (It fired at us once, some days
afterwards, with cannon fire, and we could see the little cannon
shells bursting on the ground in a line as it went by.)

The Mohawks went back, and their places were taken by three
Wellesley bombers, which flew out with a Gloucester Gladiator
fighter flying over their backs like a sparrow-hawk over some
heronshaws. Truly we were being treated to a three-ringed circus.
These aircraft flew at a dignified speed and a safe height, dropped
some impressive bombs and then flew away again. The Italian
garrison had had to put up with this one-sided air warfare for
seven months already.

When this diversion was over we had a new one—the other
half of our company came in sight on the bosky valley floor down
below us. There they were, struggling through the thorn scrub,
and although they were a long way off we could make out

individuals. We saw Mustard sit down and speak into his 'forty-eight set' (wireless transmitter). Holmes strolled across and told me that the going was very tough and there were 'plenty of bloody nettles about'. I could imagine Mustard getting in a worse and worse temper. It was hot, too, down there.

The half-company opened out and started advancing towards Deva over more open ground in open formation. Then we heard the deliberate tap-tap-tap of an Italian medium machine-gun. The line of men paused; some ran back and some ran forward until they found cover to lie behind; one Bren gunner ran up to a small tree on a hillock and put his Bren gun in a fork of the tree and opened up with it.

We could see the Italians—colonial infantry (black)—working their way down the hillside towards Mustard. An enemy heavy mortar opened up on him, but the range was too great and the bombs fell short. The colonial infantry continued to advance, although Mustard's men were firing at them (from an extreme range, I might say).

Now Mustard began to withdraw, and we saw the colonial infantry advancing again. We saw that one of our men was being carried on a stretcher. Then our men disappeared from view, and the colonial infantry retired. We had nothing to do but open our tins of bully beef and our packets of biscuits, watch the artillery duel still going on, and enjoy the sunshine.

Suddenly one of my men came and said that Mustard was at the foot of the hill. I ran down to meet him. One man only had got hit and he was lying on a stretcher with blood bubbling from his nose, having been hit in the face. He tried to sit up in a panic, then lay down again. He was now snoring heavily.

The rest were called down from the hill. Mustard and his half of the company went on ahead; our two platoons had the task of carrying the stretcher up another narrow goat track and it was hell. The track was not wide enough to accommodate two men abreast, it was hardly wide enough for one. The man was heavy and the track was rough, broken, and steep. It was dark when we got him up. An ambulance was waiting on the road—but the man was dead.

In the morning Mustard said they had lost an anti-tank rifle. A fool of a man had dropped it and not gone back for it. I asked if I could go and look for it (I wanted to get out of a day's road-making) and he said yes, provided I took my whole platoon and left at three o'clock in the morning.

So I had a pleasant and exciting day, and we found the rifle, lying on the steep side of a gully down which the man had been sliding when he let go of it. We saw no enemy, but plenty of wild flowers, birds and strange insects. It was like a delightful picnic. The poor chap who lost the anti-tank rifle (a useless thing if ever one was invented) got sentenced to a year's imprisonment with hard labour.

I describe this one patrol in some detail because it was the first of a large number. For weeks we continued to push our road ahead: every day or so some of us would drop down into the valley and probe our way near to the Italian positions, in order to draw their fire and thus locate them, and make maps of their defences. Sometimes we were shelled, sometimes shot at. Casualties began to mount, seldom more than one or two in a day though. Always there was the arduous job of getting wounded men back up the escarpment.

As for our road—the one that had been made by Peter Paez in the seventeenth century when he had gone to Gondar with other Portuguese missionaries—it became a quagmire. The brigade's transport—guns, bridging trains, hundreds of lorries—churned it into deep mud.

But on we went, and came to the edge of the escarpment again, much farther south. From here we could see a great plain, dotted with fields, farmers' round huts and threshing-floors, every little hill with a round church or a fort on it. Gondar still stood there, like a queen. And Lake Tana faded away into the blue distance. Down we went into the plain. I remember visiting a church on the way. I let my platoon go on ahead—you could do that sort of thing in the K.A.R. There was an outer circular wall, and outside this the graves of the dead faithful were clustered. Inside the wall were the priests' low huts. The priests had long white beards and wore high turbans and gorgeous robes. Great rings of stone hung on a tree—these were bells, and had a fine tone. They took me inside the church which was a circular stone building. Like all Ethiopian churches it had an inner wall, so that first one entered what was simply a circular passage. Laymen are not allowed to enter beyond the inner wall, as this is the Holy of Holies. The Tabernacle is kept there. The priests brought out tapestries to show me depicting the Trinity, Saint George killing the dragon, and various other saints. They showed me silver chalices and a gorgeous silver cross. The head priest blessed me, and I went on my way rejoicing.

We fought our way across the plain, attacking one low hill after another. When I say 'attacking', this is a bit of an over-statement. We would launch into the offensive, tremendous artillery barrage first, medium machine-guns and mortars giving covering fire, us staggering up the steep hillside being subjected to small-arms fire from the top, but when we got there we would find either a few men waving white flags on tops of long sticks which they seemed to have all ready for the purpose, or else nobody at all.

Mustard seemed to think I was good at patrolling. He sent me one day, with a 'forty-eight' set, a man from the Signals Platoon, and my orderly, to see what the Italians were doing to a certain bridge. We spent half a hot day getting to a place from which we could observe the bridge and be unobserved ourselves. We were not a hundred yards from it, and found about forty Italians at work digging a hole in the roadway preparatory to laying an explosive charge. If we had had a Bren gun we could have stopped them, but we only had rifles and a tommy, which would have been useless. We lay there for hours, sending back half-hourly reports on the wireless set, watching troops move backwards and forwards on the road right under our noses. Men and mules were passing within fifty yards of us. Then they must have seen us, for suddenly we noticed two parties of colonial infantry, one on each side of us and moving swiftly to outflank us. We sent one last rapid message back and decamped. We knew our line of retreat well enough and stood not too much on the order of our going. Before we had got far we ran straight into 'A' Company. They had been sent out to try to stop the blowing of the bridge. They were too late; there was a roar and a great column of black smoke, and the bridge was gone.

It was that night, however, that I lost my Leica. I had carried this camera right through the campaign, in my side haversack. We went on with the company, came under pretty heavy fire and spent the night huddled in a dry river bed, freezing cold, and wondering just what we were supposed to be there for anyway. During the night I took out my pad to write a message of some sort to send back to Mustard, and the camera must have dropped out.

Next day, back with the battalion, I found it had gone, and I asked Mustard if I could go and get it. He said no, certainly not. It was within a few hundred yards of the enemy positions. But, he said, a platoon from another company was going to my reconnaissance point of the day before and I was to lead them there. And then I was to come back. How I came back was my own business wasn't it? And so I got my camera after all.

The day dawned when we made a battalion attack on a strongly held position on a hill called Tadda Ridge. I remember waiting a long time squatting in a wheatfield in the dark, until, at first light, our artillery opened up most impressively, and the whole of the top of Tadda Ridge seemed to burst into smoke and flame. Over the incredible din one could hear the strange synchronizing noise of a platoon of medium machine-guns, and our own mortars were belching away from just behind us.

Then, up we went. There was some desultory fire from above. A couple of men got hit. Then we reached the flat rocky top where we found two dead mules and one dead Iti. The rest had gone. We took up positions and scraped up stones for ourselves to form tiny *sangars*, or defences. Then all hell broke loose. The Italian gunners had the range of the hill exactly, of course, and they brought every gun they could to bear on it. Most of the battalion—led, I may say, by their officers—vanished over the rear ridge of the hill. I kept mine in position (we were safer in our *sangars*), and we lay there for an hour while pieces of rock and splinters flew over our heads and shells burst all around us. We were pretty safe as long as we kept our heads down. Nothing short of a direct hit could have hurt us, and that was unlikely.

The Intelligence Officer later said he estimated a thousand shells. No one in my platoon got hurt, though a platoon from another company which had been on patrol copped it badly. They walked into an Italian booby-trap containing a lot of explosive and covered by a machine-gun on a fixed line. Half of the platoon got killed, and several of the others were wounded. One askari, a nice old man whom I knew well, came back holding his guts in with his hands. He died.

We all had a feeling that day that the Abyssinian war was nearly over. The real assault was going on, and the enemy would soon have nowhere to run to. Although they had only one aeroplane, the Italians were still vastly superior to us in numbers. We had one brigade of K.A.R., a battalion of Sudanese, and the Patriots, or Ethiopian irregulars. They had twenty-six thousand men. My friend René Cutforth (whom I didn't know then) was with the Patriots, and on subsequent meetings we have often talked about the great days of Gondar.

On Tadda Ridge I enjoyed the first sound night's sleep I had had for some time. I found myself a snug little stone hut full of teff grass, and who cared if there were fleas in it? My men were all safe behind stone walls. We were shelled during the night, off and on, but it didn't disturb my sleep.

The next morning our transport got through, and came to a sheltered position at the foot of the hill; and some of us went down to bath and shave and change our clothes, things that we had not done for a week or two. My personal servant Abdurahaman bin Fadmullah heated me some water in a petrol tin and put it in my canvas bath, which was in a hole in the ground. While I stood by it in the nude waiting for him to bring me some cold water to put into it, there was a tremendous outburst of gunfire. The Itis had spotted our transport and brought a considerable concentration of artillery to bear on it. The various Europeans present all took to holes, with the exception of Bill Cazalet, the C.Q.M.S., who sat unconcernedly leaning against a pile of ammunition boxes counting out tins of bully beef. All the personal servants fled into the bushes, except Abdurahaman bin Fadmullah who strolled happily up with a *debbi* full of cold water to put in my bath. I asked him why he was not frightened, for shells were bursting all around us. He replied tartly that he was not a soldier, but a personal servant: and that such things as bullets and shells and taking cover were the work of soldiers—his work was preparing my bath and keeping my clothes in order, and he had nothing to do with it. If I wanted him to take cover and do the work of a soldier I had better get them to enlist him in the army as a soldier and *pay* him as a soldier. Meanwhile, he poured the cold water into my bath and, although the water was still too hot, the world was getting even hotter outside it, so I got in and lay down at the risk of scalding my private parts. Abdurahaman strolled back to his fire and sat down and went on washing out my shirt.

The shells were fairly scattered, but there was a goodish noise of splinters flying through the air overhead and one shell landed close enough to me to shower me with bits of earth. Suddenly I heard a shout, and looked over in the direction of Bill Cazalet to see him lying in the arms of his old African storeman, his face paper-white, blood trickling down his cheek. He looked like the death of Nelson, in the arms of a black Hardy. I got out of the bath, pulled on my boots as I have a horror of walking barefoot, and went across to him, mother-naked except for my boots. Fortunately the M.O. was near, so I called him over and he rustled up a couple of stretcher-bearers to carry Bill away and I returned to my bath. . . . On the last night on Tadda Ridge I took over Observation Point duty at two o'clock in the morning. From where I sat I could see a great panorama in the starlight, and all the time flashes, explosions, Very lights and small-arms fire were going off around me. At about 0500 hours sounds of a very fierce battle could be heard on our right: we afterwards heard that this was some Ethiopian irregulars attacking a hill, which they did successfully. Then the day slowly dawned which was to see the end of Mussolini's Roman Empire.

Soon after daybreak our brigade went into action.

Our 'D' Company had gone off down the hill to create a diversion on our side of the enemy-occupied White House Hill, and our mortars had dug themselves in during the night ready to attack Trench Hill. A great cannonade opened up on White House Hill and we saw askaris working round the south end of it —the 2nd/3rd and 2nd/4th K.A.R.s. They attacked it from behind and the Italians put up a good resistance; the firing went on for some time before we saw our chaps running about on top of it. Then the 2nd/3rd attacked Trench Hill from the rear, while our mortars set up a continuous roar and the platoon of machine-guns made their queer synchronizing and unsynchronizing crackling noise. Very soon we saw white flags on Trench Hill—they blossomed out all over the hill face. I was taking photographs of the machine-gun platoon in action at the time, and I heard the young subaltern in command of it shout: 'White flags be buggered!

Same target—one belt—fire! And as the crackling started the flag
bearers all disappeared into their holes again.

We had orders to move, and climbed down the steep hill,
straggled through the bushy valley, waded through the river
near the demolished bridge and slowly climbed the steep bare
hillside of White House Hill. We got to the top and I saw two
dead Itis picturesquely draped over their medium machine-gun:
they at least had done their stuff. There were others, less picturesque, bloody and stiff in the long grass. It was by now very
hot. I felt hungry and tired, having missed several nights' sleep. I
was ordered to take up a defensive position with my platoon, and
this I did by discovering a small grass hut with some unleavened
bread in it and some small round tins of Iti bully beef on a little
home-made bedside table. I ate the bread and the bully beef, lay
down on the bed on a mattress of teff grass, and went to sleep for
half an hour. There is a lot of very pleasant jelly in Italian bully
beef.

I then came out and sat on the grass with my platoon watching
the battle.

Ahead of us lay the aerodrome, with Azozo village beyond it.
Armoured cars and carriers could be seen approaching the airfield.
Shells were bursting in Azozo, and the Italian guns and heavy
mortars were still firing away from the Gondar direction, and a
few shells came near us. On our right, quite close, was a steep,
conical hill with a church on top of it, and up the side of this
moved Patriots, with mortar bombs and grenades flung from the
top of the hill bursting among them. I saw one white-clothed
figure fall, his two neighbours closed in to look at him, bent over
him, but then just continued walking up the hill, carrying their
rifles over the backs of their necks as Africans often do. The
Patriots looked as if they were strolling up the hill to go to church.
Several more fell and just lay there, but the rest went on—and we
saw them charge when they got within a few yards of the top and
could hear screams and yells as they disappeared from view over
the top.

Soon a large number of Italians appeared from Azozo village,
walking like a mob, or crowd, not like soldiers, and all carrying
white flags. Then another big mob emerged from what looked
like a large underground shelter near the airfield. They trooped up

185

and surrendered to some of our battalion at the foot of our hill, and I saw Ham Holmes happily waving a gorgeous officer's sword that had been surrendered to him.

We were ordered down off the hill and we marched across into Azozo village, which looked like a little village in the Swiss Alps. Suddenly a civilian open car drove up from the Gondar direction with some Italian officers in it and white flags flying. An officer got out and handed his sword to Lieutenant Gash, of our No. Eight Platoon. This was none other than General Nazi. He had held out for eight months after the rest of Mussolini's army in Ethiopia had surrendered.

Mussolini's Roman Empire was in ruins.

Mustard was running down the hillside shouting to the rest of us to follow him. At the bottom he made us fall to in a close column of threes (we had not marched like that for months) because he had just one idea in his head: to be the first company commander to march into Gondar.

The city was still five miles to the north of us. We started marching flat out along the road. Everywhere the hills seemed to be opening up and yielding Italians; they came climbing down the hillsides in close-packed groups, each group bearing a big white flag. Some Italians would not surrender, though. There were *franc tireurs* in the mountains still. Bullets whizzed about our heads, and once we stopped and Mustard let me have a crack with one of my Bren guns at some men running away on a far-away hillside. Mustard, like a lot of regular soldiers, never seemed to grasp how ineffective small-arms fire is at extreme ranges.

Parties of Italians, close-packed and under white flags, still kept coming out of the mountains. Strings of Patriots, many of them leading mules, were streaming in too, bound for Gondar— and loot.

And we marched for all we were worth. We were well in the lead. The rest of the 3rd/4th K.A.R., which was leading the brigade, was a good way behind.

It was getting dark. We passed a shattered village, and someone had written the Spanish words NO PASARAN up on a wall. This made me feel rather good. I felt as if we were avenging Guernica

—and Madrid. I had always suffered from a guilty conscience because I had not been there and I still do. We were now busy shutting the stable door after the horse had escaped.

We suddenly marched over a ridge, and there was Gondar in front of us. It was a city of smoke and fire! Orange flames lit up great battlemented castles built hundreds of years ago by the Portuguese.

A huge ten-ton lorry was coming towards us from Gondar at a high speed. It stopped, and an Italian got out. He was frightened and desperate. He begged us to jump aboard and let him drive us back to Gondar to save the Italians from the avenging Ethiopians.

Ham Holmes jumped aboard with a platoon, and I boarded another lorry that came soon afterwards. Into the city we were rushed. We saw a huge mob of Italians in the square outside the main post office. We were driven on to the Castle of Fasilidas, the largest and finest of the Portuguese castles.

The courtyard was crowded with Italian soldiers, and a huge fire burned in the middle of it as a big tent full of medical supplies had been set alight. The flames leapt up and cast their glow on those high, castellated, inward-leaning walls. Italians ran up waving cameras and watches—even at that moment of stress they could think only of whether we might have any cigarettes to trade them. They had not had a smoke for months. I often wonder if it wasn't the lack of cigarettes more than anything that caused them to surrender. They had food, ammunition, women. All in plenty. But no fags.

Holmes and I posted our men around the walls, and a few Patriots were shot to encourage the others. (I sympathized with them and didn't take part in the shooting. They had plenty of little matters like mustard-gas bombings, castor-oil dosings and mass hangings to avenge.)

Sergeant Dagana discovered a portable gramophone and a set of records of *Cavalleria Rusticana*, and these the members of my platoon played all night. Whenever I hear it now in my mind's eye I see flame and flame-lit castle walls and hordes of beaten people and Ethiopians firing *berretta* sub-machine-guns and corpses lying about in odd corners.

I took a section of men and explored the castle. One room was a hospital ward, with a man to every bed. Each man had a hatful of hand grenades instead of flowers on his bedside table. Some of the men were wounded, and some were dead.

In the dungeons of the castle was an armoury stocked with thousands of rifles. Dagana met a 'brother' (simply a fellow Somali), who was a local trader. The man had offered him twenty Maria Theresa dollars for each rifle. Would I go fifty-fifty? I would not. Besides, we'd have got found out.

The rest of the company had come up, and C.Q.M.S. met me and said that he had found a mattress in a big hut full of beds. I went in to get one too. It was pitch dark, but I groped about and found a bed with a mattress on it—but there was a dead man on the mattress. I thought of tipping him off, then thought better of it and felt around until I found another, unoccupied mattress. I dragged this out and slept on it for what was left of the night.

The armoured cars arrived next day and managed to restore some sort of order in the smouldering and corpse-strewn streets.

As for us, we spent the next four days like robber barons. We picked the best of the castles for our officers' and sergeants' messes, we found large quantities of good Italian wine and food in the cellars, we played looted gramophones (someone had got 'When They Begin the Beguine' from somewhere, sung by a gorgeous sexy woman, and whenever I hear *this* tune it takes me straight back). We ate and we slept and we drank and, above all, we *looted*. I remember hearing a series of grenade explosions once, and I investigated—only to find a high-ranking officer dropping percussion grenades out of a high window on to a safe, which he had carried on to the ground outside. He blew it open in the end (after a number of near-misses), and I went to see what was in it. Alas— nothing but a lot of old account books and some filthy postcards!

The day came when we had to march out. And, as we did so, we were passed by a cavalcade marching out of the Middle Ages. The Crown Prince of Ethiopia at the head of his nobles and their feudal armies, the nobles wearing lion-skins and many of them carrying spears and shields, marching in to take over the capital city of their forefathers.

Chapter Thirteen

++++++++++++++++++++++++++++◇++++++++++++++++++++++++++++

Journey to Ceylon

And then we spent dreary weeks guarding the huge prisoner-of-war cages, built just south of Asmara at a place called Decamere, to hold General Nazi's men.

We relaxed by making occasional visits into Asmara, where some of the officers went to the officers' brothel and some of the N.C.O.s went to the N.C.O.s' brothel. I don't like brothels, but I found a gorgeous little semi-amateur Arab girl with whom I became quite friendly. Half the brigade got the pox. We N.C.O.s used to go to a wonderful café called the *Croce del Sud*, where there was a perfectly beautiful Italian girl who used to play the piano accordion. She used to hypnotize us with it. She loved thousand-lire notes. I have seen the folds of that accordion stuffed full of them.

Now by the time the Abyssinian war was over the askaris in the brigade that I was in had spent two years away from their homes and wives. They had marched enormous distances about Africa (it was always assumed that the K.A.R. could march much farther than white units—thirty miles a day carrying a really big load of rations and ammunition was common); they had been carted innumerable miles sitting hot and dusty, or else soaked to the skin, in the open backs of trucks over terrible roads; they had slept in desert, frost, rain and mud, sometimes under their groundsheets, sometimes under the sky: they had roughed it as certainly no other troops in the service of the British Commonwealth had had to do. And all the time we poor blighters of Caucasians set to lead them had been telling them: 'Wait till the Italians are beaten—then you will all get home leave.'

But, after Gondar, when we sat around the enormous prisoner-of-war cages on the wind-swept plains of Eritrea, even we began to smell a rat.

At first there was talk of nothing but leave. The brigade was going to Kenya and every man was to have leave. By God, they had earned it! And then strange orders began to filter down to us. Delete all marks of our units from luggage, baggage and equipment. Start packing things up for a move by sea. Bring our battalions up to strength again in weapons, men and reinforcements. It gradually filtered through the five thousand men who made up our brigade that we were going overseas to a new theatre of action.

And then one of the brigade's three battalions went on strike. Under their African Regimental Sergeant-Major (all warrant officer ranks were duplicated: black and white) the battalion, less its Europeans, paraded on the parade ground—and sat down. The R.S.M. then went to the Colonel and told him that the askaris would not obey orders until they were assured that they were going on leave.

Our Commanding Officer, an astute man, called together his own African warrant officers when he heard this, and spoke to them in these terms. 'Look,' he said, 'if you mutiny too you will render yourselves liable for a punishment which might even include being shot. If, on the other hand, you remain loyal, and the mutiny of the other battalion succeeds in its object, then you will get leave too. Either they will get white troops from somewhere and suppress this mutiny and punish the mutineers, in which case you are best out of it, or else they will give in, and you will benefit as much as the members of the battalion which has mutinied.'

This argument was effective. The 3rd/4th K.A.R. decided not to mutiny. But then it became our unpleasant duty to patrol surrounding Tigrean villages, arresting the disaffected askaris from the other two battalions who roamed about regardless, drinking *tej*, brawling and raping, and setting huts on fire occasionally. One B.N.C.O. was blown up by a percussion grenade, and a drunken Acholi aimed a loaded rifle at me and pushed the safety catch off when I went to arrest him. I walked towards him shouting 'Unload!' and he did so and got up and ran away! It was only afterwards, when the heat of my temper had worn off, that I realized how close I had been to getting a bullet through my guts. On one occasion, when my platoon and I were searching the huts in a Tigrean village where we thought some out-of-bounds askaris were hiding, I burst open the door of a hut and started looking around in the dark. I noticed a couple of dim shapes in a bed. 'Get to hell out of it, you fool!' said the voice of a very superior officer.

The mutiny was settled by the Commander-in-Chief himself flying up from Nairobi to harangue the troops, tell them what he thought of them, and then tell them that he had given in to them: they were to go home on leave, *but they had got to walk*. Just the thousand-odd miles or so.

Of course the white officers had got to march with them. But not I, thank God! After Gondar, Mustard Campbell had tried to get me a commission in the field, but, finding this impossible, had recommended that I go to an O.C.T.U. So, with a couple of other similarly favoured sergeants, I travelled the thousand miles in one of the lorry convoys which frequently went south.

In fact the brigade did not walk all the way. After they had gone a couple of hundred miles lorry convoys were sent to begin ferrying them, a company or two at a time, and thus, eventually, they were all carted down to Kenya, where they got the leave that they had so richly earned.

As for me, I enjoyed my lorry-ride across Abyssinia. Unfortunately, though, we were treated as total pariahs: we were not allowed a day or two off in Addis Ababa, for example, but were whisked straight through it, and when we got to Kenya we were kept incommunicado for a fortnight. For another brigade—the 21st—was being sent to Ceylon in our place, and it was essential that not a word of the mutiny should reach the ears of its soldiers. For if they did get wind of it, and of its success, they would certainly have mutinied too. They did not hear, though: the security arrangements really worked for once.

The four months of the O.C.T.U. (Officer Cadet Training Unit), were much like the six months' infantry training on the racecourse at Eldoret. Spit and polish morning, noon and night, terrible competition to be the bluest-eyed boy of the lot, awful sucking-up to the officers who were to decide whether we should get 'pips' or not. I was keener than anyone to get a 'pip', but I was also keenly aware of how wrong it is for any man ever to be placed in a position in which he must curry favour with another man for some promotion or advantage or other. My natural instinct always was: 'Keep away—have no part in it. Tell them what they can do with their pips.' But I didn't. I polished my buttons and doubled about the parade ground with the rest.

As near as damn it I never got my 'pip'. On the very last day—the day of the great passing-out parade—I started drinking in the canteen after lunch with two other cadets, one named Jim and one named Bert. We were on South African wine.

Various bugles blew, and we went on drinking. Then I tore myself away. I wasn't going to have done those four months of concentrated double-bullo all for nothing. I doubled off and got my rifle and staggered on to parade.

There were two gaps in the ranks. Captain Cummings, our redoubtable adjutant who had risen from the ranks of the Coldstream Guards, came and took over the parade. There were still two gaps.

Then, out of the corners of all our eyes, we saw them. Jim and Bert. They were stalking, like Indians, from the canteen to the armoury. Captain Cummings saw them too. There was dead silence. A hundred pairs of eyes were looking out of their corners. Jim and Bert made the armoury—got their rifles. Both, one after the other, tripped over the door-step coming out. Getting up, and making one last wild Indian dash, they darted to fill the two gaps in the ranks. They stood there, swaying slightly, propped up by their rifles.

Cummings burst into life. 'Sergeant-Major O'Brien!' he bellowed. 'Fall in four men! March those two off to the guard room and I don't care if their feet don't touch the ground!'

That was the end of their dreams of the King's commission, and I might so easily have been with them.

I found being an officer embarrassing. More embarrassing even than not being an officer. The truth was that I hated giving orders and I hated being ordered. I am sure that there is only one right relationship possible between men: that of equality and complete independence of each other. After these two things are secure then interdependence can come in. If there is more than one man in a boat then one man must be the captain. But this is a matter of convenience and safety. The captain should be chosen by the men, who should obey him loyally. But except at sea, or in perilous enterprises ashore, I want to have no one to order, no one to obey. I had to put up with it, though, for this was a part of the terms under which the Allied Nations were permitting me to help to fight against Fascism, which I didn't like because under it they order each other about even more, and *everybody* has to salute.

There followed a fantastic journey down Central Africa. Train to Kisumu on Lake Victoria. Steamer for two nights across the blue, island-studded lake. Those great inland seas of central Africa are infinitely romantic. How I would like to cruise around Victoria in my own little dhow. Train to Lake Tanganyika. Belgian steamer across the lake to the Belgian Congo (as it was then). Lorry to the Upper Congo River, steamer up that, more lorry, then train to the Congo–Northern Rhodesia border. Here the train's African driver, fireman and guard were relieved by a white driver, fireman and guard (for in British territory for some extraordinary reason Africans were not supposed to be capable of learning these simple duties), and we proceeded to Lusaka. And there I joined my new battalion: the 2nd/6th King's African Rifles.

I was met at the station. I was taken to the mess in the regular peacetime cantonment: good permanent huts for the men, pleasant bungalows for us sahibs. An uproar was in progress. The second-in-command of the battalion was dressed in a zebra skin, an eland tail stuck into the back of it standing up like a weird squirrel tail, a Bombay-basher on his head. He was dancing round the table. The adjutant followed beating a brass table top. Captains and subalterns either pranced around in the mad procession, or sat and drank, or lay on the floor. Dead sober, I was introduced to them all. I felt like a whore at a christening. 'We don't often have such a quiet evening here,' shouted the Intelligence Officer to me. 'We generally hit it up somewhat. I think we're all a bit relaxed tonight.'

And thus I became a member of that close, jealously guarded, clannish unit: the officers' mess of a British battalion. I loathed this immersion in a way, but at times I am nostalgic for it. We all reacted terribly much on each other: the arrival of a new officer was greeted with great interest. Would he 'be an asset to the mess'? Would he be a nuisance? Would he be posted to *your* company?

We worked enormously hard.

We knew that we had got to go to the East, to fight the Japanese. We were all terribly awed by them for up to that date they had been undefeated. Wherever they had attacked they had prevailed and so far no one had dared to attack them. They were supermen or submen, whichever way you wanted to look at it. They did not suffer from the ordinary mortal man's hopes and fears. If told to die, they would die. We knew we would only die if we simply couldn't get out of it, anyhow at all. The Japanese had swept through the jungles of South-East Asia like warrior ants, and nothing could stand up to them.

We were all frightened of them in our hearts. And so we trained remorselessly. We started training in quite a different spirit to previously. Major 'Budge' O'Hagan, the second-in-command of the battalion—the man whom I had first seen wearing the eland tail—set up a school for African N.C.O.s, at a place called Council's Farm a few miles out of Lusaka, and I was one of the three subalterns chosen to go and help him. We lived there for six weeks, teaching illiterate men from the wilds of Tanganyika such things as map-reading, compass work, minor tactics, guerrilla warfare, and the rest of it. We started doing 'battle inoculation'— firing live ammunition very close to troops on exercises to get them used to it. I made myself the most unpopular man in the battalion because, having been told to design an 'assault course', I arranged it to go over some terrible rough country, across a river, up an ant-hill, through barbed-wire entanglements, under the railway line by a horrible little culvert, up a vertical cutting-face at which a man was firing a Bren gun just to miss you, down another, under the railway by an even more horrible little culvert —a drain-pipe really—through the river again, and then a hundred yards of rough ground just as a relaxation. Every officer and man from the C.O. downwards had to do this once a week in full equipment, tin hat and rifle. One thing nobody noticed. The person who had to organize it never actually went round it. I felt it was quite enough to stand and shout at the others!

And gone were the palmy days of comfort for officers and B.N.C.O.s in the King's African Rifles. No more great fat bulky

bed-rolls that one's orderly could hardly lift—folding chairs—
canvas baths—camp beds and whisky. Those days were over. We
started, on exercises at least, to live just as the troops lived, carrying what they carried, sleeping on the ground as they slept, eating
the rations they ate. We even began to black our faces with grease-
paint! We knew that the Japanese were given to picking off
officers, and therefore it was necessary, if we were to go and fight
them, to disguise ourselves as well as possible. We put away our
silly revolvers and were issued with rifles. There was a great feeling that if the war was to be won we had got to win it, and that
this would call for our full attention.

Budge O'Hagan became a good friend of mine, in spite of the
fact that I was the most junior subaltern there and he was second-
in-command. He had been a District Commissioner in Tanganyika, spoke the most superb Swahili (he could write poetry in
it), was the only white man I ever knew who could match the
Africans at *mbau* (a game in some ways resembling chess only re-
quiring rather more skill), and he had that kind of driving force
and *élan vital* that some white Africans seem to have. He was the
real driving-force behind the battalion. He was extremely intelligent, highly cultivated, endlessly bursting with enthusiasm
and tremendously likeable. He loved Africans, and they loved and
understood him. He was the sort of man who would have been of
enormous value to Africa if he had survived the War. He was shot
dead in a senseless tragedy, as I shall later describe.

The 2nd/6th K.A.R., later under some silly re-numbering
scheme called the 26th, was recruited from the cattle tribes of
Tanganyika, but with a strong dash of Wakamba from Kenya
thrown in. I developed a strong affection and loyalty for this large
and unwieldy body of men. The officers were mostly old Kenya
or Tanganyika settlers and eccentrics to a man. Africa breeds
eccentric white people. The askaris, being from cattle tribes, were
intractable, bolshie, loyal and delightful. I stuck to my platoon as
long as I could. Later, I refused a captaincy, because this would
have meant that I would have had to leave my platoon and become
second-in-command of a company—a boring position. I loved my
bolshie soldiers. Makindi Makali, my orderly, had spent half his
life in jail, inside the army and out. He was the best soldier I ever
knew. He got the M.M. in Burma and deserved a dozen. He used

to come to me and tell me when he was going to get drunk, and I used to see that he didn't get into trouble, often by the simple means of getting drunk with him. He was with me for three years and during that time he was never 'on a charge'.

We packed into lorries and started the weary trek north again, through Northern Rhodesia and Tanganyika. One day, when we had made camp somewhere in the middle of Tanganyika, I thought I saw strong signs of buffalo. I took my rifle and walked away from the camp and sure enough came to some very thick stuff that looked real buffalo to me. It was mostly a bush called rhino thorn that is quite impenetrable excepting where big animals have forced their way through; there were tunnels and I went into it. Suddenly I heard a snort and saw a rhino charging straight at me up the narrow tunnel! I couldn't jump aside, as the bush was too thick, and to have run away would not have been useful. I didn't want to shoot the rhino at all, but I had to in self-defence. I pumped a .303 bullet into her, but it had as much effect as a pea from a pea-shooter—she came straight on. I had just enough time to work the bolt and give her another when she was three yards away. This turned her—she'd had enough. She swung round, almost knocking me into the thorns with her rump as she did so, and away she charged again. It was then that I saw the little calf at her heels squealing blue murder. I can only hope my bullets didn't kill her. But it was about the narrowest miss I had from an animal in my life.

We arrived at the foot of Mount Kilimanjaro, the highest mountain in Africa. It's a country more than a mountain—a hundred miles around the base. Some of us used to go fishing for trout at weekends, high up on the glorious green land on the lower slopes. A people called the Wachagga live there, and grow coffee and bananas and irrigate their fields from the swift little streams and keep their cows ever inside their houses; the women must go out every day to cut grass for them. The Wachagga are civilized, peaceable, political, and far too intelligent to join the army. They live high up on those verdant and wooded slopes, and look out over the mighty grass plains below where their old enemies, the Masai, roam with their cattle and their spears.

Then we went by train to Mombasa, and embarked on a troopship for Ceylon.

JOURNEY TO CEYLON

All I can remember of the voyage to Ceylon were Japanese sub-
marine scares, constant bouts of getting drunk, and one frantic
attempt to cut off the moustache of an officer named Macadoo.
His moustache was monstrous. But he fought like a man possessed, and the drunken efforts of five of us were insufficient to
hold him still. (It was ironic that he later got hit in the face by a
grenade splinter and had to have his moustache off anyway.)

We knew we were approaching Ceylon by the glorious scents
brought to us on the breeze. The first we saw of it was a cluster
of barrage balloons, like strange flowers growing out of the
empty sea. Then the hills came out of the haze—Colombo harbour.
I was landed along with a few others to guard our baggage as it
came ashore, and for several days we slept in huge hot go-downs
stinking of copra.

Asia was like another world. It knocked me over immediately.
I fell completely under its spell, and have been under it ever since.
The sights, the sounds, the smells (all right, I know there are some
bad smells, but the beautiful ones predominate), the food, the
people, the way of life, the philosophy—everything I saw was
fascinating. I felt that there was more to everything than appeared
on the surface. There was depth. In Africa everything is there to
see. In Asia the deeper you go the greater depths there are to
explore.

But we didn't have long to contemplate it. We were shoved
into a train and taken to a place called Polgahawella, which has a
little railway station modelled on a Victorian English one. A man
named Adam Beade, another platoon commander in 'A' Company, and I used to go down to this railway station every night
and sit in the refreshment room—as horrible as any refreshment
room in Outer London—and sip 'Seven-year Arak', a spiritous
liquor made from coconuts. We must have derived some strange
Betjemanesque nostalgic pleasure from the place.

As for the countryside around there, it was beautiful beyond
belief. Coconut palms climbed up the hills, emerald-coloured rice
grew in the valleys. Little houses roofed with heavy red tiles em-
bellished every vista. Snow-white *dagobas*, the shape of soap
bubbles, stood up from the green paddy fields. Every kind of
tropical fruit and herb grew around the houses and villages: a
land of fantastic plenty. And the people: the Sinhalese villagers

197

were like the Lotus Eaters—mild-eyed, gentle—and the women and children were beautiful.

It was at Polgahawella that Budge O'Hagan lost his life.

I had taken my platoon on an absurd expedition; we had constructed crazy canoes out of our groundsheets and bamboo frameworks and we voyaged for miles down the local river. When we got back late that evening, soaking wet but in high spirits for it had all been great fun, we noticed an air of gloom over the hutted camp under the coconut palms.

John Faucus, my very pleasant company commander, greeted me with: 'You've heard the news?'

I had not and he told it to me.

A sergeant (African) in 'D' Company had been put on a charge by his second-in-command. This officer had had a grudge against the sergeant (a Muslim named Sabit) for some time. I had no doubt in my own mind that he had victimized him. Sabit had been marched into the company office and sentenced to be broken to corporal. He was a regular, Sabit was, and a first-class soldier. And up with this treatment he would not put.

He saluted and marched out. He went to his lines and got his rifle. He returned to the company office, poked the rifle through the window and shot dead the captain who had charged him. The African clerk tried to rush him, likewise the African company sergeant-major, and he killed them too. He shot the company commander (a white man, of course) in the shoulder, and then decided that now he had started he might as well go and clean up the orderly room.

He started up the hill. Budge O'Hagan, hearing the shooting, was already coming down from the orderly room. He saw Sabit approaching the hospital. Budge ran in and shouted to the patients to get under their beds. He then came out and walked towards Sabit telling him to unload. Sabit shot him through the heart and he died three days afterwards. A British sergeant had by then managed to find some ammunition (nobody carried it regularly at that time) and his rifle, and he shot Sabit who died in a few minutes.

That evening our C.O. called a meeting of all the officers. One man, one of the few people who had come out to us from England, suggested that we should in future go armed. Our

commanding officer said no. On no account. For to do so would
be to lose the confidence of the askaris for good and all. We were to
continue exactly as if nothing had happened. Of course this was
by far the best decision that he could have made. We went on a
route march next day and during it one of my askaris asked me
what we *wazungu* (literally 'wizards'—meaning white men) thought
about the incident. Weren't we frightened? I said that we thought
that Sabit had gone mad and that people of all races go mad
occasionally: it was just a pity that the person who went mad on
this occasion was such an extremely good shot. 'You, Mwita
Mtende, can go mad whenever you like, for I have seen you on the
range and I know you couldn't hit a haystack at ten yards. I
certainly shouldn't be frightened of you.'

After three months in that gorgeous countryside we went on a
long march, right up to the north of the island. The northern half
is flat, jungled and practically uninhabited, except by wild elephants, bears, samba (a kind of deer), leopards and other game.
Apart from the time of the north-eastern monsoon it is dry and
terribly hot. (There are far more people in it now, though, after
the big irrigation schemes.)

For a year the 11th (East African) Division did intensive training in this jungle, with occasional periods of more training in the
south of the island. Officers as well as men slogged through the
jungle, lay sodden on the wet ground during the monsoon, carried
terrible loads for enormous distances in great heat and generally
tried to achieve the standard of toughness in the tropics that the
Japanese enemy was supposed to have. We didn't know that
somebody was going to pull an atom bomb out of a hat and win
the war for us. We fully expected a Japanese invasion of the island
and knew that if this came we would be fighting for our lives.
Sometimes we also gave a thought to the chaps behind the barbed
wire, or toiling on the Burma Railway.

I was given a new job: I had to form and train a new comic
opera unit known as a guerrilla platoon. First I was sent on a
course to the Royal Engineers, and there I learnt how to build
bridges of jungle material, but, more important, how to blow
them up again. I learnt how to use every sort of explosive, how
to make or unmake booby traps, how to 'disarm' enemy mines,
and all about sabotage and guerrilla tactics generally. The idea

was that if the Japanese invaded the island the guerrilla platoon from each battalion was to be left behind to hide in the jungle and disrupt their communications.

Back in the battalion I picked out all the toughest rogues from my old platoon, some hard cases from the rest of the battalion (I could have anyone I liked to take), and we became a sort of Robin Hood's band. I loved this. We would go away for weeks into the jungle and roam about where we would. We blew up old disused bridges in the middle of the night, and felled large trees, but above all we killed fish, which we killed in 'tanks' (surface dams) or rivers or the sea by throwing in large quantities of explosives. We practically lived on fish. Then suddenly the high command decided to disband the guerrilla platoons and I returned to 'A' Company again. But it had been a bit of fun. Ecology hadn't been invented then.

The charm of Ceylon got me hard. Even in that scarcely inhabited jungle in the north you still felt a depth of culture and weight of history surpassing anything we have in the upstart West. Wandering at random in the jungle you will come upon carved stones, old *kulams* (irrigation dams), old channels of artificial watercourses, buried cities and temples. Centuries and centuries before Christ there was a high and vigorous civilization there. And the inhabited places, whether the Hindu Tamil ones right in the very north or the Buddhist Sinhala ones of the south, seemed so deep and mysterious. Such an alien, off-beat, minor-key culture. A Sinhalese boy going around in an ox-cart beating a drum to advertise some dreadful Bombay film at the local cinema will produce a sound which has the power of thrilling me to the heart. I remember driving deep into the jungle once—right down in the south-east corner of the island—at three o'clock in the morning. I was making a reconnaissance for some silly exercise or other. Suddenly, as I drove along the track, I heard drums. I got out of the jeep and pushed into the dark undergrowth, walking in the direction of the sound. Suddenly I came to a clearing and there was a great fire, and devil-men in masks and strange clothing and sweating golden bodies dancing around it with flaming torches! I had slipped back a thousand years.

And further, as I came to know it, I loved the peasant life. The peasants sing as they work, and they work communally, and work is a joy to them. Their seasonal tasks are all religious in nature, and their religion is a joyous, laughing, happy thing. They give a significance to the seasons and the labour of the fields by marking each task with a festival and fun and pageantry.

It was difficult, in the army, to make contact with the people of the countries through which we moved. There is a natural antagonism between civilians and foreign troops. The great loyalty which a soldier has to build up for his own unit—even his own sub-unit—makes it very difficult to have any loyalty for anything else. I remember how we of the K.A.R. used to despise all other troops, from West African 'yam eaters' to 'hairy-arsed Hindis'. We were mutually exclusive. We had our own private language (Swahili)—even our private slang when we spoke English.

My mess-mates despised the Sinhalese, openly and tediously, all the time. It was funny how chaps from England who, back in Africa, had been the first to run down the Africans, now turned to praising them for their vigour, intelligence and soldierly virtues in comparison with the indolent Asians.

But when I went on leave I met Asians. I used to have to take a rail warrant to some English hill station where the climate was cool and where I would meet the sahibs and their memsahibs. But I would never get there. I would get off the train somewhere, and jump on a crowded bus, and go off just anywhere and maybe spend my week sleeping in some disused school-house in a remote village, or with a local family, or in some rest-house by the sea. In this way I soon got rid of any ideas I might have had about Asian inferiority. I found that the Sinhalese and the Tamils and the various races of India were, in fact, highly intelligent—man for man their standard of intelligence is probably higher than that of my own race. Further, they have their full share of toughness and virility. Go to sea with Sinhalese fishermen in their *orus* (outrigger sailing canoes), launching into breakers that would make even the Norfolk crabbers think twice! Then talk about the decadence of the Asians.

And, most importantly for me, I came into contact with what might be called the Hindu way of thought. I was fascinated by Hinduism. I soon learnt that this is not just the worship of a multiplicity of gods made out of wood and stone, but a system of thought that has been built up over thousands of years by a multitude of people who have devoted their entire lives to thinking. I came to see that Christianity, like the forms of Buddhism that got to Tibet, China and Japan, is merely an outrider of this vast system of thought. On talking to wise Hindus, and reading books, I came to believe that every thought of importance to be found in Christianity had been expressed in Hindu writings hundreds or even thousands of years before Christ. The Three Wise Men from the East of the Christian story brought more than gifts—they brought the whole thing.

My contact with Hinduism (in which I include Buddhism) reconciled me to Christianity. It did not make me believe in the miraculous origin of Christ (any more than it made me believe in the miraculous origin of Krishna, or in any of the miracles attributed to the Buddha), but it made me re-read the New Testament and revalue the philosophy and teaching ascribed to Christ. I came to see that very little of what he taught was false. Most is of great value. And there is no need to attribute all sorts of miracles to him to value his teachings.

But the central doctrine of Hinduism (as of Christianity) is non-attachment, and this I found completely right. All the ills of the world are due to attachment to material and foolish things. The best way for a man to spend his life would be in quiet, in thought and meditation, in the shucking off from his mind of all attachments to material things.

I would have liked to do this. I would have liked, in Ceylon, to walk out of the army and to become a recluse. I would still like to become one. But, alas, I am at far too lowly a state of development. The hot blood still runs far too quickly through my veins. If I donned the saffron robe, and then saw a pretty girl with a come-hither look in her eyes, where would my unworldly meditations go to then?

A submarine-haunted convoy took us over the Bay of Bengal and landed us at Chittagong, a place which seemed all heat and bad smells to me. I had just recovered from amoebic dysentery, and then the rains of the Arakan, on the Burma frontier, shoved me over into chronic bronchitis, and I was packed off to a Belgian Congo field hospital.

I thought I saw there the seeds of the disaster that has since overtaken the Belgian Congo.

Every morning for a week, as I sat on my balcony, often playing chess with a delightful Belgian doctor, the hundred-odd Africans who made up the field hospital used to be marched out on to the parade ground and formed up in a hollow square. Then one or two or three of their number, stripped to the waist, would be brought out, laid down on the ground, and flogged with a *kiboko* until they could hardly stand.

I asked my doctor friend why this was done. 'Oh, it's the only punishment we have in the Congo army,' he said. 'It's the only thing they understand.'

In five and a half years in the King's African Rifles I only once saw a man flogged.

I had a month's sick leave after this, and by God I needed it! I was as thin as a rake and as weak as a kitten. (Amoebic dysentery, if it's neglected for a few months as mine was, because I didn't know what it was and wasn't in the habit of going to doctors, leaves you very poorly. I had spent twenty days in Kandy hospital getting rid of mine, with the foot of my bed cocked up higher than the head of it so that I could retain the 'retention enemas' that they gave me to pickle the bugs inside my intestines. I read Tolstoy's *War and Peace* in this position, and thus claim to be the only man in the world who has read this work upside down.)

Well, a month divided between two hill stations in the foothills of the Himalayas (I really *had* to go to a hill station that time), 'Naughty Naini' (Nainital) and 'Randy Rhani' (Rhaniket), made me fit again, and I was able to rejoin my battalion, which was already beginning to feel its way through the jungle of Burma towards the Japanese.

Chapter Fourteen

❖

Journey to Burma

The journey to Burma was fantastic. There were two days in an absolutely packed troop train from Calcutta to Dimapur, in Assam: the trains at that time were crowded with men and stuff going to Imphal to the 14th Army, to the Americans with Stilwell, to China. There were British and Indian and Yankee officers, Gurkhas, Chinese, Africans, a few G.I.s. At Dimapur we got in a bus and started off along the Manipur Road. This was a tarred road that left the flat jungle country in Assam and wound into the Naga hills. A never-ceasing stream of empty trucks, driven like fury by mad Indian drivers, was coming from Imphal, while another stream of loaded trucks was going the other way. This transport never stopped, night or day; when a driver had done his spell he got out at a roadside camp to rest and another driver would jump into the driver's seat and go on. When a truck broke down a road patrol which came along at frequent intervals would get it rolling again. And there were thousands and thousands of trucks: one's head whirled with the constant swish, swish, as they passed one's vehicle. As the road was mostly hairpin bends accidents were very common.

We passed through Kohima which was the remains of a large Naga village in the hills. All these hills had been blasted by high explosive, every tree was torn to shreds and lifeless, every house and hut flattened, every old bit of corrugated iron riddled like a colander. And everywhere were little wooden crosses. Next to me sat an infantry officer of the 2nd Division (which had relieved Kohima and broken through to Imphal) and he pointed to spots all along the road where there would be a few bunkers or trenches, and a hill or two blasted by H.E., and he would tell me the story of the battle which had occurred there.

Imphal was just a large military camp. In the hills we had seen groups of wild-looking Naga tribesmen, but in Imphal we saw mild-eyed Manipuris, half-Mongolian half-Indian, most attractive people. After a night there I went on with a lorry convoy towards Tamu, and the open Manipur plain gave way to high jungle-clad hills again, scars of battle became frequent, and fresher—for the tide of battle had only just passed—a nasty smell began to be evident near caved-in bunkers everywhere and the road became worse. Then the road ran abruptly out of the hills and into the flat but still jungle-filled Kabaw Valley and we drove through the hideous ruins of Tamu where the charred remains of every house were full of the blackened bones and bodies of dead Japanese. We spent a night in the valley, and everywhere one wandered one came upon ant-cleaned skeletons in Japanese uniforms, and little shallow graves with flies buzzing over them. Jackals and vultures didn't seem to have disturbed them much—I suppose because there were so many that these scavengers satisfied themselves on a few.

We crossed three swollen rivers on ferries improvised by East African engineers and after that the track became appalling; a morass of deep soft mud through the jungle. No ordinary car could have looked at it and even jeeps were useless, but we had Dodge 6-by-6 trucks which were able to churn through for a few miles. All along this road lay corpses and skeletons: you got so used to them that after a while you no longer noticed them.

We climbed into the hills again and came to the road-head, and thereafter had to walk.

We slushed along through the mud. Wherever there was a suitable bit of hillside there would be a camp of askaris: maybe a troop of 25-pounder guns, maybe a rifle company, maybe a field company of engineers, or supply chaps, or field ambulance, or brigade headquarters. There were no tents for anybody—even the brigadier lived under a groundsheet. Everyone slept under his groundsheet, which he carried on his back when not sleeping under it. A camp consisted of hundreds of beds made of bamboo, each one with a groundsheet over a stick over the top of it, and a slit-trench just beside it for the occupant to flop into when shelling started. The jungle was bamboo growing thickly under large trees, many of them teak. The ground was a series of very steep ridges, all running north and south—like waves breaking on a beach.

Eventually I reached my battalion, was given my old platoon, and in ten minutes was off on a patrol. The officer who took over my groundsheet space had his arm blown off by a Japanese mortar bomb ten minutes after I said goodbye to him.

As soon as you got off the track in those jungled hills you found that you were in very difficult country. The hills were all steep— so steep that you had to clamber up them and pull yourself along by the bamboo, whose leaves were sharp and apt to cut your hands. The bamboo was very dense and you had to push your way through it. It was constantly wet and dripping, and so were you. It was mostly raining, though so finely that you didn't know whether it was raining or not, but it didn't matter. The bamboo had a sort of slightly prickly fur on it which came off on you, like a not very virulent form of itching powder. Over the bamboo were the high teak and other cover trees, their tops meeting overhead to form a canopy.

If you were walking north and south it was far easier. If you were able (for tactical reasons) to stick to the ridge of one of the waves of that solid sea (for that is what those hills are like) you could walk quite fast, for along the narrow hog-backed ridges the bamboo was much less dense, and you could see the sky above. If you were forced to travel in the valleys it was worse, but not too bad either. There was always a *chaung*, or small swift-flowing stream, often with nice fish in the rocky pools. (A grenade in one of those pools would provide fresh fish.) But if you had to walk *across* the grain of the hills, as of course you often did, it was terrible. You hauled yourself up from one clump of bamboo to the next, weighed down by sixty or seventy pounds of equipment. Your pack got entangled with the blasted bamboo, your boots slipped and slithered in the wet mud.

As I look back on it now it seems amusing, but at the time I know it was horrible. Every European amongst us (except me—I seemed immune) got skin trouble: ringworm, 'crutch rot', 'foot rot', prickly heat, ear trouble. Officer after officer went sick. The askaris stood it better. During that first advance down to the

Chindwin River we got little fighting. The Japanese who were around there at that time were a defeated army. The three enemy divisions that had invested Imphal and Kohima, depending on seizing the stores of rice in these places, had failed to do so and were falling back sick, wounded, starving, sodden with rain and mud, dying, and their places had not yet been taken by fresh troops.

My company, however, was the first to march into Sitaung, the port on the River Chindwin, and as it happened my platoon was the first to reach the river.

Before we got into the riverside village I noticed our brigadier and his staff close up behind us. 'A' Company was the leading company. To the left of the track we came to a broken-down Burmese hut built up on high stilts. Under the hut sat two Japanese. I thought they were dead when I first saw them—dead but they wouldn't lie down—but when I looked at them I saw that they were alive. Their eyes were following me. I noticed (and it was like a biff in the solar plexus) that maggots were crawling on their lips and out of their nostrils. They were, of course, living skeletons, and their rain-stiffened trousers were stained with the blood that they had been passing due to dysentery. I went on and left them but very soon heard two shots from a Sten gun. I turned round and saw that the brigadier had just shot them. I was sure that he did not do this out of any blood-lust, but simply because it was the humane thing to do and he did not like to order somebody else to do it.

John Faucus told me to take the lead with my platoon and I led them into Sitaung. We were the first members of the Fourteenth Army to reach the river. We picked our way through the bomb-shattered village over a carpet of corpses. Most of them were thin and wasted with hardly enough meat on the bones to rot, but I saw one fat man floating in water in a bomb crater and he was blown out like a balloon. This horrified me somehow, for I had got used to my corpses being thin. An askari put a shot into it and you could hear a great hissing of gases. Some of the corpses were not corpses—there were a number of live men lying around—but they might just as well have been dead for there could be no question of reviving them. The maggots had already got to work on their living features. They had become too weak to brush the blowflies away any more. Eyes, mouths, nostrils, gnawed away at by maggots, and still life in them. And to keep breathing ourselves we had to keep our hands constantly moving in front of our faces: the blowflies were like a dense cloud.

These were the Japanese soldiers who had left the Chindwin three months before, each man carrying a month's ration of rice. These were the men who had fought on trying to take their objective until food had gone, ammunition had gone, hope had gone, senior officers had gone. They had been left to themselves— sixty thousand of them—to get back to the Chindwin as best they could. They had been the strong ones who had hobbled or crawled all the way back to Sitaung where a boat should have been waiting to take them away. But no boat was waiting. The RAF had seen to that. All the boats were sitting on the bottom of the river.

Many of the skeletons we had seen back along the track had been lying on home-made stretchers—their comrades had staggered with them as far as they could. They would not have weighed much, except to weakened men who could hardly move themselves. Most had died beside the long sticks which they had been using to help them hobble on their lacerated feet. Few still had their rifles. Napoleon's retreat from Moscow might have been on a bigger scale, but I am sure that it was no more horrible than the Japanese retreat from Manipur. I know the Japanese were our enemy. I know they were not of the Caucasian race. But they were men. They were among the bravest soldiers this world has ever seen, and send not to hear for whom the bell tolls.

We withdrew from that place of pestilence, leaving the R.E.s to come in later with their flame-throwers and complete the work of the flies, and we camped on a hill overlooking the Chindwin. When I say camped, we followed our usual drill when not in contact with the enemy. Each pair of men built a bamboo double bed, put their common groundsheet over the top of it to keep at least the full force of the rain off, and hung their joint mosquito net underneath. (This was before the stuff called 'Skat' was invented and came to relieve us of the need to carry nets.) By the side of the bed each man would then dig his 'grave'. This was just that—a narrow slit in the ground into which the man could drop should the Japanese start mortaring or shelling. And that was the camp. If we were in contact with the enemy, or liable to be, we would just dig the 'grave'. In this we would spend the night, rifles and Bren guns at the ready, rain pounding down on us. Many, many times on patrols we did not even have 'graves'. We would sling our packs off to use as pillows, put our hats over our faces to keep the rain from filling up our ears, and sleep like birds in the wilderness. And one thing about the African soldier: he can light a fire in a few minutes in the middle of a wet jungle in the biggest downpour that ever was and boil a mess-tin of tea over it. Don't ask me what we would have done without tea. We ran on it.

Next day John Faucus called me and told me to take my platoon five miles down river where I would come to a village. There I was to look for a Burmese intelligence officer and escort him across the river in a canoe.

This was fine.

We picked our way through Sitaung again and followed a good track which skirted the swamps along the river there. We duly came to the village, which was unbombed and consisted of about a dozen large houses, well built of split bamboo (bamboo is used for everything in that country, just as coconut fronds are in Ceylon), and there we found a fat man wearing a *longhi* (Burmese sarong) sitting in an old chair and smoking an enormous cheroot.

Supposing that he was the headman of the village, I went up to him—everybody else had run away at our approach—and said: 'I want English officer. You know—English—English officer—things like this here!' And I indicated my shoulders. I had never talked to a Burmese before.

The man looked at me. He took his cheroot out of his mouth. 'If you happen to be looking for Major Robinson,' he drawled, 'I am the man you are looking for.' I felt I had walked into the middle of one of those silly spy thrillers.

He was a great man, this Major 'Robinson' (that was not his name). He shouted for the headman of the village, who approached timidly (he was a *thin* man), and a few of the other villagers crept out, and soon the askaris were handing round cigarettes and making friends. The Burmese had never seen Africans before and at first were sure that they were cannibals and would eat them. But askaris are marvellous at making friends and they soon had the little yellow children running round their feet and sitting on their laps. We climbed the ladder into the head-man's hut (after I had stuck pickets out) and were entertained to curried chicken and rice, bamboo shoots, and green tea. And it seemed the best food I had ever tasted.

'Shall we go across the river?' I said, after we had eaten.

The major gave a curt laugh. 'In daylight? And the RAF bomb-line this bank of the Chindwin? No, no.'

'But there are no planes about. It wouldn't take us long.'

'Certainly not. We'll go as soon as it gets dark.'

Some arak was produced. The major and I got down to it.

He was a sort of Burmese Walter Mitty. He told me the most wonderful stories of daring. At first I believed him, and thought he was the most extraordinary man I had ever seen. Then I began to suspect. Then I knew. These stories were all made up. Later I met a man from divisional intelligence and he told me the man was famous for it. But it was interesting to hear how he had held up an entire Japanese division for three days single-handed with a Sten gun.

We finished the bottle and I said: 'It's dark now. Let's go.'

'What? In the dark? Why, man, we could never find the way! We'd land up in a swamp somewhere. You don't know the Chindwin—I can see that.'

'When do we go then?'

'Dawn.'

'What about the RAF?'

'Blow the RAF! We'll slip across quickly.'

We lay down on the floor and went to sleep.

Dawn came, as it always does.

'Major Robinson!' I said. 'Dawn!'

The major rubbed his eyes. 'Oh—er . . .' he said. 'Look here, old man—I've decided not to go. Risky, you know—RAF and all that.'

'Well, you can do what you like, sir,' I said. 'But I am going. If you like you can come with me. If you like you can stay behind.'

And he decided to come with me. I think he realized that it would look a little bad if I went back and said I had crossed but that the major was too windy to come with me.

The river is five hundred yards across there, with a swift

current, but some of my Watende were brought up in canoes and we soon got across. There was another village there, likewise inhabited by Burmese. The headman treated us again to a good meal of curried chicken and rice. 'Robinson' questioned him about the Japanese. There were no live ones within several miles. It would certainly be safe for my battalion to make a landing. And as I had taken care to be the first man to step out of the canoe I claim (and no one has *yet* ever disputed me) to be the first man of the Fourteenth Army to set foot east of the Chindwin.

When we got back across the other side again I found that the men I had left there had captured a prisoner. They had been taken to him by the Burmese. He was the first Japanese I had seen who could walk. He was in quite good order, but was terrified because he thought the Africans were going to eat him. As soon as he saw me he shouted, 'English mester! English mester! Come quickly!' He had been a schoolmaster and could speak some English. The askaris were terribly proud of him and gave him cigarettes and bully beef and tea, and I talked to him about his home, and we put him in a canoe with two Burmese paddlers and two askaris and sent him back to the battalion. They would want to ask him questions.

We fought a 'naval action' there. A canoe came shooting down on the current with two Japanese aboard her. We opened up from the bank but they lay down in the bottom of the canoe and it was hard to see them. I jumped into a cranky little canoe by the bank and an African intelligence sergeant who had come with me on this jaunt got into another and we set out after them. I would have let them go, but one thing that our high command desperately wanted was live prisoners. My canoe rapidly filled up and sank, but the other got to them and found them both dead—our fire from the shore had been effective. The 'I' sergeant brought back their regimental badges, numbers, etc. Every Japanese carried a thing like a pencil box with two chopsticks in it, an ink pad at one end, and a stamp with his own name carved on it. This was to sign his name. Every section commander had a little rising sun flag signed by all the men in his section. Every officer lugged a sword.

A few days later 'A' Company crossed the river in assault boats with outboard engines, and we stayed on the other bank for a fortnight. I remember this stay as remarkable in that for five days and nights it never stopped raining once—not for the period of a minute. I also remember it because it was there that I first met James Thurber. Someone had given me a book of his. I shared my bed at that time with a cannibal—a very old man who was my 'platoon runner'. He had fiercely cicatrized cheeks, teeth filed to points, ear-lobes hanging down to his shoulders. He admitted that he had eaten human flesh, and said that when he got home after the war he intended to eat some more. It gave you strength. This man and I lay under one mosquito net and one groundsheet for five days and nights, while he sniffed snuff and sang little cannibal songs to himself and I read Thurber, shaking with laughter most of the time. We all have the pleasure of discovering Thurber once in our lives. I feel I was lucky to have discovered him under such Thurberesque circumstances.

When it stopped raining James Gascoigne, another platoon commander and a very great friend of mine, and I used to go down to what we called our 'club'. This was the house of some Burmese fish-trappers down by a small river. They worked a huge fishing machine—a kind of weir that they lowered into the water to entrap the fish. We would take them the odd tin or two of 'soya links' (disgusting vegetarian sausages that they used to give us sometimes as a change from bully beef) and they would cook us delicious fish and vegetables and rice, and supply us with arak. First we would bathe in the river, then we would eat and drink, then James would start going: 'Ah-da-diddy-da-da! I want—some —sea—food—de—mama! Ah-da-diddy-da-da-cha-er-cha!' Noises like that. Because he was a mad keen jazz man, of the furthest out kind. We were short of ordinary food over there, for not much got to us. It had to be dropped by parachute some miles the other side of the Chindwin, transported on mules to the river, ferried across in assault boats, and carried to us by Burmese porters.

We then recrossed the river and marched back all the way we had come through the rain to Tamu in the Kabaw Valley. Near that town of the dead we rested for a week to fit out again. Indeed we needed to—we looked like an army of scarecrows. In rags and tatters, equipment tied together with pieces of bark, weapons rusty, half the chaps with no boots, everything rotted through constant wet.

Then we set off down the Kabaw Valley, up which we had

heard that the Japanese were sending reinforcements. The real
war was about to begin.

We set off southwards down the valley, each one of us carrying
a groundsheet or a mosquito net, a jersey, a spare jungle battle
dress, spare socks, a mess tin, a water bottle, two or three grenades
per man, four full Bren magazines; officers carried a Sten and five
full mags, other ranks a rifle and a hundred rounds ammo, also
two-inch mortar bombs, smoke grenades, and a dozen kinds of
pills and potions to ward off malaria, tick typhus, etc., etc. Besides
this we generally had three or four days' food on us. I do not think
that any troops except African ones could have stood up to this
without many of the men falling ill. Instead we got lighter sickness
casualties than a British battalion gets when out of the line in
India. Before we made contact with the Japanese the rain had
slackened off, for which we were very thankful.

For some time we were not in the leading brigade and therefore
saw no real action. We just patrolled the hills to the flank and held
various defensive positions. The Japanese did send small parties
to worry us at night—'jitter parties'—and they would shoot off
blindly hoping that we would answer. We slept in our 'graves'
and could therefore ignore them. Other units were not so well
trained and one battalion blazed off thousands of rounds one night
—and hundreds of grenades—and hit nobody. Our men had been
drilled not to shoot at over two yards' range at night, and we
surrounded our positions with lines of *panjis*—sharpened bamboo
stakes.

A couple of times Japanese fighter-bombers came over and
strafed us—exciting and not very dangerous. I also stood on a hill
and watched five of our 'bully bombers', i.e. supply-dropping
planes, shot down by Japanese fighters, one by one, and there was
no means of warning them that the enemy was about. We saw
several ground battles from the tops of hills; other units were
attacking strong positions across the road in the Kabaw Valley
and we would sit on the hills to guard the flanks. Our attacks
were often prefaced by an 'air strike' of Hurribombers—250-
pound eggs which shook the ground like earthquakes—followed
by cannon strafing and then heavy mortar and artillery concentra-
tions. It looked as though nothing could survive it, and yet the
Japanese were generally safe in their bunkers and ready to

welcome our infantry. These attacks began to cause us heavy casualties, particularly among officers who—being white—were conspicuous.

I vividly remember the first time I lost a man on one of our flanking patrols.

There was some sort of a battle going on down in the Kabaw Valley—that was the day that the 11th K.A.R. lost every one of its officers and white N.C.O.s and ended up under the command of the African regimental sergeant-major. We were quite peaceable though. We were ordered to clear some hills in the jungle along the flank. My platoon happened to be in front and we stooged gently along, with me frequently changing the leading section so as to give everybody the same chance of getting shot, and each section commander, while in front, frequently changing his leading man. In the jungle the only practicable way to walk is in single file—no matter how you tried you could not get men to spread out. So there was always one man who was the first. The platoon commander was never very far behind him. In fact, on this occasion I was right behind him. It was strictly against the rules for the platoon commander to be in front: he was supposed to keep behind the leading ten-man section, but this was impossible. You see, these men were mercenaries, after all—it was not *their* war. And the leading scout was not in a very good position. If he did strike the Japanese, they would be lying down in a hole, concealed, motionless, watching. He would be standing up or walking in the open, clear for all to see. The Japanese would let him come quite close and then let him have it with a light machine-gun. For this reason scouts went more and more slowly. If they could creep along slowly enough they could often sight the enemy before the enemy sighted them, for these men from the African bush have fine eyesight and can move like cats. But we were always in a hurry, always being driven on from behind. And so the platoon commander tended to be right up in front, shooing his leading scouts on.

My leading section commander had just detailed a youngster named Ngombe to take the lead. Ngombe was no more than a kid, and I had doubts about letting him go but, after all, each man had to take his chance. Ngombe was woefully slow. I think he sensed something. I kept telling him to get a bloody move on, and even once called him back to me and told him that I thought he was a damned coward and I would make him do a double shift as scout if he did not hurry up. He went forward again just after this—and the air was rent with the crack of a light machine-gun. I threw myself flat on my face—no doubt we all did. I could hear Ngombe screaming. The crack of bullets over my head seemed to be terribly close and I turned my head and looked upwards. The bamboos were splintering not six inches above my head. We had learned to crawl like snakes in the army and that was the way I crawled up to Ngombe. My platoon had begun to return the fire, and I hoped that the enemy's firing would become more erratic. My man with a grenade discharger had begun to lob grenades over our heads. Ngombe held his hand towards me—it was nearly off. The wrist was a bloody and splintered mess. He was weeping and screaming *mama*! The word for mother in most Bantu languages is the same as our own. I tried to comfort him—told him to keep calm—told him he would be all right once the doctors got him. He took no notice of me. I took out the field dressing from the little pocket in his tunic where this was kept and wrapped it tight round his upper arm to try to stop the bleeding. He cried something about his *tumbo* (tummy), so I looked at him and found that a bullet had gone clean through him. I started fumbling for my own field dressing. I reflected how cowardly it was of me to do what I was doing, using the body of the wounded man as cover. For there was no doubt that I was keeping behind him—and my head down—and I was well aware that a bullet would hit him first. The Japanese could see us and were trying to hit us but their aim was too high. They were rotten shots. Also my own chaps behind had mostly by then crawled to better positions, and three Brens and seven Sten guns and twenty or thirty rifles were cracking back at the enemy. A body suddenly flopped beside me and I saw it was Makindi Makali, my orderly. He had run forward in a lull and made a dash for it. He had had no business to get off the ground.

Together we turned Ngombe over and got the field dressing right round him. He screamed with pain as we moved him. There was just a tiny little mouth of a wound each side, hardly bleeding. Makindi told him that he would be all right; he wept and said he wouldn't—he would die—look at his arm—look at his poor arm!

I said to Makindi: 'Now!' Makindi grabbed Ngombe's legs and I grabbed his shoulders and we got up and ran with him. Makindi even remembered to pick up Ngombe's rifle. We made a dirty dash and flung ourselves into a little *donga*, or depression. I called two men and told them to carry him back to the rear—they could do it in fairish safety from there.

John Faucus came up. He told me to withdraw. I said: 'What about me staying here and keeping up covering fire and you attacking from the flank?' I was sticky with Ngombe's blood. John said no, I was to withdraw and he would take the whole company round to the left flank where there was higher ground.

James Gascoigne led, and we blundered off through the jungle. Suddenly there was a great burst of firing again and I left my platoon and went forward to find that James's platoon was pinned down under heavy fire. John Faucus was obliged to order him to withdraw. And, with the third platoon leading, we blundered even farther round to the left. We came to the ridge that the Japanese were on, only higher up on it, and John told me to lead. 'You might as well have the fun of attacking,' he said. I could have done without it.

My platoon opened out (the jungle was not too thick there) and we started forward. Suddenly little Japanese mortar bombs began to burst amongst us and one man was hit on the hand by a splinter. A light machine-gun opened up and we got down. We were surprised to find that we were very close—only about twenty yards from a little nob of a hill from which the fire came. The Japanese were well hidden.

'Attack!' shouted John.

'I can see a bunker!' shouted one of my corporals. I had heard James say that he had definitely seen bunkers when he had been fired at.

Bunkers were a Japanese invention. They would dig a deep hole on a hill-top, cover it over with five-foot-thick teak trees, and cover these over with several feet of earth. They would leave a tunnel to get in by, and a long and wide but very low slit in front to fire out of. It took a direct hit from a 250-pound bomb to open one of these up. I knew that if there were bunkers on the hill our attack would be hopeless—particularly as there was no possibility of any covering fire. For there were no troops on the flank to provide it. Also there was open ground between us and the supposed bunkers, and a frontal attack like that with no covering fire to make the Japanese keep their heads down would be disastrous. I had no ambition to be a hero—least of all a dead one. I had a dread of killing any more of my own men. Also I had a suspicion that were I to get up suddenly and rush forward shouting 'Charge!' my men would go on lying just where they were and I should look a terrible fool. So I shouted to John that I would, of course, attack if he insisted on it, but that I thought I ought to have some covering fire first.

He asked me to crawl back to him. I did so and we had a bit of a discussion about it. James came up and said that he definitely thought it would be wrong to attack without artillery preparation —he had certainly seen at least two bunkers—was sure of it. John said, 'All right. You're quite right. We'll go back and ask for some artillery preparation in the morning and attack them then.'

So back we went. And the C.O. (he was the great Colonel 'Cobber' Carne, of the Gloucesters—later to be captured on the Imjin River in Burma) 'laid on' an artillery concentration for dawn next day. John again said that my platoon could have the honour of leading the attack. (I would have been perfectly happy with the honour of staying behind, but I didn't say so. Has honour skill in surgery?)

In the middle of the night we blundered again, in single file, through the black darkness of the jungle, until we got to where we had been before. We lay down and waited. After a terribly long time we heard a banshee screaming, and a hundred shells from a hundred guns came rushing towards us and fell on top of that bunkered hill. The noise of them all going off was quite earth-shattering. The whole hill seemed to leap and bound in front of our eyes with flame. Then it stopped, John blew a whistle, and we all got up and lumbered forward. It was just light. It was difficult to move forward once we got to the hill, for the place was a tangled mass of blown-down trees and branches. Great white scars showed everywhere on the rocks, and every trunk was pock-marked with splinter holes. One shot came from the hill-top. Some of my men later said they saw some Japanese running away. When we got to the top we found no one there. Just two small bunkers, one pair of field-glasses left behind by someone in a hurry. One caved-in bunker with flies buzzing about it—a quick way of burying honourable comrades. They had probably been buried some time. Anticlimax. And Ngombe was dead.

After this our battalion was ordered to make a deep left-flanker, down a stream valley known as the Bon Chaung. This would bring us down into the Kalemyo Gorge, which runs at right angles to the Kabaw Valley and connects it with the Chindwin. So off we went into the mountains with some mule transport.

This job took a week or two—I forget exactly how long—during which time we were never out of contact with the enemy, and we attacked so many of their positions that I lost count of them.

The drill was generally much the same. The leading scout copped it. The leading platoon got down and returned fire, and then got out of it. Next morning artillery fire—and very often an air-strike with Hurribombers. Never again any question of a direct frontal attack unsupported. A few casualties—but a few casualties time and again over a long period make a lot of casualties, and men's nerves got touchier and touchier. It began to be harder and harder to get your leading scouts to go forward. I remember another subaltern (a Rhodesian farmer with a wife and family at home) coming to me as we lay on top of some hill somewhere and almost weeping with strain. It was just after James Gascoigne had been shot through the leg. This man confessed that he was frightened, scared stiff. He didn't know if he would be able to go up another hill. And he pointed out that officer after officer had been picked off and there was only a handful of the original ones left. How long could we last? I didn't know what the hell to say to him. I hated to see my fellow officers go, but I seemed to hate losing askaris even more. The officers knew what they were fighting for. What were the askaris fighting for? It wasn't their quarrel.

They blundered on with a sort of cheerful persistence. They had got beyond grumbling. They laughed. They were light-hearted, somehow—perhaps a little light-headed. I remember my lance-corporal, Kidombo. He was a merry, tough little man. I once told him to take two men and climb a little hill on our flank to make sure there were no Japanese on it. I told him to take his time, to stalk it, to take no risks—and to avoid becoming engaged.

A short while afterwards there was a burst of Sten gun fire. While I was wondering whether to go and see what had happened Kidombo came back with his two men and the lapel badges of five Japanese. He had surprised them sitting round in a circle having their meal, and had killed them all with one burst of his Sten gun.

I saw a corporal from another platoon come back after a similar patrol, and he stood by the fire talking about what had happened, when somebody handed him a mug of tea. He took the mug in one hand and plonked his Sten gun butt-downwards on the ground with the other. There was a shot. He looked surprised, then glanced down at his hand and found that a bullet had gone through it! Sten guns are a bit like that. He finished his tea before walking off to the field dressing-station.

As the road dried up behind us and more and more artillery could be got along it, the Japanese resistance began to go. They used to start nipping off before the artillery concentration ('crump') was brought down on them. And by God, I don't blame them! We used to climb up a hill to find complete chaos—the country absolutely shattered. Not a leaf or a piece of bark left on any tree, half of them knocked over, great branches ripped off, everything covered with dust and leaves. Some ammunition, odd helmets, odd sacks of rice or tins of food lying about, letters, sometimes some dead soldiers. Never any thrill of victory to reward us.

We hit the Kalemyo Gorge at last, ambushed some Japanese and captured a supply dump, and after a day or two the rest of the division broke through to us along the road, with some tanks.

Progress was quicker after that, but I think even harder for us—or maybe we were getting tired. The main force went along the road with the tanks, and whenever they bumped anything we, who kept to the hills on their left flank, would outflank it. We had one or two rare old battles and not all of them give me pleasure when I remember them.

Then just when we began to think that it was going on for

ever the Japanese simply melted away. And we could march flat out into Kalewa.

This turned out to be a large area of heavy bomb craters on the confluence of the Mittya and Chindwin Rivers. There was practically no trace of where the buildings had been, with the exception of an artificial hill on which stood several large pagodas and temples which had only received a few direct hits from 500-pounders. The pagodas showed traces of having been covered with gold leaf. There was one fine marble Buddha, almost unscathed, serenely ignoring the homicidal stupidity going on round about him.

We sat in the dust at Kalewa for a few days, and every afternoon the Japanese shelled us from across the river, with some casualties. Then 'A' Company crossed the Mittya River and I took my platoon up some big hills overlooking the Chindwin to sit and observe the Japs on the opposite side. We stayed up there for several days, and it was very restful, and we often saw parties of Japanese, passing up and down, and we sometimes managed to call artillery fire down on them and see a crump of shells land in their midst. One of our brigades crossed the Chindwin in assault boats and began to clean up resistance over there. And one night we heard a peculiar rumbling sound, which did not stop, and which turned out to be our relieving division (the Second British), crossing the new floating Bailey bridge—the longest military bridge in the world—which our East African engineers had thrown across the Chindwin, but which I had not yet seen.

Then it was back to an air-strip in lorries, a delightful ride in a 'bully-bomber', and Christmas and a rest in the cool hills of Assam.

I still declined—as far as one can decline anything in the army—a third 'pip' with second-in-command of a company, and so 'Cobber' Carne sent me off to a mortar course, at Saugor, in central India. The three-inch mortars, those miracle weapons of the British infantry, were being brought into line with artillery practice. We were taught to fire them as artillery: map-shooting, ranging several platoons of mortars from the firing of one weapon, all the rest of it. I became lost in the sheer technical fascination of it. The chief instructor at the mortar school was an old actor.

Epilogue

✦✦✦✦✦✦✦✦✦✦✦✦✦✦✦✦✦✦✦✦✦✦✦◇✦✦✦✦✦✦✦✦✦✦✦✦✦✦✦✦✦✦✦✦✦✦✦

Liverpool in November in the rain. A brass band playing 'Colonel Bogey' on the quayside and a general up on a rostrum making a speech to welcome us which could hardly be heard because of the ribald comments of the returning heroes, who only wanted to be let off the ship.

The culmination of thirteen years of exile—of longing—of romantic dreams of England. For twelve years I had imagined the green pastures, the bosky woods, the cool bracing climate, the mellow fruitfulness, the honest yeomanry. As my train sped across the flat and muddy Midlands, with rain streaming down the windows outside and stuffy air steaming up the windows inside, I began to have doubts. Were my romantic memories and imaginings the images of reality? Perhaps it was my youth that I had felt homesick for rather than any particular country.

At the details camp at Gravesend I did not distinguish myself by my soldierly bearing. It was the first time that I had soldiered in a 'Home' establishment, and I could not reconcile myself to the bull. I had got hold of a British-style battle-dress but still wore my filthy old bush hat. I was told by the adjutant that I would have to equip myself with a beret and I just grunted. Beret indeed—what did they think I was, a Basque? Coming down bleary-eyed to breakfast I happened to sit down at the table opposite the adjutant and the commanding officer. I should, of course, have said: 'Good morning, sir!' I didn't. I addressed myself, not to my commanding officer, but to my porridge. The adjutant reprimanded me by saying, significantly: 'Good *morning*, sir!' Meaning, of course, not that he was saying good morning to me, but that I

'Rain them down, gentlemen!' he used to drawl. 'Rain them down! When you've got a good target, and have the range—rain them down! Don't let them get away with a dusting!'

I never had a chance to rain them down—at least not in anger.

I rejoined my battalion—this time with the third 'pip' after all —at what I imagine could well be the hottest place in India—a sun- and dust-stricken camp in Bihar—where we suffered in our tents as British soldiers had suffered in the hot seasons of two hundred years. I taught my mortar platoon the new techniques. I took them into the jungle with the mortars on mules and got them so that we could have 'bombs on the ground' within seven minutes of my blowing a whistle. We were all ready—ready for the promised landing in Malaya. We were eager to try out our mettle. On the way back from my jungle training, walking in single file along that jungle track, men and mules strung out behind me, I heard the cuckoo—the first time I had heard him since leaving England a dozen years before.

Shortly afterwards I met a fellow officer leading his men *out* for jungle training.

'Have you heard?' he said. 'The war's over.'

And he told me of the new bomb which the Americans had dropped, which made all the mortar bombs in the world look like fire-crackers. And I walked back to camp feeling bitterly disappointed. There would be no landing in Malaya. The war had come to an ignominious end.

supposed to be working I drove around, met farmers, drank beer with my foremen, became an Englishman and an East Anglian again.

I did not like the changes that had occurred in English farming. The farmer was becoming just another dyspeptic businessman at the end of a telephone. The farm worker (the few that were left) just another factory hand, clocking in and clocking out. There was coming to be less and less chance for a farm worker to get a little farm of his own. Farms were being knocked together into huge factory units, run by high finance. The land was becoming just something to exploit, to make money out of. The English countryside was becoming a rubbish-dump for the refuse from the towns. And the great wens themselves were spreading out into the country like cancerous growths.

I suddenly decided 'to be a writer'. I gave a month's notice to the 'War Ag.', and lived at home in my trolley bus or sailed the seas in my smack, often with beer-drinking friends. I began to give 'talks' on the wireless. Then the BBC gave me a hundred and seventy pounds to go overland to India with, using whatever transport I could find on the way, and I went and came back and gave a series of talks and wrote a book. Drawn strongly still to India I went there again, and roamed about for a year, and wrote another book.

I sold my trolley bus and bought a 'Dutch barge'—the kind of vessel that I had dreamed about in the heat and dust of Africa. I lived on board her, met Sally, got married, sailed around the coasts of England and up the rivers and canals, and wrote another book. Went back to Africa and wrote another book.

Then I lived on five acres of Suffolk ground, with Sally and our daughters Jane and Anne and Kate. And we tried to be self-supporting. We tried, as far as possible, to 'contract out' of an economic system which we did not like, because we felt that it was motivated by greed. Sally is a potter and an artist, I did enough 'radio journalism' to make enough money to conduct a very limited and controlled trade with the rest of the world. We milked our own cow, killed our own pigs and poultry, grew our own potatoes, drove our own pony and generally worked our way into the practice of self-sufficiency. We were very happy and it did us good.

should have said good morning to the commanding officer. I looked up from my porridge, looked at the white faces opposite me—faces which had obviously never been farther than the Mediterranean in their lives—and muttered: 'Oh, good morning —good morning,' and then went back to my porridge wondering vaguely why the adjutant had called me sir.

When I was finally let out of the army I had to purge myself of the state of mind that one gets into after having engaged for five and a half years in a war. I wanted to get so that I could look at a hill without wondering if it would make a good mortar position; could see some people on the skyline without wondering whether it would be practicable to engage them with a light machine-gun. I wanted to cut my way back to some sort of sanity, some serenity. I wanted to forget the people whom I had ordered to get a move on in Burma, and who had never gone home again to their wives and cattle on the shores of Lake Tanganyika. I wanted to rediscover the countryside and the ancient peace and sanity of England, and find in it some place for myself.

I certainly did not wish to make money. The idea never occurred to me.

I went for a walk. I got a train to Ipswich and then walked north, and east, into the part of Suffolk where I later lived, near the coast. I crossed a heath and walked to within a hundred yards or so of my future home and didn't see that it was there, for the cottage is in a dip and you can pass close to it and not see it. On the way back I came to Melton and saw there a notice saying 'East Suffolk War Agricultural Executive Committee'. For fun I strolled into the office and asked them if they had a job for me, say as a tractor driver.

They had a job, not as a tractor driver but as 'district labour officer'. I bought an old trolley bus and dragged her up a hill at Pin Mill, overlooking the River Orwell, and in it I lived, having a lady down in the village to give me meals; and I drove about in a little car and made contracts with farmers for work which was to be done with German and Italian prisoners.

I enjoyed my work with the 'War Ag.'.

I bought an old Colchester smack which had been washed up high on the saltings by a gale, got her afloat, and sailed her in my spare time up and down the coast. During the hours when I was